Advertising the Black Stuff in Ireland 1959–1999: Increments of Change

Reimagining Ireland

Volume 95

Edited by Dr Eamon Maher,
Technological University Dublin

PETER LANG
Oxford • Bern • Berlin • Bruxelles • New York • Wien

Patricia Medcalf

Advertising the Black Stuff in Ireland 1959–1999: Increments of Change

PETER LANG
Oxford • Bern • Berlin • Bruxelles • New York • Wien

Bibliographic information published by Die Deutsche Nationalbibliothek.
Die Deutsche Nationalbibliothek lists this publication in the Deutsche Nationalbibliografie; detailed bibliographic data is available on the Internet at http://dnb.d-nb.de.
A catalogue record for this book is available from the British Library.

A CIP catalog record for this book has been applied for at the Library of Congress.

Library of Congress Cataloging-in-Publication Data: A CIP catalog record for this book has been applied for at the Library of Congress.

ISSN: 1662-9094
ISBN 978-1-78997-345-7 (print) • eISBN 978-1-78997-346-4 (ePDF)
eISBN 978-1-78997-347-1 (ePub) • eISBN 978-1-78997-348-8 (Mobi)

Cover image:

Cover design by Peter Lang Ltd.

Published by Peter Lang Ltd, International Academic Publishers,
52 St Giles, Oxford, OX1 3LU, United Kingdom
oxford@peterlang.com, www.peterlang.com

In memory of my cousin, Nicola Walker

Contents

Figures

Foreword by Patrick Guinness

Selling beer is different from selling *a* beer, as it depends upon consistent brewing. Until the late 1800s the family sold Guinness only within 10 miles of Dublin, requiring consistent agents to take it far beyond the city. The business grew but its centre remained at St James's Gate, a vast but intricate clock serviced by several thousand Dubliners.

My first memories of the brewery in the early 1960s as a little boy were of huge brick walls, pipes, tunnels, steam and smoke, smiling faces, grubby overalls, a small train, barrels everywhere, a place with no centre. My genial tweed-suited grandfather Bryan was somehow involved in managing it all, and everyone said that it was special to Dublin. Gilroy's zany animal posters selling the stout also made sense because I knew that Grandad was a sponsor of Dublin Zoo. I didn't know that Bryan, as Lord Moyne, had argued against television advertising in the House of Lords in 1953–4, seeing it as an expensive and Orwellian method. Thankfully he was voted down, and Guinness ads were the second to be broadcast in Britain. He and the board also sponsored the Book of Records from 1955 as another marketing tool that has proved to be a huge success in its own right.

Aged 10, in 1966, I had my first full tour, which took three hours, and emerged onto the tall white grainstore roof from which the entire capital could be seen. Also in 1966 came the 1916 commemorations, so along with the Beatles and Percy French, I learned songs from a darker past. Other Dubliners had not prospered as we had, but still expected a better future. My parents' friend Máire Comerford, a doyenne of 1916, pronounced that I was ready to join the Fianna scouts. To me, and perhaps my family, the brewery running its own bank, fire service, water, ships and trains, theatre, pool, pensions, sports fields, security, post office and health centres, was prospering and semi-independent long before 1916. Did I mention the zoo?

As we had no television at home in Kildare, childhood was face-to-face, local and unfiltered. Thankfully the wooden TV advertising of the 1960s passed me by. By the mid-1970s I was a student in Dublin, and beer and colour television became new aspects in my life. Everyone felt that Guinness was a good product, if not as edgy as lagers like Colt 45. Guinness TV advertising was indisputably funnier and more original than the rest. Each campaign resembled an art film or mini-series, using a soft-sell technique. This is the world that Patricia Medcalf captures so thoroughly, charting the evolution from the staid 1950s and working up to that magic moment when the brand name disappeared. The colours, sounds and *mise-en-scène* all whispered: 'this must be the new Guinness ad'. The brand became implicit. The product vanished, as it was being sold in the subconscious. The brewery shrank from 3-D to a trickle of electrons between our ears. Co-founding the brand manager Diageo was the obvious next step. This magic was easier when there was one screen per household and only two to six channels, watched by millions of families. Recognising the latest Guinness ad before it ended became a family parlour game. Will this marketing focus ever be possible again? It was much easier than the internet, but thanks to the web those electrons have trickled backwards, and now millions want to see, smell and touch the 3-D brewery.

Dr Medcalf also skilfully weaves emerging Irish social themes around these evolving advertisements. Ireland had its real revolution in about 1990, and her timeframe of 1959–99 encompasses that moment. If the State often looked to the past, the people wanted a future, and Ireland suddenly outgrew herself, much as the brewery had outgrown Dublin. Yet in newer campaigns, traditional music and stout can still dreamily complement and adorn our elemental island. Desire, beauty, heritage; what more do we need?

Acknowledgements

The genesis of this book stems from my PhD, which was skilfully guided by my supervisor, Dr Eamon Maher. He encouraged me to embark on that journey and has been a source of encouragement ever since. Thanks also to Dr Brian Murphy for his frequent words of encouragement and for his feedback on my work. I am also very appreciative of the wider AFIS community in Ireland and France. Sincere thanks to Dr Eugene O'Brien and Dr Neil O'Boyle for recognising the book's potential and for offering suggestions that would enhance it.

I am extremely grateful to Eibhlín Colgan and Fergus Brady at the Guinness Archive. They have been most generous with their time, expertise and resources. Without them, this book would not have been possible.

I would like to extend my thanks to Tony Mason, Senior Commissioning Editor at Peter Lang, who was prepared to give me the opportunity to publish my work. Special thanks to Patrick Guinness for agreeing to write such an evocative foreword.

I really appreciated meeting up with Ian Young, former chairman of BBDO (Dublin), who shared his own views on Guinness advertising with me. His insights were invaluable and reassured me that my analysis was on the right track.

I would also like to thank my Heads of Department at TU Dublin, past and present, Adrian Payne and Glenn Mehta, who supported my endeavours.

Last but not least, my sincere gratitude to my long-suffering husband Dave for his unwavering support throughout. He encouraged me all the way and it would have been much more difficult and lonely without him.

Unless otherwise stated, all copy from print and TV ads cited in this book are reproduced with permission of the Guinness Archive, Diageo Ireland. Guinness adverts have changed over the years and they are continually evolving to take into account the changing society, advertising rules, as well as the internal standards, that make Diageo a responsible business.

These adverts may contain historical product claims that are not now endorsed by Diageo. In making those adverts available, the intention is not to promote the benefits of drinking, but to show Guinness advertising over more than forty years.

Introduction

First encounters

For more than thirty years, I have worked both as a marketing practitioner and an academic in the disciplines of advertising and marketing. Due to the nature of my profession and my innate curiosity regarding happenings past and present, I have always been fascinated by advertising's ability to serve as a social commentator. Before commencing my PhD research, upon which this book is based, I had been exposed to enough advertisements to conclude that some really can tell us about society, its people and popular culture at a certain point in time. Similarly, much can be inferred about a country's legislative structures, the state of its domestic economy and its inclination, or disinclination, towards globalisation.

In order to test the validity of this belief, I kept thinking of one brand in particular: Guinness. For me, there were many reasons for its drawing power. As someone who grew up in Dublin, I was aware of the brand long before the point in my life when I reached the legal drinking age. Indeed, one of my earliest memories of Guinness dates back to the early 1970s, when I was no more than 7 or 8 years old. I was returning from a family holiday in Donegal and, to save time, my parents navigated a shorter route through Northern Ireland. Of course, this meant that we had to pass through customs and a British Army checkpoint. Regardless of the fact that we had done nothing wrong, it was a tense encounter, particularly for my parents, who were fully versed in the border's politics. The mood in the car lightened considerably when we left 'The Troubles' behind and my father's relief was palpable. To this day, I still remember him expressing a desire for a pint of Guinness as soon as we crossed the border into the much less oppressive environs of the Republic. Looking back, I realise that it was a subconscious, visceral reaction, and although I did not understand its significance at the time, it lodged in my memory. Years later, I was able to discern that his desire was highly symbolic. For him, Guinness was synonymous with home, and being in the safe and familiar environs of twenty-six-county Ireland. It represented a sense of identity and it was an integral component of what is commonly referred to as habitus.

Why was this so? When one ponders the question of Irish patrimony, time and again drinking and Guinness enter my mind. Their status in Irish heritage is well established, going back hundreds of years and, in many instances, their paths are intertwined, often deliberately so by writers and musicians. The Department of Health felt compelled to acknowledge alcohol's long-standing status in Irish society when it conceded that:

> The drinking of alcohol is an integral part of Irish social life and is accepted as such by most people. It plays an important role in our social, cultural and sporting activities ... Historically, the Irish have often been described as having a legendary and unenviable reputation for drinking.
>
> (1996: 11)

In the mid-nineteenth century, Ireland's love affair with alcohol began in earnest when drinking became commonplace across all strands of society. Such was its ubiquity that it would become one of the defining features of the nation's identity, a constant presence at all stages in an Irish person's life. Christy Moore's 1979 ode to the Irish patron saint, 'Patrick's Arrival,' would lead one to believe that drinking was a national pastime as far back as the fourth century:

> That day with a barrel of beer, he was drinking away with abandon.
> Says Patrick, 'It's grand to be here.'
> And they drank till they fell, yet by Jingo, the pot it still frothed o'er the brim.
>
> (Connolly, 1984: 66)

In his analysis of Irish drinking, Richard Stivers (2000) draws on a 1944 study by Robert F. Bales in order to explain why drinking is inextricably intertwined with Irish identity. As in other countries, the rise in popularity of alcohol was associated with celebration and rites of passage such as baptisms, marriages, wakes and emigration. However, Stivers foregrounds the unique forces present in Ireland that made alcohol's relationship with the Irish different to the one that existed with its nearest neighbours in England and Scotland. For example, in Ireland's largely agricultural economy, it was used as a social lubricant at marts in order to secure business transactions. A more worrying reason for drinking's widespread popularity was the Catholic Church's encouragement of fasting, which incited many of its congregation to substitute drink for food.

Stivers (2000) explains that the single most important societal factor that contributed to Ireland's drinking culture was the low marriage rate that prevailed between 1870 and 1940, an occurrence that can be attributed to the single inheritance farm economy. This gave rise to a disproportionately high number of bachelors. Unlike their married counterparts, they had few responsibilities and their desire for company and comradeship was very strong. Consequently, they spent much of their free time in the pub where their masculinity was judged on their ability to hold their drink. Here they were part of a community, a group of individuals who lived in similarly harsh circumstances. Married men joined them in the pub too, perhaps in the hope of re-capturing their freedom and of 'proving' themselves in this most male of environments. Henceforth, the pub became a focal point in Irish society for socialising, doing business and grocery shopping.

Guinness was founded in 1759, which means that it was already well established by the time the drinking habits of the Irish took off. According to Guinness (2009a: 30), its 'heraldic heritage' was first used on its earliest bottle label in 1862 and with uncanny foresight the harp was registered as its trademark in 1876. It has the same visual identity as Ireland's official national emblem, thus aligning itself firmly to the nation's DNA. The only difference is that Guinness's harp always appears with its straight edge to the left, whereas the straight edge of Ireland's harp is located on the right. To this day, the harp, along with the beverage's name, Guinness, and the signature of Arthur Guinness, remain integral elements of the brand's identity.

Rory Guinness (2009b) explains that the brewery's attention to the logistical side of the business in its formative decades meant that its barrels of porter became commonplace on the country's canals, which conveyed their contents beyond the pale. When rail became the preferred mode of transport for moving merchandise, Guinness even built its own onsite railway, which linked the brewery to the national rail network. Never a company to stand still, it went on to acquire its own fleet of ships in the twentieth century and boats like the *Miranda Guinness* became landmarks on Dublin's city centre quays, thus establishing Guinness in the hearts and minds of inhabitants and visitors to the capital city (Guinness, 2009a).

For several decades now, it would appear as if prominent writers, musicians and artists conspired to consolidate Guinness's place in Ireland's cultural heritage. Indeed some, like Brendan Behan, gained notoriety for consuming copious amounts of the beverage, all the time reinforcing the links between Guinness, creativity and identity. Despite his predilection for wine, in *Ulysses*, James Joyce refers to Guinness as a signifier of what it means to be Irish when he cites the Guinness brewery alongside a long list of ancient treasures and landmarks (Guinness, 2009a). Carl O'Brien's report on the 2009 Bloomsday celebrations also gives prominence to the link between Guinness and Joyce's classic novel, which, like the beverage, is part of Ireland's cultural heritage. The Irish proudly adopt it as one of the nation's treasures, regardless of whether or not they have read it. Similarly, they confer the same honour on Guinness, even if they don't drink it. One of O'Brien's (2009) interviewees emphasises Guinness's role in *Ulysses*, which is part of a ritual, steadfastly mimicked in the annual celebrations by domestic and international tourists. In other words, Bloomsday without Guinness would be incomplete:

> 'And the Guinness,' said Ena Smyth. 'The Guinness for breakfast, that's in it too. It's the only time of year you're allowed to have Guinness at eight o'clock in the morning.'

Meanwhile, Alan O'Riordan (2009) reminds readers that such is its reputation and infamy that writers do not even need to mention Guinness's name in their writings.

> As Brendan Behan wrote in his Irish Sketchbook, 'Guinness is universally drank in Ireland'. Thus, the Irish poets can be familiar. 'Pint' means a pint of Guinness; 'stout' and 'porter' (a distinction little appreciated nowadays) similarly take the same brand in the mind of the reader.

This is borne out in Flann O'Brien's classic poem, 'The Workman's Friend', in which he coined the phrase, 'A pint of plain is your only man.' Similarly, Christy Moore could only mean Guinness in his 1983 track, 'Lisdoonvarna', when he concludes: 'I don't need to worry about the weather. Ramble in for a pint of stout, you'd never know who'd be hangin' about' (Connolly, 1984: 110). In a much more overt reference to Guinness in the 1985 ballad, 'Delerium Tremens', he muses, while all the time strengthening the link between Guinness and Irish popular culture :

> As I sat lookin' up, the Guinness ad I could never figure out,
> How your man stayed up on the surfboard after fourteen pints of stout.
>
> (<http://www.christymoore.com>)

Guinness became important in my own life when I entered adulthood in the 1980s and embarked on student life at Trinity College Dublin. Unlike students from Generations Y and Z, my preferences for particular alcohol beverages were formed against a relatively simple vista of brands. Gateway drinks like Smirnoff Ice and Bacardi Breezer had not yet been created, and many of my peers, male and female alike, soon acquired a taste for Guinness. Apart from the occasional party in a bedsit, a dwelling now consigned to history, alcohol was largely consumed in the sociable confines of city centre pubs, many of which were affiliated to Guinness. In these establishments, we received our 'education' on this most Irish of drinks. Most importantly, we became acquainted with its colourful backstory and the ritual that surrounds the pouring of a pint. These are recurring themes in this book and their relevance to any analysis of Guinness advertising should not be underestimated.

Guinness's presence in my formative years was copper-fastened in the summer of 1985 when I was very fortunate to secure a summer job at St James's Gate. I was consigned to work on an administrative task that was menial and repetitive, but integral to the construction of a computer system that would help transport Guinness into the information age. Depending on the wind's direction, the aroma of hops brewing meant that the brewery's presence in Dublin's city centre was inescapable. This most sensory of triggers is still capable of transporting me back to that time.

Despite my very limited experience of corporate Ireland, whilst working at Guinness I was struck by my employer's largesse towards its workers and the local community. Each day, all employees, including myself, enjoyed a fully subsidised three-course lunch. In addition, a daily allowance of two bottles of beer from the company's portfolio was available to all staff. The beneficiary could consume them at lunch or they could be taken home. Meanwhile, senior management dined in a separate restaurant, where waiters served them high-quality fare. Sports facilities, including a swimming pool, were provided for staff at various locations throughout the city. All full-time employees and their immediate families were given free access to Guinness-affiliated general practitioners.

Of course, these perks were by no means new. Guinness's reputation as a benevolent employer differentiated it from most other employers. According to Rory Guinness, by the end of the nineteenth century it was estimated that one in every thirty people in Dublin depended on the brewery financially. By then, employees were very highly paid, and unusually for that time, they received benefits such as pensions and medical care. In addition to the brewery's pioneering approach to employee welfare, housing was built and provided for workers and their families by the Iveagh Trust, which was funded from Lord Iveagh's personal resources. Another example of his largesse is evident on the Guinness Storehouse website, which states that he established a charitable organisation in 1915 and it touched the lives of many local children with the daily provision of cocoa and currant buns. At Christmas, the charity staged parties for these children. Consequently, the standing of Guinness and Lord Iveagh in Dublin went way beyond the commercial sphere. Their philanthropic philosophy infiltrated the lives of Dubliners and secured a place in their hearts and minds, regardless of whether or not they drank its porter.

The question at the heart of this book

The over-arching question at the heart of this book is the extent to which Guinness advertising responded to and/or initiated change in Ireland between 1959 and 1999. Aspects of this question bear similarities with the tenor of Marchand's (1985) study of 1920s and 1930s adverts in the United States, which investigates whether or not they might be viewed as *social tableaux*, capable of portraying a realistic representation of society. On the basis of his research, Marchand concludes that the ads under scrutiny focused less on reality and more on consumers' social aspirations. However, they did reflect many of the social norms that prevailed in the 1920s and 1930s, most noticeably the obvious demarcation of the social classes, the status of women, and the treatment of ethnic and racial minorities in advertising. His findings concur with the widely accepted truism that advertising practitioners frequently draw on societal reference points when creating advertisements. This inevitably leads to the creation of ads that inform onlookers about the range of issues and characteristics that are peculiar to individual nations. According to O'Boyle (2011: 123), Irish advertising agencies are no exception: 'As cultural producers, advertising workers mediate and intervene in the circulation of meanings about Irishness, arguably routinising them much more than contesting them.' Therefore, depending on how well executed an ad is, it might propagate particular national characteristics, as evidenced in many of the Guinness ads in this book, which often depict Irish people as sociable and fun-loving.

More than forty years ago, Williamson (1978: 11) boldly declared that: 'Advertisements are one of the most important cultural factors moulding and reflecting our life today.' This suggests that, as well as advertising being responsive to cultural trends it might actually exert influence over them. Fox (1997: 272) seems intent on admonishing such claims:

> Advertising – which sometimes claimed to foreshadow and direct social change – actually lagged behind the general course of events. The advertising mirror itself, the reflective devices that the trade held up to Americans, remained stable, with the usual cyclical adjustments. What changed was American society and culture, the objects in front of the mirror. Slowly, stubbornly, the mirrored image changed too. But the time lag remained. Advertising never quite caught up.

Fox's scathing attack was aimed at American advertising executives of the 1960s, a period when they enjoyed reverential status. Essentially, he is challenging those who claim that advertising is capable of instigating societal and cultural change.

Goldman (1992: 61) holds a similar view and in less acerbic language, he maintains that: 'Advertisers draw sociocultural meanings from viewers' life-worlds and the mass media themselves, and embed these meanings in images, which are then returned to viewers.' In her study of graphic design pertaining to Aer Lingus in the 1950s, King (2000: 16) argues that graphic design pieces are often 'cultural signifiers' because they are capable of painting a picture of society at a particular point in time. This is also captured by Leiss et al. (2005: 2), who, like Marchand, see advertising as 'a useful interpretive key for tracing aspects of our consumer culture.'

Perhaps these views are understandable, as one participant in Cronin's (2004: 354) collection opines, which is close to Fox's view, that rather than leading cultural change, 'advertising is reactive and relies on siphoning off ideas from culture – practitioners strategically raid new cultural trends they see appearing across a range of sites ... and put selected elements of them to work in their campaigns.' Thus, advertising tends to exploit the yearnings of consumers by blending realistic scenarios with their aspirations. An advertising executive articulates this technique in an interview with Jhally (2003: 251): 'Advertising doesn't always mirror how people are acting but how they're dreaming.' Many of the Guinness ads that were analysed in this study depict aspirational imagery, which reflected the most appealing and desirable facets of Irish society when they were published or broadcast. From river cruises to a journey aboard Concorde, the ads contained visual triggers that served as cultural signifiers, regardless of whether or not the target audience was ever likely to experience them first-hand.

Fanning (2006) acknowledges that brand communications are usually more effective when they reflect the social constructs of the time. However, in order to achieve cut-through in a cluttered environment, hyperbole in advertising is commonplace. It serves to underline a brand's understanding and appreciation of societal trends, while at the same time cultivating stronger relationships with consumers. O'Boyle's (2011: 4) pronouncement suggests why many ads end up being cultural signifiers when he casts a light on those responsible for creating ads:

> Ireland's advertising industry can to some extent be viewed as a microcosm of wider Irish society increasingly under the sway of exogenous forces. In this context, culture remains a vital source of competitive advantage or 'soft power', for both the advertising industry and the State alike.

This statement acknowledges the fact that the Irish advertising industry is extremely open to the vagaries of global forces but that in many instances, it presses home on its clients the importance of local culture when communicating with audiences in Ireland. This gives Irish-based agencies, most of which are owned by global giants, reasons to convince clients that they should continue to produce bespoke campaigns.

However, this study does not just set out to examine the extent to which Guinness drew on Irish culture and society in its first fifty years of advertising in Ireland. It also aims to examine the extent to which Guinness's ads might have helped shape Irish culture and society. The question of whether or not ads are capable of triggering societal and cultural change is much more contentious than the largely uncontested view that advertising is shaped by culture and society. Having posed the question to Ian Young, former chairman of BBDO Dublin, he is of the opinion that advertising reflects culture as opposed to shaping it. In putting forward this judgement, he appears to support Marchand's (1985) depiction of advertising practitioners as mere mediators as opposed to being apostles of modernity, which is how many of them would like to be considered. At best, Young is of the opinion that some campaigns are built on cultural trends before they become mainstream, which gives the impression to many consumers and commentators that the advertiser is ahead of the curve. Hence, this often works to the advantage of the brand in question because it can confer on it an air of leadership.

Some academics, including Leiss et al. (2005: 13), hold a much more nuanced view and they see advertising as 'a channel through which social change is constantly mediated – both a discursive practice contributing to cultural and economic change and a representational practice wherein such changes can be witnessed and interpreted.'

Therefore, while they agree that social change might be observed in advertising, they are of the opinion that it is capable of contributing to changes in culture and society too. Hesmondhalgh (2012: 4) is of a similar mind-set and his work focuses on three related elements that determine the importance of modern-day cultural industries, a sector to which advertising agencies belong:

> Their ability to make and circulate products that influence our knowledge, understanding and experience (texts); their role as systems for the management of creativity and knowledge; and their effects as agents of economic, social and cultural change.

Leiss et al. (2005: 70) strengthen their argument with an exploration of the evolution of advertising. They argue that: 'In consumer society, advertisements became an important means for transmitting cues, in specific forms consistent with product messages, about new styles of personal behavior.' This makes them the ideal lens through which to explore a country's social history. The authors (2005: 63) highlight the relevance of what they refer to as 'landmark events in the constitution of a consumer society.' Such events trigger social change and in the case of Guinness, the advent of a commercial television network in Ireland in 1961 was one such occurrence. It coincided with a time when Irish people started to migrate to urban districts in greater numbers. Ironically, despite the close proximity of their neighbours, they often felt isolated. Television was a powerful way of bringing people together, and from the start, Guinness recognised its significance. It was an early adopter of this potent technology, utilising it to further ingratiate the brand with Irish consumers. As is evident throughout this study, other triggers such as internationalisation and globalisation, gender issues, the switch to off-trade alcohol consumption, and popular culture all formed the backdrop for many of the ads in its extensive catalogue.

When analysing advertising across a forty-year time span, the evolution of the levels of advertising literacy amongst a country's consumers is of particular relevance. It helps explain the approach taken by advertisers and their agencies when creating ads. Inevitably, advertising literacy is shaped by economic developments and the socio-cultural make-up of a country. Hence, it influences the degree of sophistication that is evident in advertising across different markets. Goodyear (1991) identifies a number of factors that impact on a country's rate of development in advertising literacy. They include levels of exposure to television, film and advertising, and whether or not a society thinks about products as brands as opposed to commodities. She classified five levels of literacy, each one suited to a different advertising approach. The key thing is that they are not static and evolve over time in tandem with a population's increasingly sophisticated visual literacy (Goodyear 1991; Lannon 1992).

Levels of advertising in Ireland burgeoned quite dramatically in the 1990s, which helped bring the Irish population up to speed in terms of advertising literacy. From 1959 up until the early years of the twenty-first century, Guinness's advertising in Ireland was specially created for the domestic audience. This may have been due to the different levels of advertising literacy that existed among British adults when compared to Irish adults, thereby necessitating a different approach. Lannon's (1992) succinct categories of advertising styles can be applied to the evolution of Guinness's advertising in Ireland. The first category 'The Manufacturer Speaks,' relates to many of the ads in the first decade (1959–70), when Guinness concentrated on providing audiences with factual information about the stout and the brewery. Then there is the second category 'The target audience consumes with pleasure.' In this style of advertising, ads are often created using a slice of life approach, real life situations to which the target audience can relate or aspire. This approach became more commonplace from the mid-1960s and through the following two decades, when ads presented scenarios like parties, holidays and first dates. The third stage involves 'Hyperbole and exaggeration,' a method that was used by Guinness in the 1990s 'Big Pint' series of ads. However, even by the 1980s, Guinness appeared to have made significant progress because many of its ads adopted the fourth of Lannon's categories, 'Brand appropriate symbols and metaphors to express personality.' In the 1990s, three categories of advertising literacy are catered for in Guinness's ads. They are levels three, four, and towards the end of the decade, the fifth whereby: 'Brand creates own language code.' Rather than focusing on the product and its features and attributes, as is typical when audiences are at the first three stages of advertising literacy, arrival at the fourth and fifth stages enables advertisers to create stories about brands. For brand managers, advertising becomes a way of starting or joining conversations with their target audiences.

Carefully orchestrated conversations between brand owners and consumers have the potential to propagate what Muniz and O'Guinn (2001: 412) define as a brand community, which is:

> A specialized, non-geographically bound community, based on a structured set of social relationships among admirers of a brand. It is specialized because at its center is a branded good or service. Like other communities, it is marked by a shared consciousness, rituals and traditions, and a sense of moral responsibility … Brand

> communities are participants in the brand's larger social construction and play a vital role in the brand's ultimate legacy.

At the heart of this definition is an underlying cult-like devotion to the brand, similar to that which is evident in followers of religion. An essential by-product of this is the sense of community that ensues. Durkheim's (cited in Sheffield 2006: 39) definition of religion bears many similarities to Muniz and O'Guinn's concept of brand community. 'A religion is a unified system of beliefs and practices relative to sacred things, that is to say, things set apart and forbidden – beliefs and practices which unite into one single moral community called a Church, all those who adhere to them.'

The term 'sacred things' is replaced by brands and 'beliefs and practices' are likened to a brand's values, rituals and traditions. Sheffield (2006) suggests that advertising has assumed the role of celebrant, capable of using its special powers to breathe life into a brand and transform it into a symbol that is worshipped by like-minded individuals. She deploys the term totems to describe the objects of consumers' desires and posits that in developed consumer societies, 'totems are objects to be consumed. The objects are imbued with an image of the sacred by the meaning advertising gives them' (Sheffield 2006: 54). Within this study, religious analogies are apt when analysing some of Guinness's most distinctive qualities, such as the pouring technique and the time it takes for a pint to settle.

When it comes to understanding how advertising works, the seminal works of Shannon and Weaver (1949) and Schramm (1955) in the field of Communications are still widely used by advertising practitioners and academics more than sixty years after their publication. The simplicity of their Communication Process Model belies the complex process that underpins advertising but it facilitates a structured approach to its planning and analysis. The analysis of the actual ads in this book focuses on the sender (Guinness); the receiver (the target audience); encoding (what Guinness was trying to say and how its agencies codified the message); and the message itself (what did Guinness say?). 'Noise' (any external force that conspires to distract the target audience from the message) was also considered in this study when identifying the historical contexts in which the ads were created.

In order to decode the meaning in the advertisements, semiotic analysis provides a framework against which they can be deconstructed and interpreted. Barthes (1972: 220) explains that 'semiology is a science of form since it studies significations apart from their content.' For instance, why do audiences understand that a swirling, crashing wave signifies a pint of Guinness being poured? The reason is that they have been guided by the producers of cultural content, be they advertisers or film-makers, so that the more 'fluent' an audience is in the language of advertising, the less literal the ads need to be. Consumers' understanding of the signs used in advertising makes it easier for a brand to communicate because 'having made these links and created symbols of exchange it can use them as "given"' (Williamson 1978: 12). So, while it is perfectly acceptable to encode messages in an obvious and literal way, it is possible to create more cryptic ads as consumers become more advertising literate. Barthes (1972: 219) sums this up when he states that: 'Pictures become a kind of writing as soon as they are meaningful.' Therefore, in order to decode most adverts, the analyst must look behind that which appears in the ad. For example, using Barthes's (1972) and Williamson's (1978) terminology, what is signified (meaning) by the dancer and the barman (the signifiers) in the 1994 ad 'Anticipation'?

Lawes (2002) suggests that such questions might be answered by deploying a semiotic toolkit. In it, she places 'tools' such as visual, linguistic and aural signs; the communication situation; structure of text (particularly relevant to print ads and the final frame of television ads); visual emphasis; and genre. They help to ensure that a rigorous approach to analysing ads is undertaken. Meanwhile, Gadsby (2010) takes a less formulaic approach and looks beyond the mechanics of semiotic analysis, preferring instead to focus on the advantages that are conferred on advertisers when signs are assembled in such a way that they transcend the unwritten rules of advertising in a particular product category. He postulates that:

> There are certain iconic brands, such as Coke, Google and Nike, that have so great an appeal that they cast a spell over consumers; it would be a genuine insight to understand how they achieve this. Semiotic analysis is perfectly situated to do this, because it is capable of decoding the signs of these brands' communications – it can literally identify the formula for magic. (Gadsby 2010: 40)

It is evident that many of Guinness's most memorable ads fall into this category. Semiotic analysis can still be applied but in order to come up with answers, the researcher might have to delve deeper into the meaning behind the signs. However, being different or obscure does not necessarily guarantee success, as was evident in Guinness's 1990s 'Big Pint' campaign, which is discussed in Chapter 4. Therefore, when analysing ads and forming an opinion about them, it is advantageous to keep in mind Prue's (1998) advice on what it takes to create good advertising. As well as making ads in such a way that they will appeal to the target audience, they should be relevant and inextricably connected to the brand. Again, as is evident in this book, this was not always the case, particularly in the second half of the 1990s when consumers were sometimes left wondering what the ads were about.

In many ways advertising producers might be likened to magpies because they borrow from a variety of sources such as television, cinema, art, music and literature when creating ads. Williamson (1978) highlights the concept of Referent Systems, which give meaning to ads and are derived from influences outside advertising. This is an accepted phenomenon in the world of advertising and according to O'Donohoe (1997: 235): 'The substance and images woven into advertising messages are appropriated and distilled from an unbounded range of cultural references.' Such appropriation is referred to as intertextuality, a theory that Fiske (1987: 109) explains as being when 'any one text is necessarily read in relationship to others and that a range of textual knowledge is brought to bear upon it.' However, in order to understand the text, the viewer does not have to be familiar with the text from which it is borrowed. This is because audiences have what Fiske (1987: 109) refers to as 'a cultural image bank', which enables them to understand the signs and symbols that are used. Chandler (1994) and Fiske (1987) refer to the work of Julia Kristeva on intertextuality when they distinguish between horizontal and vertical relations between texts. The former refers to explicit links between texts by virtue of genre, character or content. The latter refers to relations between the primary text and other texts of an unrelated type, such as Guinness ads, that make overt reference to it.

Therefore, to conclude, the question that was posed at the start of this section emerged from the writings of a range of academics including Marchand, O'Boyle, Fox, Goldman, Cronin, Jhally, Fanning and Hesmondlagh. While all of them agree that advertising is shaped by cultural and societal influences, many of them do not extend this certainty to the question of advertising's ability to initiate societal and cultural change. Indeed, Fox is unequivocal in his rejection of such a premise but the conviction of other authors to the possibility of such powers make it a question worth exploring.

Exploring the Guinness Archive

In order to assess the extent to which Guinness advertising responded to and/or initiated social and cultural change in Ireland between 1959 and 1999, an in-depth analysis of Guinness's body of advertising work from that period was undertaken. An initial visit to the Archives at the Guinness Storehouse in Dublin to review the extensive range of ads preserved there, convinced me that Archival Research would enable me to answer the question. According to Moore et al. (2017), an archive is, quite simply, a repository for a variety of documents that can be held in various formats, both official and unofficial. The UK's Archives Task Force (2004: 12) contends that the growing interest in archives in recent decades is due to the fact that many of them are a 'direct, uninterrupted and authentic voice of the past.' Moore et al. (2017: 4) underline the potency of this attribute when they state:

> 'The past' is a shorthand for everything that has come before and made us, our lives and the societies we live in, what they are. So understanding even small parts of the past can give us a handle on things in the present and possibly aspects of the future too.

This quote summarises what I envisaged when I first visited the Guinness Archive to evaluate the quality of the range of ads preserved there. They were established in 1998 and contain many diverse documents, including its extensive collection of advertisements. Therefore, an archival research methodology would facilitate a thorough investigation of the significant trove of print and video ads that had been catalogued. More specifically, a historiographic archival research method was used. Ventresca and Mohr (2002) explain that this method places the focus on archive material from just one or a few organisations. Depending on the amounts of data available to the researcher, it often facilitates an ethnographic approach. However, when finding answers, this alone would not suffice because I did not experience first-hand the early decades of Guinness advertising in Ireland. Also, my memory of subsequent decades has been dulled with the passage of time and biases would be inevitable. Nevertheless, I read and viewed a large number of ads from the archive in order to 'gain insights, make discoveries and generate informed judgements about the character of historical events' (Ventresca and Mohr 2002: 815) in Guinness and Ireland. This concurs with the view of Leiss et al. (2005), who believe that advertising can be used to explain historical happenings.

According to Ventresca and Mohr (2002: 806), archival research is an unobtrusive methodology, which allows the researcher to analyse 'organisational change in increments of time that captures significant institutional processes.' Similarly, Salter (2017) advocates time as an excellent way of organising archive records and that this enables the researcher to look into the future by analysing the past. Foucault (1972: 147) enthuses that: 'The analysis of the archive, then, involves a privileged region: at once close to us and different from our present existence.' He approaches the archive with reverence, almost in awe of its ability to take the researcher back in time. The four decades identified for analysis in this book are as follows:

- 1959–69: 1959 was the 200th anniversary of Guinness and celebrated the launch of its first ads made specifically for the Irish market. It was a period of immense economic and societal change, as marked in Guinness ads, which were strongly influenced by heritage, the advent of Irish television, sport, the rise of travel and tourism, and the changing role of women in society.
- 1970–9: The Guinness ads in this decade bore witness to an increasingly cosmopolitan population that yearned for aspirational lifestyles. Alcohol consumption patterns changed and were influenced by greater choice. Women's changing role in society was gathering pace

and a more outward-looking sense of identity among Irish people was evident, brought about by greater exposure to external cultural influences.
- 1980–9: The economy and emigration dominated the news but this did not stop an explosion in the influence of popular culture from abroad. Ireland's internationalisation gathered pace and the start of the standardisation/globalisation debate took centre stage. Ireland's island status was a recurring theme in Guinness ads and the use of celebrities and testimonials in its ads became commonplace.
- 1990–9: The arrival of the Celtic Tiger dominated this decade. The impact of structural changes and greater regulation in the advertising industry, the formation of Diageo, and the appointment of London ad agencies were reflected in many of the ads. The decline of the Roman Catholic Church and the rise in sexual liberation inspired more risqué storylines in some of the ads.

It is up to the researcher to surmise as to the context of the archival records, which are not stand-alone pieces of communication; rather they were created for a reason. Referring to her research on an archive of letters, Stanley (2017: 54) maintains that they 'put across a particular message in a particular voice, and intend (but do not necessarily produce) a particular desired effect on their reader/s.' This is equally applicable to the ads in the Guinness Archive, which is why it was imperative that they would be analysed in the context of those aspects of Ireland that were relevant to Guinness and its consumers between 1959 and 1999. This rigour was vital as Stanley (2017: 63) explains that strong archival analysis:

> Requires having a feel or a 'nose' for what is interpretationally interesting. However, this is not magic or a special gift, but results from close familiarity with the archival sources, carrying out detailed analyses of specific documents, and working across things to discern the wider picture.

This quote captures the essence of the research activity and explains how archival research is not just about looking at the contents of an archive. Instead, it is about taking the contents and bringing them to life by attempting to get inside the minds of the people who created them. Elder et al. (2011) endorse this view when they advise archival researchers that the content in an archive reflects the originator's point of view, as well as themes from the period in question. They advocate the need to place content, in this instance the ads, in a historical context, all the time taking into account the likely concerns, viewpoints and aspirations of the creators.

An initial scan of some of the print ads that were created for the Irish market unearthed a number of emerging themes. The year in which each ad was published or broadcast is clearly identified in the Guinness Archive so this proved crucial when locating the ads in a historical setting. Information and commentary about the period from 1959 to 1999 was extracted from articles, reports and books written by social commentators, historians, economists and journalists. The main themes identified in ads included advertising regulation (or lack thereof), agriculture, cultural, demographic and social change, the economy, globalisation, heritage, migration and sport.

To conclude, Guinness's advertising provided a lens through which I could examine the extent to which cultural specificity can be enhanced, rather than occluded, by advertising. It enabled me to question how effectively Guinness made use of backstory and a sense of place when promoting the brand in Ireland, from the time that it first started advertising in Ireland in 1959 up until 1999. Consequently, this book focuses on investigating four key areas:

- The influence of the Guinness brand's provenance on advertising campaigns aimed at consumers living in Ireland;
- The evolution of cultural signs used in Guinness's advertising campaigns aimed at consumers in Ireland between 1959 and 1999;
- The extent to which Ireland's social and economic history might be recounted through the lens of Guinness's ads;
- The extent to which Guinness's advertising might have influenced Irish culture and society.

Coming from particular backgrounds can mean that researchers are likely to apply self-reference criteria when analysing the data. I lived through most of the decades identified in this study, and in 1984 I entered 'official' adulthood. I worked in Guinness for a few months in 1985, and my impressions of the brand were formed before 1997, the year that the company was subsumed into the newly founded global entity, Diageo.

These admissions might explain the tenor of some of my conclusions but they are inevitable because 'people are products of their time' (Stanley 2017: 39). At the outset, I was aware of this but even though I endeavoured to maintain an objective and non-partisan approach, most likely there are nevertheless instances where my own backstory might have influenced and informed my analysis.

Furthermore, according to Moore et al. (2017), most archives are incomplete, which means that by necessity, archival research entails an ethnographic approach because the researcher is forced to make assumptions about the missing information. Moore et al. liken this activity to being akin to a balancing act between facts and stories. This applies to the analysis of the Guinness Archive's contents in this study because I was required to somehow infiltrate the minds of the creative teams that conceived the ads, thereby putting my own interpretation on the meanings contained in them. In order to reduce the likelihood of bias, my assumptions were not only based on personal views but were considerably strengthened by the inclusion of information gleaned from authors who wrote extensively about the decades under investigation.

Even though the Guinness Archive is very comprehensive, the Archive Manager, Eibhlín Colgan cautioned at the outset that it was by no means 100 per cent complete. Also, despite the Archive being incomplete, its collection of Irish ads is very extensive and hence I used temporal (categorisation into four distinct decades) and thematic maps based on pertinent elements in Guinness's macro environment in Ireland to select some ads from the Archive while discarding others. This is bound to introduce some bias because a different researcher might have identified alternative themes and consequently, might have omitted or included certain ads that do not feature in my thesis. Weber (1990) highlights the data-reduction process as one of the main problems when engaging in research that focuses on content analysis. Some ads were discarded from this study because they were not deemed to be relevant to the themes. Perfectly valid data might be eliminated because 'of the ambiguity of word meanings and category or variable definitions' (Weber 1990: 15) but if a coding scheme has been tested and implemented, such problems should be significantly reduced.

Nowadays, archive data is not confined to the medium of paper or microfiche. Most of the print ads analysed in this study were produced between 1959 and 1982, and while they were made available to me in paper format, it is evident that some of them are faded and fragile. Consequently, the archivists at Guinness have digitised a significant number of its paper documents including many of its print ads. However, the migration to electronic formats can change the way in which the material is analysed. Craven (2008) argues that paper records contain important signs that are usually absent from electronic versions, thus changing the way in which researchers analyse the material. For example, an ad taken directly from a newspaper that was published in the 1960s accentuates its age because of the faded, fragile state of the newspaper. Such clues are often airbrushed from the digital version, thus making it 'feel' less old. Deterioration of archive data is not confined to paper formats. For the purposes of this study, from the 1990s onwards, the television ads in the archive were more pertinent to the research questions. This switch in focus reflects TV's prominence in the final decades of the twentieth century.

To conclude, archival research is an inexact science and often requires the researcher to exercise judgement in order to fill in some gaps that might exist in the data held in the archive. To fully appreciate its worth, it is vital to comprehend the context in which the data in the archive was created. If this is not documented alongside each piece of data, the researcher is required to draw on secondary sources and personal recollections (where applicable and appropriate) in order to set the scene. Therefore, when analysing the ads in the Guinness Archive, it was imperative for me to make certain assumptions about the intent behind the ads and the societal and economic context in which they were created.

CHAPTER 1

1959–1969: New beginnings

The late 1950s: Laying foundations for economic and societal change

The end of the 1950s and the 1960s signified the start of immense change in Irish cultural identity. It was an era when the country opened its doors to outside influences. At the same time, one of Ireland's most established and iconic companies, Guinness, adopted a more formalised approach to marketing and advertising in its domestic market, with the intention of creating a distinct brand identity in Ireland.

Up until the late 1950s, Ireland's formative years as a republic were characterised by protectionism and an ambition to go it alone. However, despite efforts to build and assert its own identity, the country's language, justice system and trading orientation ironically gravitated towards its old adversary, the United Kingdom. According to Thornley (1964), some aspects of Irish culture did move on as the old class structure disappeared, and the Anglo-Irish aristocracy faded into the background. In its place, the GAA flourished, an Irish literary revival took place, and the majority of the population adhered to the Roman Catholic religion. Government policy was formulated by many of the key players in the War of Independence, a cohort of extremely nationalistic politicians who believed that Ireland could succeed as a self-sufficient, independent nation. This merely resulted in an extended period of economic stagnation and, as observed by Haughton (1987: 34), protectionism meant that Ireland in the 1950s had become 'too inefficient to export successfully.'

One politician with impeccable Republican credentials was Seán Lemass, but as Minister for Industry and Commerce between 1957 and 1959, he consciously decided to adopt a radically different approach to that of the protectionist era. The 1958 economic programme entitled 'First Programme for Economic Expansion' was largely informed by the then Secretary of the Department of Finance, T. K. Whitaker's policy document 'Economic Development,' which is credited with being the catalyst for Ireland's transformation into a small, open economy, enthusiastically securing business contracts with its European neighbours. Also, it marked what might be described as an irreversible disruption to Irish society as its workforce increasingly found employment in the industrial and services sectors of the economy as opposed to agriculture. In their analysis of the Central Statistics Office (CSO) data, Kennedy and Giblin (1987) observe that in 1961, 34.5 per cent of the Irish workforce was employed in agriculture and that by 1971 this had fallen to 25.9 per cent, despite the labour-intensive nature of the work. Nolan's (1987) assessment of the CSO's data on sectoral growth between 1961 and 1973 shows annual growth in the industrial and services sectors was 6.2 per cent and 3.7 per cent respectively, while agriculture grew at a rate of just 1.7 per cent. This shift in production and employment led to a very different way of life for many, a life influenced by urban backdrops and the challenges and opportunities that they presented. Lee concluded (1982) that this era marked the start of a societal evolution as Irish people were faced with many of the same problems and opportunities encountered by people in other countries, while Rottman and O'Connell (1982) go so far as to describe 1958 as a watershed in the structure of Irish society.

As the government's new policies took hold in the 1960s, the economy grew stronger, and the tide of emigration that had dogged Ireland in the 1950s was stemmed. In what he referred to as Ireland's demographic transformation, Walsh (1972) drew attention to some very significant changes that took place between 1958 and 1970. The annual rate of marriage increased steadily from 15,000 to 23,000, a trend that he attributed to greater prosperity and economic stability. He discovered that while the rates of first and second births rose steadily, 1964 was the year when births to women with already at least three children fell. Even as early as 1972, he surmised that as a result of the rise in the number of women having no more than two children, an opportunity existed to exert greater influence on society and the economy. Improved prospects opened up for many people, and the class structure changed markedly in the 1960s. Rottman and O'Connell's (1982) analysis of the censuses conducted in 1951, 1961 and 1971 showed a marked increase in the numbers of upper-middle-class Irish people (higher and lower professions, managers, and salaried employees) from 47,780 to 58,934 to 84,512 respectively. Similarly, the lower middle class and skilled manual classes all rose significantly, while, as already stated, numbers working in agriculture fell. Much of this change can be attributed to the strengthening economy, and the implementation of the second Programme for Economic Expansion of 1963 that set out to improve educational opportunities for everybody.

It was against this backdrop that Guinness officially started advertising in Ireland for the first time in 1959. Until then, it had relied on its bottlers and public houses to advertise its product, an approach that could only lead to inconsistencies. In addition, Guinness Headquarters engaged in smaller scale promotional activities such as the Doctor's Books. According to the Guinness Archive, these books were the brainchild of Bensons, Guinness's advertising agency in Britain. The books were inspired by the many testimonials that the agency had sought, and received, on behalf of their client from doctors so as to give credibility to the 'Guinness is good for you' proposition. Bensons aimed to produce a branded gift for doctors from Guinness in order to strengthen the relationship between the two parties. The books were sent to doctors each Christmas between 1933 and 1939, and again from 1950 to 1966. As described by the Guinness Archive fact sheet: 'the themed, lavishly illustrated books notable for their whimsical charm and overt literary parody, contained many lateral – and often ingenious – references to Guinness, both visual and verbal.' In many ways, the Doctor's Books series was ahead of its time. They were geared towards a very influential and revered target audience and placed the Guinness brand at the heart of some very entertaining material. They were beautifully illustrated and contained poems that had the potential to appeal to an audience far wider than the doctors receiving the gifts.

1959 was thirty years after the first national ad for Guinness was published in Britain, but due to a confluence of factors, it was considered the right time to start advertising in Ireland. 1959 marked the 200th anniversary of the brewery's foundation, a remarkable feat for any company and one that was deemed to be worth celebrating. More significantly, the company was entering an era of competitive pressures – up to that point government protectionist policies had provided Guinness with considerable shelter from competition. It enjoyed a 75 per cent market share in its home market as against a paltry 5 per cent in the United Kingdom, where it faced stiff competition from British breweries (Yenne 2007). Just as Guinness would benefit from a more open regime from an exporting perspective, it would probably have to face up to competition from lagers in its Irish market, thereby necessitating advertising in order to keep its name to the forefront of its customers' minds.

Guinness set out its stall in its very first ads published in the Irish press. By highlighting its long heritage, it seems to be saying that having survived 200 years, it would be around for a long time to come. The years 1759–1959 are used to frame the ad in a stucco-style decoration, and a defiant and celebratory headline declares '200 years of Guinness – What a lovely long drink!' (see Figure 1).

It seems to warn potential competitors, who would inevitably arrive in Ireland that the famous brewery has been around for a long time and would be there for many years to come. The ad poses the question: 'Do you imagine that our great-great-great-great grandfathers when they tasted their first Guinness two hundred years ago, realized that it was to become Ireland's favourite drink?' A framed portrait of Arthur Guinness flanks the copy, his attire and wig bearing witness to the brand's longevity. Interestingly, the copy evokes a time when 'Irish brewing was suffering severe competition from abroad,' a situation that was destined to return due to the policies of Lemass. Again, Guinness seems to be saying that it has nothing to fear from competition. Pride in its Irish heritage, the use of home-grown ingredients, and the employment of an Irish workforce are emphasised – 'brewed by the Irish for the Irish, almost entirely from Irish barley, Guinness caught the fancy of the Irish people.' The ad signs off with the iconic phrase, 'Guinness is good for you,' a declaration that would not be allowed in later years.

In another press ad from 1959, two men feature, one from the 1750s, wearing pantaloons, jacket, waistcoat, scarf and hat, and the other dressed in a contemporary (for the 1950s) suit and trilby hat. Both men clutch a Guinness, one in a ceramic tankard and the other in a glass. The text proudly recalls how 'just before the advent of Guinness … Ireland was being flooded with English porter. But Guinness soon altered all that. Within a few years, the tables were turned, and England was clamouring for the infinitely superior Irish brew.' Again, the copy highlights Guinness's confidence in its ability to capitalise on the radically new economic policies of Lemass when it states:

Figure 1: The first Irish ad from Guinness

> Today, the St James's Gate Brewery in Dublin supplies the world with Guinness, and many thousands of Irish men and women are engaged in the good work. Yet in spite of this great export industry, Ireland is the home of Guinness, and it is here that it is truly appreciated.

Very tellingly, the concluding line of the copy in this ad demonstrates a real desire by Guinness to stake its claim as an integral part of Irish society and identity when it concludes: 'the people of Ireland who found

Guinness so much to their liking when Arthur Guinness first brewed it, 200 years ago, still enjoy it as much as ever today.'

Another ad in the 200 years of Guinness series celebrates Guinness's connection with the farming community in Ireland (see Figure 2). This time, the years 1759–1959 are decorated with a garland. The style of the ad simulates a newspaper article and features a quote from the barley harvest: 'I expect you're off to Guinness as usual.' This underlines the importance of Guinness to the Irish agricultural economy at that time and reflects the assumption held by barley growers that Guinness would buy their crops. The ad copy allays any doubts that might have been held by farmers and says:

> Today, 800,000 tons of malted barley – including the roasted barley that gives Guinness its unique colour – are needed to brew over 2 million barrels, that is one year's supply of Dublin stout.

Figure 2: 200 years of Guinness – What a lovely long drink (agriculture)

Guinness signals its continued commitment to barley farmers when it states in the ad: 'to satisfy the ever-growing appetite of the huge kieves at St. James's Gate, Irish farmers have now under cultivation over 70,000 acres. And the acreage is increasing all the time.' The rural scene in the ad features two farm workers aboard a combine harvester, bringing in the barley harvest. Despite the fact that Ireland's dependence on the agricultural sector was set to diminish in the 1960s, the ad clearly shows that it still had a significant contribution to make to Guinness and a changing Irish economy.

Guinness: A key player in Ireland's economic success

Throughout the 1960s, Guinness continued to support the agricultural sector as evidenced in the 1965 press ad that depicts a conversation between a cattle breeder and a Guinness drinker:

> 'It's a fine head' the breeder exclaimed.
> 'Wait 'til you taste it' I said,
> taking a deep drink …
> 'Taste the head?' he said, looking surprised.
> 'I don't know what he thinks the head on a pint is for!'

In the background of the ad, there is a poster for an annual livestock show featuring a bull, while various glasses and two bottles of Guinness are in the foreground. In 1966, a number of press ads feature images of malting barley blowing in the wind. The accompanying headline in one states proudly: '75% of Ireland's malting barley goes into Guinness.' The body copy concludes: 'So Guinness does the farmer good in more ways than one.' Later that same year, a similar press ad is published but this time the headline is '80% of Ireland's malting barley goes into Guinness.' Both versions highlight Guinness's importance to a sector that was no longer as dominant in the Irish economy. A vibrant Guinness brewery had the ability to provide security and a steady income stream to barley farmers.

Also in 1966, Guinness advertised its support of the Cork Summer Show, and the Kildysart Agricultural Show. The same year, a TV ad 'Country Kaleidoscope' was broadcast. It depicts a typical agricultural show, and focuses on men viewing the equipment on display. One scene features a demonstration, showing how the machine can process a raw material such as barley, into a finished product that can be used by a brewery such as Guinness. The ad concludes with a bar scene, populated by men who attended the show. The deals are done, the cheques are written, and they are at various stages of consuming Guinness. The voiceover at the end reassures the viewer in soothing tones: 'Guinness – the most natural thing in the world,' thus implying that Guinness is an integral part of the types of rituals encountered at an agricultural show. However, as with many advertising themes, more than one meaning can be elicited from the words used. In this case, Guinness's natural properties are foregrounded, reinforcing the narrative that the ingredients in Guinness are natural, and that the drink itself is very much embedded in the Irish way of life. This tagline was used in twenty-four TV ads between 1965 and 1970, and was reproduced in many print ads at that time.

Another TV ad in 1966, 'Royal Dublin Horseshow', features one of the nation's most prestigious shows. It was first held in 1868, and although the ad showcases horses and show jumping, it includes images of farmers who attend the show in order to view agricultural equipment, and cattle. Yet again, the social aspect of such shows is underlined by interspersing scenes of show jumping, horses, and cattle, with images of a Guinness bottle being opened and poured into a Guinness glass, and images of men drinking Guinness in a marquee. The voiceover concludes the ad with 'Guinness – the most natural thing in the world.'

By publishing and broadcasting these ads, Guinness reassured farmers and rural dwellers that unlike many policy makers, it would not turn its back on them, despite the fact that the economic importance of urban centres was gathering pace. Workers are consumers, so by creating copy aimed at farmers, farm labourers, and their families, Guinness displayed a willingness to invest in maintaining this important customer base. It is likely that the ads would have resonated with a growing cohort of urban dwellers too who had migrated to the cities in search of work. Their identities had been defined by their rural upbringings, and many of them had parents, siblings and friends still living in rural Ireland.

It is evident from many of its press ads in the 1960s that Guinness wanted to position the brand alongside the rising fortunes of the Irish economy. Due to its prowess in the alcohol sector, it was ideally placed to do so in a very credible manner. According to Conniffe and McCoy (1993), alcohol was the largest non-agricultural export in the first thirty years of Irish independence, and in 1960 it accounted for more than 4 per cent of Irish exports. While this share had declined by 1975, the fall was due to the fact that a significant proportion of exports were accounted for by a new but highly influential sector, the multinational. In 1966, one ad proudly states: 'Every day well over five million Guinnesses put new heart into who knows how many Guinness drinkers the world over.'

That same year, other press ads, this time in the style of newspaper articles, draw attention to Guinness's contribution to the Irish economy: 'They [Guinness] are proud to be the largest private employer in the Republic, with almost 4,000 staff and employees. It is their policy to buy Irish materials and services where possible.' One of the 'articles' underlines Guinness's credentials as a global force, and recounts in journalistic style how travellers in the nineteenth century had found the drink in places like Brazil, Madagascar, and Russia (see Figure 3).

Another ad boasts how Guinness is 'The Best Selling Drink in Ireland, The Biggest Beer and Stout Advertiser in Ireland, The Biggest Exporter of Beer in the World.' These accolades tied in perfectly with the outward-oriented economy that Ireland had become, and they placed Guinness at the heart of its revival. In 1966, the business journal, *Statist*, published an ad that features a Guinness bottle with a tag attached stating £7 million, and body copy recounting how 'Guinness products account for 26% of all excise revenue. Guinness is Ireland's largest industrial export worth £7 million a year. Guinness is good for Ireland.' A 1967 press ad asks: 'Who sells over half a million bottles on average daily in Ireland?' while a 1968 ad declares, 'In over one hundred and thirty countries, six million Guinness are enjoyed every day.'

Figure 3: Guinness – that's a drink and a half (1)

At a local level, Guinness sponsored the Galway Junior Chamber of Commerce, and celebrated the alliance in a press ad. This underlined the growing importance of the business classes in Ireland at a grassroots level. As previously highlighted, before the implementation of Whittaker's economic policy, the agricultural sector employed more workers than industry. However, from the 1960s onwards, CSO figures show that the industry and services sectors accounted for almost three-quarters of Irish employment, rising to more than 80 per cent by 1981 (Kennedy and Giblin 1987). This shift is clearly depicted in the 1968/9 TV ad 'Working Ireland' which in some ways could be mistaken for an Irish Industrial Authority (IDA) ad, aimed at attracting manufacturers into Ireland. The ad opens with aircraft engineers working on a plane, and subsequently switches to a generic factory setting. Positioned in the middle of the ad is a bar scene that shows men and one woman at a bar, drinking Guinness. The final factory shown in the ad is a carpet factory, and improving TV production techniques are evident when a roll of carpet morphs into the head of a newly poured pint. Yet again, Guinness is shown as an integral part of working life and in this ad, it aligns itself with Irish workers. Guinness believes that it contributed to the transformation of the Irish economy and working life, and uses this belief to create this narrative in some of its adverts, thereby enabling the brand to connect with a new type of worker.

Guinness and early TV advertising

On 31 December 1961, Ireland's first TV service was launched. Since the late 1950s, TV set owners in some parts of the country, in particular Dublin, already enjoyed access to British channels and their cultural influences. Ferriter (2005) reckons that by the late 1950s, 40 per cent of the Irish population was able to access British television broadcasts, thereby exposing viewers to diverse, non-national influences. Allied to this, from the beginning, Irish TV relied on importing much of its content which, according to Fisher (1978), meant that it was subjected to criticism by Church authorities, in particular the Roman Catholic Church, and

Irish-language supporters, dissatisfied with what they considered to be a low level of Irish-language programming. In a scathing attack, Thornley (1964: 13) comments that: 'no greater barrier has ever been imposed upon any attempt at either moral censorship or cultural discrimination against foreign influences than the sheer inability of the native TV network to produce enough material to fill its own schedules.' Perhaps this criticism is unfair since RTÉ lacked the budget, resources, and expertise enjoyed by the BBC, at that time acknowledged as the world leader in the creation and provision of excellent programming. Therefore, it was inevitable that insufficient home-produced programming would necessitate the buying in of programmes from channel owners in the UK and the US.

Guinness was quick to recognise the power of TV and cinema as a way of taking advertising to a new level in Ireland, and of bringing its messages to a more diverse audience. By the 1950s, it had already broadcast its inaugural TV and cinema ads in the UK, made by the British advertising agency SH Bensons Limited, first appointed in the UK in 1929. Ironically, in a debate in the House of Lords in 1953 on television policy, Bryan Guinness (Lord Moyne) argued vehemently against the introduction of commercial television. In a speech where he positively declared his nationality, he delivered a searing attack against the proposed policy (HL Deb 25 November 1953):

> I believe that the majority of manufacturers would prefer this expensive and extravagant race never to begin; they say very little about it, because if it does begin they realise that they may be forced by the snowball effect of competition to participate, and they do not want to have to eat their words. I, being Irish, have a logical mind, and I see no difficulty at all in saying that I do not want this expensive race to be run, but that if it is run we might be obliged to go in for it and would acquit ourselves creditably. I do urge on the Government the advisability of seeing whether industry as a whole wants this thing started. I am told that it is the most expensive form of advertising in existence in proportion to the results obtained.

Despite his protestations, television policy to allow for advertising was passed into law and Guinness proceeded to engage in this new form of communication with enthusiasm.

Many of its early TV ads fell under the theme, 'Yes, Guinness goes so well with food.' Due to the drink's fulsome characteristics, this seemed counterintuitive, but it is an approach, which was pursued with great enthusiasm. While the ads were created for a British market, 40 per cent of the Irish population would have been exposed to them due to the rise in ownership of TVs with access to British channels. The ads were unambiguous in their intent, and that was to forge a link between food and Guinness.

The visual and aural signs in many of these TV and cinema ads were very significant in the context of the mid-1950s and subsequent years in both Ireland and the UK. In 1940, the British and Irish governments were forced to impose years of food rationing. It impacted to a far greater extent in Britain because Ireland's stronger agricultural base meant that meat and eggs were not rationed at all. Rationing remained in place for some years after the Second World War had ended, and even then, was only lifted on a phased basis. A news report from the BBC in July 1954 announced the end of rationing in the UK with the headline: 'Housewives celebrate end of rationing.' The headline provides an interesting perspective on society in the 1950s, and is quite categorical in its view that the end of rationing was of most relevance to women. Throughout the years of frugal supplies, it was the women of Ireland and Britain who were forced to stretch out their supplies in order to put together family meals. Avoiding the tedium of repetition must have been challenging, so the use of the word 'celebrate' in the headline was no exaggeration. The report goes on to chronicle the removal of the restrictions, starting with flour in July 1948, canned and dried fruit, chocolate, biscuits, treacle, syrup, jellies and mincemeat in May 1950, sugar in 1953, butter in May 1954, and finally, meat and bacon in July of that year. *The Irish Times* published a number of articles in the lead-up to the cessation of rationing in the UK, and like its British media counterparts, it looked at things from a woman's perspective. In a piece written in the lead-up to July 1954, the newspaper surmised that:

> British housewives, and especially the inexperienced younger ones who have never had an opportunity of getting to know the difference between a good joint of meat and a poor one, will get a 'break' in a month's time when meat rationing ends for them. (*The Irish Times*, 1954)

Mennell (1996) surveyed two women's magazines, *Good Housekeeping* and *Woman's Own* (both published in Britain but available in Ireland), just as rationing came to an end. He found that the narrative was about variation, cookery as a hobby, and as a method of showcasing social status to peers. As rationing neared its end in Britain, a consumer revolution was occurring. According to Winterman (2012), the wider availability of labour-saving white goods like washing machines in the home made it possible for housewives to devote more time to home baking, and the preparation of family dinners. These tasks were made easier with the arrival of specialist appliances, thus allowing women to create dishes more quickly and efficiently.

Some TV ads in the UK in 1950s, depicted the culinary repertoire of a 'typical' housewife, made possible with the acquisition of new devices, and the availability of a wide range of ingredients again. For Irish housewives with access to cinema and British TV channels, ads of this nature would have resonated. They celebrated the end of more than a decade of deprivation by featuring many of the products that had been rationed. Of particular relevance was the array of meats on show; roast leg of lamb, cocktail and chipolata sausages, fresh ham, joint of beef and roast Surrey fowl. The ingredients required for many of the featured foods included flour and butter, and here they were, resplendent in a feast-like setting, all topped off with creamy glasses of Guinness. Having endured years of rationing, images such as those presented in the ads, must have been uplifting, and suddenly attainable.

This theme was utilised in a number of Irish print ads in the 1960s with copy like 'Lunch isn't lunch without it (Guinness),' 'And food goes with Guinness,' 'The simplest of snacks is twice as tempting with a good creamy Guinness,' and 'It's the appetising taste of Guinness that makes it go so well with food.' The testimonial from the chef is symbolic because of his expert status. Even though Guinness and food together might have seemed unlikely, the seal of approval from a chef lends credibility to the claims. Borrowing from this idea, in 1965 and 1966, a number of press ads in Ireland feature the illustration of a chef with the accompanying headline: 'A good chef will tell you Guinness goes so well with food'.

When Guinness commenced advertising on TV in Ireland in 1963, it was the same UK-based ad agency, Bensons that was charged with creating ads specifically for the Irish market. The first TV ad in Ireland, 'Bar', went on to form part of a campaign known as the 'Sporting Series', which ran until 1965. The series featured hurling, Gaelic football, cross-country running and cycling. By the 1960s, cycling had woven itself into the fabric of Irish society, largely due to the popularity of the long-distance cycle race known as the Rás. Daly (2003) explains how the Rás was initially named Rás Tailteann in an effort to associate it with the Tailteann Games, and that it consciously tried to associate itself with nationalism. In 1952, the inaugural route started at the GPO, and Daly recounts how a group of cyclists laid a wreath at Cúchulainn's statue, a legendary hero who had died defending Ireland. The cyclists were members of the National Cycling Association, a group of nationalists who refused to recognise Ireland's partition. This stance ensured that they were banned from international competition. Cycling may not be as synonymous with Irish identity as hurling or Gaelic football, but this story, together with the sport's obvious popularity, may explain why Guinness wanted to associate with it. Meanwhile, Ronnie Delaney's gold medal at the Sydney Olympics in 1956 had sparked interest in athletics in Ireland. In the 1960s, the middle distance runner Noel Carroll became a very successful, high-profile athlete when he won a number of European Championship medals, as well as representing Ireland at the Olympics. Therefore, Bensons' decision to feature cycling and athletics, alongside the more traditional Irish sports portrayed in the 'Sporting Series', tapped into the love that Irish people have for several sports.

The 'Sporting Series' of TV ads lived up to its name, and variously feature athletes from hurling, Gaelic Football, cycling, and cross-country running, competing hard before retiring to the bar for what the ads describe as a well-earned Guinness. They were produced in fifteen-, thirty- and sixty-second formats, and in the sixty-second versions, a caption appears after six seconds: 'Inside sport with Guinness,' a clear signal that Guinness was keen to align its brand with sport. For approximately forty seconds, the focus is on the athletes as they compete in landscapes that are evocative of Ireland.

The cross-country and cycling routes take the viewer through scenes of rugged Irish countryside. The Gaelic football and hurling matches are played out in what appear to be country clubs, and the soundtrack to the sports scenes of the ads consists of feet running, the breathing of the athletes, the clash of the ash, the bicycle wheels rotating and some spectators urging their teams or men on. The ads suggest exertion and effort as the athletes compete to win, an early sign of intent that the Guinness brand imbued excellence.

The ads then cut to a bar scene. In one of the ads, the barman brings two glasses of Guinness in Wellington, tulip-shaped glasses over to two customers, most likely two of the cross-country runners. Interestingly, one of the men smokes a cigarette, something that would never be associated with sport today or, of course, permitted in an ad. One of the men puts down a newspaper before picking up his Guinness – it might be the *Irish Press*, a Dublin-oriented newspaper that is a good fit for Guinness's heritage. The voiceover declares dramatically in one version, 'And now, the best moment of all – a Guinness. That puts the strength back into a man. You've earned that Guinness' or in another version, 'When you've worked up a real thirst, you need a Guinness.' Throughout, the imagery and the copy are overtly masculine, and play on the relationship between sacrifice and reward. It is interesting that the bar in the ad is the domain of men only, thus reflecting the lowly status of women in Irish society at that time, especially when it came to pub culture. It was not until the second half of the decade that women appeared in Guinness's TV ads set in bars.

In 1964, the copy in Guinness's press ads reinforces the messages in the 'Sporting Series' of TV ads, and features head and shoulder shots of individual males bringing Wellington or tankard-style glasses of Guinness towards their mouths. In all cases, their attire reflects the social change that had gathered momentum in the 1960s, the migration from rural to urban dwellings, the growing numbers of the middle class, and the move away from agricultural work. In this particular series, the men are dressed like office workers, (sometimes) with glasses, tweed jacket and shirt and tie. In the 1960s, this would have been considered a very contemporary image, almost like a uniform for Irish men (see Figure 4).

Figure 4: Guinness – that's a drink and a half (2)

In 1964/5, and running in parallel with the 'Sporting Series', a series of cartoon ads was broadcast. They all show workers that might have been more or less associated with a changing Ireland – a bricklayer, an office worker, a sculptor and a window cleaner. All are shown surveying their completed work, be it a brick wall, an emptied in-tray, a sculpture or a high-rise building of clean windows.

The voiceover directs his chat to the cartoon figure throughout: 'Done a good job? Done a job and a half? Well then, you need a drink. You need a drink and a half.' At this point, the ad switches to a real person, a man clad in a jacket, shirt and tie, picking up a glass of Guinness stout, and bringing it to his lips as the voiceover purrs: 'Guinness – mmm-marvellous! That's Guinness.' With eyes closed, he takes a generous sip of the stout, before putting the glass down again, and licking his lips in a satisfied manner. The closing shot shows a pint of stout and the tag line, 'A drink and a half,' also uttered by the voiceover artist. The music is jaunty and light, bearing no cultural relationship to Irish musical references.

The occupations featured in the ads could be carried out in any urbanised society, and are not peculiar to Ireland at that time. Perhaps that is what Guinness is trying to convey – by 1964, Ireland's economic and social transformation had taken hold, and its population was just as comfortable in urban surrounds as it had been in a rural Ireland. The sculptor ad features a happy looking craftsman leaning happily against a completed piece of work that resembles Rodin's seminal piece, 'The Thinker'. This work is often used in philosophy books, and symbolises deep thought. Although the execution of the ad has child-like qualities, the underlying meaning and symbolism is perhaps aimed at connecting with a more educated audience, thus reflecting the growing importance of education at that time.

While the accent of the voiceover artists in the TV adverts is Irish, it is typical of the type of trained voice adopted at that time by newsreaders and commentators on the fledgling national broadcaster. Taking its lead from the experienced BBC, RTÉ coached its staff in a delivery style that imitated the intonations and inflections used by its British counterparts. It is clear from these ads that Guinness followed suit, and employed voiceover artists capable of reproducing the 'RTÉ accent.' This enabled the ads to fit in with environment in which they were being viewed.

Travel and tourism

Television was not the only significant cultural influence in Ireland in the 1960s. Ferriter (2005) refers to the democratisation of travel and notes that in 1964 visitors to Ireland from Continental Europe and the United States increased fourfold. Similarly, at the same time, Irish people embraced the concept of holidays, and as well as the rise in popularity of the foreign package holiday, domestic tourism grew. Changing employment patterns facilitated travel because, unlike agricultural jobs, industrial and service jobs did not tie the worker to the workplace. Therefore, this growing cohort of domestic and international tourists was looking for attractions to enhance their holidays in Ireland, so Guinness used this as an opportunity to promote visits to the St James's Gate Brewery.

The 1965 ad, 'Ireland is famous for', identifies some of Ireland's most famous exports, including 'Tweed from Donegal,' 'Linen from Belfast,' 'Crystal from Waterford,' and, of course, 'Guinness from Dublin,' before alerting tourists to the fact that 'the Guinness Brewery in Dublin is a famous sight' (see Figure 5). By associating with other famous Irish products, Guinness positioned itself strongly as an essential inclusion on any tourist's itinerary, be they domestic or foreign.

The following year, the company published more press ads in domestic and international newspapers, inviting tourists to visit the home of Guinness. They feature a cartoon drawing of the brewery, and a couple standing outside saying 'So this is where the Goodness comes from,' or in the case of the German version, '*Daher kommt also die Gute!*' (see Figure 6).

In 1968, more press ads inviting tourists to visit the Guinness Brewery at St James's Gate were published in Ireland, France and Germany. Depending on where it is published, the headline is 'Guinness (just look at it!),' 'Guinness (*Mais regardez-la donc!*),' and 'Guinness (*Sieh' dir das an!*).' The decision by Guinness to promote St James's Gate Brewery as a tourist attraction was both insightful and lucrative. It was already a well-established fixture on the tourist trail by the 1990s when Ireland and Dublin enjoyed an explosion in the numbers of overseas visitors. According to Pope (2018), the Guinness Storehouse remains the most popular fee-paying attraction in Ireland and in 2017, a record 1,711,281 visitors passed through its doors.

Figure 5: Ireland is famous for

Figure 6: *Daher kommt also die Gute!*

Guardians of Irish culture

Numerous efforts were made by the authorities to curb the spread of outside influences. There was what Ferriter describes as Archbishop McQuaid's crusade against 'foul books,' and the GAA's ban on what they perceived as foreign sports, which remained in place until 1971. The Irish language was languishing, as evidenced by the Commission on the Restoration of the Irish Language in 1965 (Brown, 2004). So, in 1966, De Valera used the fifty-year commemoration of 1916 to try and revive it. Once again demonstrating its awareness of current affairs, press ads published by Guinness that year supported Irish cultural events, while others contained Irish text. For example, the brand advertised its support for the Sligo *Feis*, an event that is committed to protecting Ireland's language and cultural heritage.

One advert in 1966 assertively states 'Guinness – *gan dabht*,' meaning 'Guinness – without doubt.' Another ad, aimed at theatre enthusiasts advises audiences in Irish '*Cosaint Tine – Síos le Guinness amháin i rith gach léiriu'* – which, when translated, means, 'Fire protection – down a Guinness during every performance.' It is worth noting that before and after the year of the attempted revival, Guinness published Irish-language ads. Once again, this supports the argument that it did not merely follow trends. Instead, in some instances, it was a trendsetter. In a 1961 press ad, a glass of Guinness is featured with the accompanying headline '*An leann dub as dublinn* – Guinness', which means 'The black beer from Dublin Guinness.' In 1968, another Irish-language press ad was published simply stating 'Guinness *maitheas ó fhréamh*,' which means, 'Guinness, goodness from the roots.'

Also in 1968, two versions of the TV ad 'Festival' were broadcast, one featuring a voiceover at the end: 'Guinness – the most natural thing in the world.' The Irish-language version uses the same imagery but signs off with a voiceover in the Irish language saying, '*Dúchas d'ól duit*,' which can be translated as, 'The homeland of drink'. This line emphasises Guinness's sense of place and deep association with Ireland, whereas the English-language version focuses on the product and its ingredients. As the name given to the ad suggests, the ad itself is set at a festival in a rural Irish town, and it features people participating in various games, typical of that time. As well as incorporating the Irish language into the ad, the visual imagery celebrates Irish culture, and the importance of community to the rural population at that time. Again, women are cast in a passive role, mere spectators at the festival, whereas the only participants in the games are men. To the twenty-first-century viewer, this seemingly blatant sexism arouses indignation, but at that time, it was the norm and would not have raised an eyebrow.

Breaking down barriers: Portraying women in the pub

In the latter half of the 1960s, tentative signs of women's changing societal status emerged. Female membership of trade unions rose, ownership of domestic electrical appliances became more widespread, and between 1966 and 1971, the numbers of married women at work rose by around 60 per cent (Ferriter 2005). Conversely, Ferriter stresses that various political and legislative roadblocks frustrated the pace of change, not least a refusal by the 1968 government to adopt the 1952 UN convention on the political rights of women by not waiving the law preventing married women from working in the civil service. As if to reflect these tentative changes, Guinness began to reach out to women with their ads. A press ad in 1966 highlights Guinness's support of the Soroptomist Club, founded in 1966 to advance the lot of women in management and professions.

A number of TV ads in Guinness's 'Irish Life' series between 1965 and 1970 attempted to make women part of the narrative. Some of the bar scenes include at least one woman, and, in 1965, 'Young Man – Dublin' features a young couple going up to a bar to order drinks. The woman follows the man's lead, and asks for a half pint of Guinness. The presence of women drinking in bars in Ireland was a relatively new phenomenon, and reflected a change in Irish social mores. Nevertheless, an air of subservience is maintained (the man ordering the drink and influencing the woman's choice, in his case a pint, and in hers a half pint), thereby perfectly reflecting the slow, deliberate pace at which women were being liberated. An analysis of the remainder of the ads in the series underlines its adherence to the social mores of the 1960s in some instances, while in others, its intent to pre-empt, and possibly drive, change is clear.

Many of the ads in the series reinforced the gender stereotypes that prevailed at that time. In the 1965 ad, 'Friends', no women are present in the bar. It tells the story of three male friends who gather in a pub, and as well as socialising, their *raison d'être* is to repair and pump up a deflated football. The ad captures the close bond that exists between the men, and their mutual love of sport is evident. They all drink Guinness and throughout the ad, there are shots of bottles of Guinness, a Guinness tap, and Guinness in tankard and tulip-style glasses. Throughout, the bar is depicted as a sanctuary for men, a place where they can meet and indulge their interests, unencumbered by the presence of females. As previously mentioned in the introduction to this book, Stivers (2000) identifies the low marriage rate that prevailed between 1870 and 1940 as the most important societal factor that contributed to Ireland's male-dominated drinking culture.

Five TV ads from 1966, 'Golfer', 'Long Bar', 'Round Bar', 'Race Meeting' and 'Party', underline Guinness's contrasting approaches when it came to developing advertising themes. In a few instances, the themes challenge, in others they reinforce the status quo. 'Golfer' re-enacts scenes from a golf club, most likely on a Saturday when women were not permitted to play golf at private member clubs. The ad alternates between shots of male golfers teeing off and putting, and players enjoying glasses of Guinness in the clubhouse bar. It concludes with a still-life composition consisting of glasses of stout at various stages of consumption, alongside the all-important score cards from a day's golf. Of course, at that time, the bar in a private golf club was off limits to women on any day of the week, so Guinness is merely communicating in a realistic style. To include women in the ad would have been fantastical, and may have caused offence to some of its loyal customers.

As its name suggests, 'Long Bar' features a very long bar, and the camera pans along it to show men and one woman sitting and standing alongside it. With the exception of the woman, everyone is either drinking or being served Guinness. She appears to be drinking a soft drink, which is presented to her by a male companion. On close examination, the glass might carry the Guinness logo, but the liquid is clear. Conversation at the bar is lively and convivial, but the clothes worn still depict formality, in keeping with the times. The barmen wear white overcoats, which were typical workwear in bars in the 1960s. Unlike the 'Young Man' ad, there is no attempt to promote Guinness to women. However, there is a sense that her inclusion at the bar symbolises an attempt to remove women from the background.

Meanwhile, in 'Round Bar', women are seated at tables near the bar, and well-dressed men in shirts, ties and jackets place their orders. Many of the men drink Guinness and while the women do not, there is a suggestion that at least one of them may be about to imbibe when one of the men is heard ordering: 'Two pints and a glass.' Like 'Long Bar', there is an air of conviviality as the people engage in conversation and some smoke cigarettes. The soundtrack to the ad is the same as that used in other ads in the series, but this time it is played in a relaxed, yet sophisticated, lounge style. There is no sense of Irishness in the music but the voiceover at the end is in an Irish accent: 'Guinness, the most natural thing in the world.'

'Race Meeting' opens with two women dressed in twinsets and hats, standing at the side of a racecourse. They focus on setting up a small picnic table, and their servile role is underlined when a man's arm appears, placing a six-pack of Guinness on the table. His work is done whereas the implication is that the women are responsible for ensuring that the accompanying food and utensils will appear on the table. Further imagery of a race meeting, including a jockey, a punter ticking a betting slip, and a race are interspersed with images of Guinness being poured from a bottle, and men taking drinks from a glass. In the midst of the vignettes portraying stereotypical behaviour for men and women, a man and woman enjoy a Guinness together in an outdoor bar. Perhaps it is the temporary nature of the drinking establishment that makes this proposition socially acceptable, but the concluding scenes of the ad revert to men drinking Guinness. In the closing scene as the voiceover says: 'Guinness, the most natural thing in the world,' a man's hands tear up a betting slip before he picks up a glass of Guinness. Like drinking in public, betting was an activity deemed more socially acceptable for men at that time.

Based on his study of advertising in the US in the 1920s and 1930s, Marchand (1985) concluded that it was acceptable for women to be portrayed in advertising as 'modern' and enjoying 'male' activities, as long as their domestic responsibilities were not neglected. This double standard is evident in 'Race Meeting' because at the start, the women are responsible for setting up the picnic but because they have fulfilled this task, they are rewarded with a Guinness. This type of 'modern' representation of women was probably acceptable at the time because 'it threatens neither patriarchal nor capitalist hegemony' (Goldman 1992: 131).

While there is nothing particularly radical or ground-breaking about the portrayal of a race meeting, the 'Party' ad from the same year takes a much more liberal approach, and seems in keeping with the Swinging Sixties. The setting is a house party, attended by men and women. The gender divide is less evident, and both sexes mingle and engage with each other on an equal footing. Their behaviour and appearance seem to symbolise the change that is starting to take hold in parts of Ireland, and while the men are dressed in shirts, ties and jackets, their female counterparts are wearing very contemporary (for that time), fashionable clothes, including above-the-knee dresses. One woman sits with her legs curled under her on a sofa, and she has discarded her shoes. This pose is in stark contrast to the formalities typically portrayed in Guinness ads at that time. While there are no shots of women drinking Guinness, they are not peripheral to the scene, and are enjoying the party just as much as the men. A woman hosts the party, and at no point in the ad is the viewer led to believe that she is doing so on behalf of a man. Instead, she is portrayed as a confident, independent woman, most likely with a career of her own, who greets one particular new arrival bearing a take-out pack of Guinness with a mixture of relief and enthusiasm: 'Don, oh good – you've brought the Guinness.' The implication is clear: the party cannot truly commence without this very important ingredient.

Another ad in the series, 'Take Home', in 1968/9, portrays a couple in a bar having a Guinness before going home with a takeaway pack of the same libation. Again, the man orders the drinks but the woman sips from a glass of Guinness. The woman's clothes are very fashionable and she appears to model herself on one of the decade's most famous style icons, Jackie Kennedy. This suggests that she is at the forefront of societal trends, including the consumption of take-out alcohol brands.

However, most of the ads in the series focus on men drinking Guinness, and the overwhelming majority of the bar scenes that include women show them either drinking soft beverages or nothing at all. Guinness might have alienated some of its customers if it had given women more significant roles. By taking an evolutionary approach that involved their gradual introduction, the concept of women in bars was not considered too shocking, and viewers grew used to the idea in the ads and in pubs themselves.

Conclusion

The first decade of ads created by Bensons for Guinness in Ireland helps paint a picture of Irish society in the 1960s, a time when Ireland and Guinness were coming to terms with a rapidly changing environment. The moment Lemass turned his back on the protectionist policies of his predecessors, he gave Irish businesses the opportunity to expand into foreign markets. In doing this, he opened Ireland's borders to foreign companies and the competition that accompanied them. Previously unavailable job prospects opened up to Irish workers and in some instances these were enhanced as educational attainment among the general population improved. Societal structures evolved as more workers joined the ranks of the middle classes and found employment in the manufacturing and services sectors. Guinness's ads reflected Ireland's newfound prosperity by depicting well-dressed, professional workers in many of their ads. Nevertheless, in the 1960s, agriculture remained the mainstay of rural Ireland, as regularly represented in Guinness's ads throughout the decade. However, armed with education, many young people migrated towards the opportunities afforded by urban settings.

While it might be claimed that Guinness's ads merely mirrored changing societal norms, it could equally be argued that Guinness might have had a role to play in bringing about some of these changes. As if emboldened by the decline in births to women with more than two children, Guinness might have helped their quest for equality by showing women socialising in pubs, or drinking Guinness. This gradual acceptance laid the foundations for Guinness to print ads in the 1970s that portrayed women-only groups enjoying a sociable drink together, thus revealing a considerable shift in societal norms.

By featuring indigenous sports like hurling and Gaelic football alongside internationally accepted sports as diverse as cricket, cycling and bowls, Guinness reflected a softening of the attitude of GAA officials towards the ban on foreign sports. Meanwhile, Guinness's decision to publish and broadcast Irish-language ads revealed its understanding of the challenges facing Ireland's fledgling republic at that time. In order to grow and prosper, Ireland had to, and did become more outward-looking. While, as demonstrated in this chapter, this was a positive move, it posed challenges to the survival of Irish culture. Guinness's willingness to draw on themes peculiar to Irish culture is evident in many of its ads in the 1960s – indigenous sports, language, cultural events and past-times. In those early days of Guinness's advertising in Ireland, the provenance of the brand was clearly aligned to Irish culture, but it exhibited an ability to use themes that represented Ireland's transforming societal landscape.

Having been around for 200 years, Guinness possessed the confidence to draw on its own past, and Ireland's rich heritage, while in many instances being able to embrace the changes of the 1960s. It went even further than this, and at times it used its advertising narrative to influence Ireland's future.

CHAPTER 2

1970–1979: Emerging voices

The 1970s and change is afoot

The 'Irish Life' series of TV ads continued right up until 1970, and by the end of the series, they really start to mirror and promote the more significant societal and cultural shifts in Ireland. In a sense, the ads mark the beginning of a metaphorical abandonment of the shackles that had kept Irish people and hierarchies in check. A more relaxed, informal air begins to emerge in the ads, and in many instances, men and women interact freely. As if setting down a marker for the 1970s, the 1968/9 ad 'Sport' focuses on sports that are aspirational and not particularly associated with the general Irish public – water skiing, boating and stock car racing. Participants need money and in the 1960s, they would have evoked images of a glamorous and previously unattainable lifestyle. In a lakeside scene, a group of men and women is served Guinness from a tray that holds two pints and one glass. Nothing in the ad suggests that the glass is not intended for the woman. Their clothes symbolise a freedom that is not evident in many previous ads. Gone are the shirts, ties and jackets for the men, and in their place are turtleneck jumpers, while the women wear fashionable, tight-fitting trousers. They are confident and relaxed with each other, and the air of servitude appears to be gone, at least in the ads.

In 1970, one of the final ads from the 'Irish Life' series, 'Cruising' continues to promote Guinness as part of an aspirational lifestyle. Images of a cruise boat ploughing through the water, a relaxed woman sitting at the helm, and a group of smiling men and women mingling on a boat, signify an attempt by Guinness to position the brand as a drink that is central to leisure time. While it is not stated in the ad, Guinness's acquisition of the Emerald Star boating holiday venture enables the company to turn the ad into reality for some viewers. The voiceover is soothing and plays on the brand name: 'Anchors away, it's a great day, far, far away – Guinness is there. How's that for neatness. Something to eatness.' At the mention of eating, the boat is moored, and the occupants (male and female) run energetically ashore to a table laden with food and a six-pack of Guinness. Even though the setting is in Ireland, the camera switches to an outdoor swimming pool, with a woman lounging beside it. A pint of Guinness appears in the foreground, and the voiceover purrs: 'So up on your feetness' accompanied by a shot of a man's feet in a pair of plimsoles resting on the side of a rowing boat. When the man in question brings a tankard glass of Guinness to his mouth, the smile on his face exudes happiness and satisfaction. The sun is shining and this adds to the air of wellbeing in the ad. As well as being the drink of the working man, this ad places Guinness at the heart of leisure activity for Irish men and women, providing the ideal springboard for a less formal, and more inclusive style of advertising in the 1970s.

Still part of the 'Irish Life' series, the 'Now you're OK' TV ad from 1970 portrays an Ireland that has assumed a less provincial demeanour. A man with a suitcase enters a crowded Irish bar, and his light coloured suit sets him apart. He appears well travelled, cosmopolitan, sophisticated and wealthy. However, the voiceover in the ad clarifies for the viewer that he is most likely Irish when he says: 'You've noticed the change.' At this point, the camera focuses on the women in the pub as the new arrival surveys the scene. In many of the previous ads from Guinness, pubs were the domain of men, so the presence of women might be surprising to someone who has been out of the country for a while. The voiceover reassures him: 'But it's really the same,' as an older man pouring a Guinness comes into focus. 'Well, that isn't so strange – Guinness is here.' The voiceover continues in comforting tones and plays on the word Guinness when he says: 'But when you've been awayness and you're back home to stayness, you know what to sayness. Guinness is here.' Fellow customers greet the visitor, and he holds a pint aloft, using the universal sign to signal 'Cheers' to his new companions. The soundtrack to the ad is very generic and does not draw on Ireland's rich musical heritage. However, the harmonious humming is warm, welcoming and comforting.

Unlike Irish emigrants from previous decades, the new generation of travellers could leave and return, thanks to the improvements in the economy and transport links with the rest of the world. Those who came back to Ireland brought with them diverse cultural experiences. They were no longer consigned to a life away from Ireland but their return in the 1970s presented challenges for established drinks companies like Guinness. Before leaving Ireland, many emigrants would have been familiar with Guinness, and would have consumed it, because there were not many alternatives. As stated earlier, this changed at the end of the 1950s when the government dropped its protectionist policies, thereby opening the door to new, imported drinks.

It was not just in Ireland that Irish people were exposed to new drinks. According to Ferriter (2005), more than 110,000 Irish people took holidays abroad by the 1970s, and this gave them the opportunity to sample many aspects of the different cultures that they visited. Likewise, emigrants would have been able to try alternative products. Therefore, in the ad 'Now you're OK', Guinness reminds the well-travelled drinker that: 'There's more than goodness in Guinness.' It is an integral part of being Irish, and the moment the man in the ad takes a sip from his Guinness, he feels at home again.

In 1970, another TV ad from the series once more acknowledges the existence of a cosmopolitan, well-travelled cohort of Irish people in 'Friendships'. The ad is set in a busy pub, filled with people of various ages. The voiceover asks: 'Travelled all day? Well … stop on the way. You know what to say.' At that point, a group of young, vibrant men and women dressed in casual but fashionable attire explode into the pub, and the atmosphere livens up. Guinness is poured and the voiceover says: 'Guinness is there.' A man moving in time to the backing track plays a flute, and a young woman dances enthusiastically. Her movements lack the constraints of previous decades, and she shows no sign of self-consciousness. The voiceover continues: 'We'd stay until darkness but best friends must partness,' once again playing on the 'ness' in Guinness. The young people leave the pub but their brief stay has energised those who remain. The focus switches to an older man at the bar, perhaps an attempt by Guinness to stand by its traditional customer. The voiceover addresses him when he says: 'Don't take it to heartness. Guinness is here – more than goodness.' Throughout the ad, men and women are represented as equals, and this equality applies to their drink of choice too, Guinness.

While the approach can seem trite to a contemporary viewing, these ads enjoyed success at the time. Even the emphasis on 'ness', which may grate on the ears, did achieve its purpose of linking the ideas being propounded to the product.

Evolving economic landscape and changing alcohol consumption patterns

The export-led, outward-looking policies of the 1960s continued to gather pace in the 1970s. According to Haughton (1987) by 1974, 60 per cent of Ireland's industrial output was accounted for by new, IDA-subsidised, foreign companies. Nolan (1987) analyses the importance of these companies for the Irish economy, and states that three-quarters of the increase in total employment in manufacturing between 1960 and 1973 was accounted for by foreign-owned subsidiaries based in Ireland. He highlights the fact that the Irish economy grew by a robust 4 per cent per annum between 1961 and 1973, but that this rate weakened somewhat as a result of the global economic slowdown that came about after the first of the oil price shocks that occurred in late 1973. This coincided with Ireland joining the European Economic Community (EEC) on 1 January 1973, a decision that Haughton says raised expectations of greater prosperity, and a more European outlook. The effect of Ireland's sustained and growing involvement with countries in Europe and the rest of the world was palpable. However, Haughton reveals that their impact was not as significant a factor on Irish growth rates as they might have appeared because from 1977, the government embarked on a politically motivated policy of borrowing in order to stimulate the domestic economy, and maintain economic growth. He notes that real expenditures on building and construction increased by 9.7 per cent per annum between 1977 and 1981. While this fiscal policy helped create jobs and prosperity amongst those in employment, it would prove to be unsustainable in the longer term. Meanwhile the growth rate in agricultural output remained relatively stable between 1973 and 1986 at 1.5 per cent. However, employment in the sector continued to decline, decreasing by a further 3.5 per cent in the same period (Nolan 1987).

Declines in other sectors were less pronounced, and Conniffe and McCoy's (1993) analysis of the CSO Census of Industrial Production reveals that employment in drinks manufacturing between 1975 and 1979 was fairly stable. Numbers involved in the production of beer in Ireland peaked at 4,800 in 1975, and while they declined to 4,590 in 1977, they were back up at 4,789 by the end of the decade. According to sources at the Guinness Archive, numbers employed in production at St James's Gate were around 3,600 in the late 1960s, and by the late 1970s, they had fallen to around 2,500. Despite the decline, St James's Gate accounted for just over 50 per cent of the employment in the Irish beer production sector. In 1977, a £7 million brew house was opened at St James's Gate (Yenne 2007). Most likely, this entailed labour saving automation equipment, thus contributing to a decline in employment levels at the brewery. However, the author singles out the new bottling line in 1977 at Guinness's brewery, Irish Ale Breweries in Dundalk, which exceeded previous sales records.

As stated by Conniffe and McCoy (1993), overall alcohol consumption per adult in Ireland increased very significantly between 1960 and 1991. It rose by 83 per cent, and within that, beer consumption went on an upward trajectory throughout the 1960s up until the early 1970s. In referring to these authors, and the work of Walsh (1980), some of the opportunities and threats faced by Guinness at that time are identifiable. Significantly, Walsh examines the trends in alcohol consumption in Ireland and illustrates a changing competitive landscape. He finds that in 1950, only 28 per cent of alcohol consumption was in the form of spirits and wine, whereas this had risen to almost 40 per cent in 1978. Taking data that he compiled from the Annual Reports of Revenue Commissioners, the changes in consumption patterns since Guinness's 200th anniversary in 1959 are clear. In that year, alcohol consumption per head of population aged 15 and over, in litres of 100 per cent alcohol, was 4.67. Beer enjoyed the lion's share of this (3.43 litres) whereas consumption rates of spirits and wine were just 1.08 and 0.16

respectively. By 1969, overall consumption per head had jumped to 6.80 litres, and beer, spirits and wine consumption had risen to 4.59, 1.93, and 0.28 litres respectively. By 1974, overall consumption had increased significantly to 9.44 litres, and of this beer, spirits, and wine consumption were 6.19, 2.82, and 0.43 litres respectively. By 1978, consumption was 9.64 litres per head, and the growth in popularity of spirits was more pronounced, standing at 3.35 litres, while intake climbed to 0.56 litres per head. While beer consumption grew to 5.79 litres, by then its share of consumption had declined from 73.4 per cent in 1959 to 60 per cent in 1978. Over the same period, the share enjoyed by spirits and wine had grown from 23 per cent and 3.4 per cent, to 34.75 per cent and 5.8 per cent respectively. Consumption by visitors to Ireland is included in Walsh's figures. This in itself is significant because, as in the 1960s, income from tourism doubled, and in 1964 alone, there was a fourfold upturn in continental and American visitors to Ireland (Ferriter 2005).

Walsh (1980) contends that the surge in alcohol consumption in Ireland resulted from the higher incomes enjoyed by Irish people during the economic revival of the 1960s and early 1970s. However, Conniffe and McCoy (1993) identify a disparity between rural and urban consumption patterns in this period, a difference that they attribute to lower incomes in rural areas. McCoy (1991) suggests that Irish alcohol consumption rates started from a relatively low base because of the growth in national and international movements espousing temperance and abstinence from alcohol. In this regard, he points to the role of the Gaelic League and the Pioneer Total Abstinence Association in the late nineteenth century. From an international perspective, he highlights the more extreme measures adopted in countries like the United States and Finland between 1919 and 1933 where prohibition was imposed. The post-Second World War period saw a reversal of this trend, which led to an increase in the consumption of alcohol. McCoy (1991) finds that Ireland lagged behind the trend for higher consumption, and that abstinence was still practised in large numbers in the 1950s. Based on Walsh's (1980) contention that alcohol consumption levels relate to income levels, the growth in the intake of alcohol from the 1960s onwards might have less to do with temperance than with economic prosperity.

As shown in the statistics above, throughout the 1960s, the market for beer in Ireland was very dominant when compared to the alternatives, spirits and wine. When Guinness commenced advertising in Ireland in 1959, the themes of many of its ads suggest that it feared the government's outward-oriented economic policies would result in much greater competition from foreign beer manufacturers. Previous analysis in Chapter 1 reveals that the purpose of many of the ads in 1959, and much of the 1960s was to remind audiences of Guinness's longevity and contribution to the Irish economy. In my opinion, their aim was to pre-empt the arrival of new competitors, and to position the Guinness brand and its beer as being a very important part of Irish life. However, Conniffe and McCoy's (1993) analysis of the CSO's trade statistics reveals that by 1975, just IR£300,000 worth of beer was imported into Ireland, whereas IR£14.2 million worth of beer was exported. While a 0 per cent tax on profits from exports remained in place until 1980, Irish breweries benefited from the export-driven regime, and until the 1980s, the proportion of imported versus exported beers remained low. However, this did not mean that Guinness could rest on its laurels. As outlined above, in the 1970s opportunities existed for Guinness and its competitors to increase sales in the domestic market as beer consumption among Irish consumers continued to grow, but so too did consumption of spirits and wines.

As a response to the changing competitive environment, Guinness published a number of press ads in the 1970s, which focus on the product's point of difference. This is in marked contrast to many of the print ads in the 1960s, which concentrate on the strengths and longevity of Guinness the company. In 1970, one particular print ad tackles its direct competitors head-on with the headline: 'If all these new ales and lagers confuse you – here's something that won't.' The copy that follows aims to make purchase decisions easier: 'Guinness. The dark fantastic. In these changing times, at least one thing hasn't changed. Guinness. In a bottle. Nothing new. No gimmicks. Strong, dark and reliable.' Guinness empathises with the reader, and recognises that Irish people are living through a period of significant change. For some people, this can be daunting. The body copy in the ad continues with its reassuring tone: 'So when all these ales and lagers confuse you, there's still something that won't. Guinness. The same as ever. Don't keep it bottled up. Enjoy it.'

Other print ads draw the reader's attention to key visual, taste and ritualistic attributes associated with Guinness, attributes that help set the drink apart from its rivals. For some consumers, these so-called features might explain their reticence to drink Guinness. It is known as an acquired taste, and with the arrival of more instantly palatable options on the market, some people may not have been prepared to persevere with Guinness. The challenge for the advertising agency, Arks, was to write copy that would transform these negatives into positives that might appeal to wary, sometimes impatient consumers. The tone in a 1972 print ad is educational, and breaks the pint of Guinness down into its constituent parts. It introduces the 'lesson' by telling the reader: 'But for those who would like to know a little more about Guinness – and cannot spare the time to visit our brewery at St James's Gate – we'd like to point out a few things about this pint.' The ad explains that the head 'is cunningly designed to stay with the drink right down to the last drop.' An air of mystique emerges when the copy debates the intricacies of the body of a pint of Guinness:

> You must drink this mysterious darkness up through the head. This is part of the Guinness ritual. Because only by drinking it this way are you able to savour fully the unique Guinness taste – and isn't that why you bought your pint in the first place?

The language used about the body is emotive, almost sensual, and invites the uninitiated drinker to persevere with the prescribed ritual, which will reward them in the end. The concluding section in the ad, headed 'The purpose' empathises with those reluctant to drink Guinness when it says: 'Most of this may seem a little fussy when all you really want is simply to enjoy a good pint.' Without actually saying so, Guinness acknowledges the fact that its competitors' products are less complex. They are easy to pour, and do not require a particular methodology when consuming them. The ad moves quickly to assuage worries about this inconvenience, and promises that those who persist will be rewarded:

> But remember, everything has a purpose. That purpose may become clear only when you have finished the whole pint. Maybe not even then! But don't give up. It could

> be clearer the next time you order a pint. Rest assured, you will discover it. That is the moment when you suddenly realise that the pleasure in a pint of Guinness is a pleasure no other drink can equal. It is unique. And *that* is the whole point of a pint.

A 1977 print ad admits that drinking Guinness is challenging when compared to other drinks. In order to convey its message, the ad builds its theme around the very popular movie, 'Jaws', which was released in 1975. The headline: 'It bites' is positioned above a cage containing a pint of Guinness in a tankard-style glass. Subsequent text belittles competing ales and lagers, and presents the reader with a challenge: 'Almost anybody can tame an ale or a lager. But a Guinness? That's different.' Guinness's natural ingredients are emphasised, establishing them as a point of difference: 'Some people will tell you Guinness has a bit of a bite. That's the kiss of the hops. Refreshing. It brings out the true zest in the brewing barley. And it's one of the things that makes a Guinness a Guinness.' The acknowledged challenge of drinking Guinness is addressed: 'Once you master that smooth sharp flavour, no ordinary beer will do. So tell your taste buds they're growing up. Who knows – they may even enjoy it.' Like many of Guinness's ads in the 1970s, the ad concludes with the tagline: 'You're at home with a Guinness.' These words have an emotive charge, and aim to establish a bond with drinkers, whether they are in Ireland or abroad.

Also in 1977, a print ad was published bearing the headline: 'The beginner's guide to goodness' (see Figure 7). Due to increased competition, many drinkers chose more palatable options that did not require much time before the taste for them was acquired. Clearly, the ad is aimed at the lucrative young drinker segment, and the copy adopts an amicable, empathetic tone: 'Remember when "a shandy" was as close as you'd come to ordering a drink? Then you moved on to lagers and ales. But sooner or later your taste buds blossom and grow up.' These words endeavour to make drinkers question their choices heretofore, at which point the ad assures the reader:

> And you're ready for a Guinness.
> The creamy head looks appetising.
> The drink down under is deep and dry and surprisingly refreshing.

With a bit of a bite that's just right.
Before you're very much older, you'll probably order another.
It could be the beginning of a beautiful friendship.

Figure 7: The beginner's guide to goodness

The copy in a 1972 ad, 'Get close to your Guinness (it looks even better)', has sexual nuances, and compels the audience to get to know their pint of Guinness intimately (see Figure 8):

> When you get really close to your Guinness, close enough that it's almost touching your lips, pause briefly; look at that tender creamy head poised delicately at the rim of the glass. Then close your eyes and swallow. There's a feast for the eyes, too, in Guinness.

Figure 8: Get close to your Guinness

It might be inferred from the copy that the bond formed with Guinness is more satisfying than that which comes from the instant gratification experienced when drinking competitors' products. By getting close to Guinness, consumers might enjoy a lasting bond, one that will satisfy them at every encounter. The overflowing pint supports the language in the ad and might be construed to symbolise a sexual climax.

In 1973, the print ad that advises readers to: 'Start at the top and work your way down,' concentrates on the ritualistic behaviour associated with drinking Guinness.

> Building a career usually means starting the hard way at the bottom and working your way up. It's different with a pint of Guinness. You start at the top and work your way down. It's so much easier. And much more fun.

A cartoon character holds a pint of Guinness in one hand and a thick cigar in the other. His pinstripe suit and the image of his bowler hat, which hangs on a coat-hanger in the background, identifies him as one of Ireland's growing number of professional, urban managers.

Meanwhile, a pithy print ad that same year reassures drinkers who might be considering a switch: 'Familiarity breeds content.' Its candour challenges readers and the twist on the familiar maxim causes them to stop in their tracks. In a wordier ad, Guinness admits that it might have a rival, but it is from within its own ranks: 'Draught Guinness has only one real rival.' It transpires that the rival: 'comes in a bottle. It's black. And it's called Guinness.'

By 1970, Guinness had appointed Arks, an Irish advertising agency, to create and produce all of its ads for the Irish market. Between 1971 and 1974, they created a number of TV and print ads known collectively as the 'Get together with a Guinness' series. One of the ads entitled 'The first one' brought the theme of drinker uncertainty to the TV screens, thereby reinforcing the message contained in many of the print ads. The ad focuses on two men standing at a bar, looking over at a young, attractive woman. The barman hands them two pints of Guinness, and at that point one of the men sees a familiar figure reading at the bar. He exclaims, 'Hey, there's Fergus,' and orders another pint. They announce to Fergus: 'It's about time you had a pint of Guinness,' while at the same time presenting him the pint. Fergus appears nervous and unsure. In portraying this, Guinness acknowledges the fact that the drink challenges the uninitiated. Fergus takes a tentative sip, after which he says: 'I like it.' He takes another sip, and offers the same positive reaction, and after another sip, he declares very enthusiastically: 'I like it.'

The tone in these ads is both nurturing and educational, at once drawing parallels with observations made in Ewen's (1976) book on advertising. In it, he introduces the views of American businessman Edward Filene who, in the 1920s and 1930s advocated the need for producers to use advertising to educate the masses in order to sell their mass produced products. It was only when Ireland's economy opened up to the outside world in the late 1950s that manufacturers like Guinness saw the need to 'educate' Irish consumers. In these ads, it is quite literally educating young drinkers in an attempt to distract them from competitors' less complex offerings.

The rationale behind campaigns like 'The first one' explains why Guinness deemed it necessary to develop a less 'challenging' stout in order to discourage young men from sampling competitors' beers. In 1979, Guinness Light was launched and according to Gluckman (2017), it was specifically aimed at 18- to 24-year-old males. He explains that before its launch, extensive market research was conducted and the feedback was extremely positive. It looked just like Guinness but it was not as heavy, a characteristic that won overwhelming approval from those who participated in the research. An expensive advertising campaign accompanied its launch, bearing the infamous line of copy, 'They said it couldn't be done,' and along with matching merchandise, it was distributed throughout Ireland. However, to the surprise of Guinness, it seemed that no amount of marketing could make the beer a success so they commissioned David Gluckman and his business partner to find out why. In an interview with one young man, they uncovered a problem with the new product that would prove impossible to solve. The interviewee explained what happened when he went to the pub:

> I walked into my local bar and it was decked out with Guinness Light material. It was everywhere: posters and beer mats. There were even special Guinness Light pint glasses. It all struck a chord. I remembered seeing a TV advert for it and I decided to order a pint. It appeared in its special glass and looked pretty tasty. But as I put it to my lips a hand tapped me gently on the shoulder and a man said 'You're cheating. You're drinking ladies' Guinness.'

Based on this young man's experience, the promotion of the product could not be faulted. The TV ad had made an impression on him and this was reinforced with the point-of-purchase material in the pub. However, the intangible properties of a brand are often more important than the tangible manifestations. This is because a brand says something about the person using it. However, if it does not say the right thing, people will not buy it. The original Guinness beer was associated with strength and for many Irish men, it was worth the effort of acquiring a taste for it because once initiated, it bestowed kudos on the drinker and the right to be admitted to an Irish club. Therefore, Gluckman surmises the main reason why young men rejected Guinness Light: 'Who wanted openly to advertise that they couldn't manage "the real thing"? Not in the 1970s and not in Ireland.' In spite of all the societal changes that occurred in the 1970s, Ireland was still a very male-oriented society where masculinity and stoicism were expected of men and such expectations extended to their capacity for alcohol. The failure of Guinness Light proved that in 1979, Guinness and Irish manhood were inextricably linked, so much so that a lighter version of the famous stout could not be countenanced. Upon reflection, it was clear that Guinness made a fatal error when attaching the word 'Light' to a brand that had come to mean strength.

The 1970s: A seminal decade in redefining women's role in Irish society

Despite the economic improvements that came about in Ireland from the late 1950s onwards, they did not precipitate a noticeable change in the status of women. Their position in society was sustained by legislation dating back to the 1920s, and a Constitution that according to Scannell (1988: 127) relegated women to 'domesticity and powerlessness … Laws based on the premise that women's rights were inferior to those of men survived in and indeed appeared on the statue books.' Based on research conducted by the United Nations in 1995, O'Connor (1998) concludes that improved economic activity does not necessarily hasten the prioritisation of gender equality among the political classes. This view is supported by her analysis of the CSO's 1997 census. She found that by 1971, only 27 per cent of women of working age were at work, compared to 76 per cent of eligible men, and just 13.6 per cent of married women formed part of the work force. Kennedy (1989) reveals that just over 60 per cent of the women not participating in the labour force in 1971 were engaging in what the CSO describe as home duties. In her analysis of the sectors that employed women, she found that in 1961, agriculture accounted for 15.1 per cent of women at work, compared to 22.2 per cent and 62.7 per cent in industry and services respectively, while by 1971 the percentage of women employed in agriculture had decreased significantly to 9.2 per cent, a figure that would more than halve to 4.3 per cent by 1986. Meanwhile, the number of women working in industry had risen slightly to 24.5 per cent by 1971, and in services to 66.4 per cent. With the exception of agriculture, the changes between 1961 and 1971 are not very large. However, they mark the beginning of an irreversible trend, the trajectory of which was set in the 1970s. By 1986, 74.6 per cent of women in the labour force were employed in the services sector. Significantly, this sector includes nurses and clerical workers, careers that would have been closed to married women up until 1973.

The reasons for low female participation rates can be attributed to a number of legislative, economic and social factors. As far back as 1925, the Civil Service (Amendment) Act was enacted due to what Galligan (1998) describes as a crisis in male employment. Crucially, it allowed the government to limit employment opportunities solely on the grounds of gender. An equally punitive and regressive edict was enacted in 1932, which excluded married women from public and civil service employment. In 1957, married female teachers were exempt from this ban, but the Act was not rescinded completely until 1973. O'Connor (1998: 8) identifies solidarity among men as:

> An important element in maintaining the position of men relative to women in society. At an informal level, such ties might be associated with an unwillingness to challenge certain kinds of behaviour towards women and children.

In Ireland, this solidarity manifested itself in many walks of life, such as the exclusion of women from employment opportunities, from some sports clubs, most notably golf clubs, and limited access for women to bars in public houses. Trade unions were reluctant to take up the gender equality cause because, according to Galligan (1998), they were concerned that if the battle for equal pay were won, male pay would decline. One of the most influential forces in Ireland throughout much of the twentieth century, the Roman Catholic Church was a patriarchal hierarchy, which prohibited (and still does) the ordination of women priests. In tandem with the family values embedded in the Constitution, the Church promulgated a moral code that was observed by large swathes of the population. This fostered a conservative, sometimes fearful population that upheld the teachings of the Church. These teachings helped maintain the patriarchal society, which in turn sustained the type of Ireland set out in the Constitution, an Ireland that treasured the ideal of family and motherhood within the confines of marriage.

For a while, the dominance of the agricultural economy in Ireland conspired to maintain a labour market that was more suited to men. With the change in direction in government policy at the end of the 1950s, the manufacturing and services sectors grew, and consequently there were more clerical jobs available, jobs that could be done by women. The transformation of the Irish economy created an environment where, according to Kennedy (1989), women could enjoy greater earning power by engaging in the labour force. She acknowledges that a reduction in fertility resulting from the wider availability of contraception for married women in the 1970s meant that the time spent rearing children was reduced. This phenomenon, allied with the growth in women's participation in education, meant that by the 1970s, there was a greater likelihood that women would want to enter the labour force. However, without political will, and radical legislative change, this would not be possible. While not written specifically about Ireland, Yuval-Davis's (1993: 626) research is applicable to the status of its women at that time when she posits:

> There is one characteristic which specifies women's citizenship. That is its dualistic nature: on the one hand, women are always included, at least to some extent, in the general body of citizens of the state and its social, political and legal policies; on the

> other hand, there is always, more or less developed, a separate body of legislation which relates to them specifically as women.

The ban on married women in the civil service is just one example of a law that perpetuated the dualistic nature of women's citizenship. Legislation can of course be implemented in such a way that it positively discriminates in favour of women, but such policies were not evident. Yuval-Davis (1993) concedes that since women are not often depicted as the agitator, this positions them as outsiders to the political domain, thus making it difficult for them to influence societal change. As previously mentioned, by the end of the 1960s, some women had begun to challenge the status quo, and were agitating for change, buoyed by domestic and international supports and events that magnified their voices. From an international perspective, the United Nations (UN) and the EEC advocated and legislated for greater gender equality but the Irish government chose to ignore UN guidelines, and as Ireland was not yet a member of the EEC, it was not bound to introduce its legislation. However, Ireland wanted to join the EEC, and if its application were to be accepted, it would have to change its draconian laws that prevented women from participating fully in the labour force.

The Irish media was very influential, and television in particular exposed Irish viewers to cosmopolitan influences. As will be illustrated later, these influences were often captured in advertisements, which were broadcast during domestically produced, and imported programmes. O'Connor (1998) suggests that television offered the general public a more outward looking viewpoint than the one predominantly given by the Roman Catholic Church. A number of female journalists were prominent in the women's movement, and gave it access to the media. It was against this backdrop that the women's movement gathered pace in the 1970s, a decade that Connolly (2003) considers a period of advancement in Irish feminism. She posits that the movement mobilised along two opposing ideological constructs. They were women's rights, which pursued gender equality through legal and political paths, and the other was women's liberation, which was more radical and espoused a social stance.

For reasons outlined above, the government was forced to pay more attention to the gender equality issue, and in 1970, Jack Lynch established the First Commission on the Status of Women. According to Connolly (2003: 97), its purpose was to:

> Examine and report on the status of women in Irish society, to make recommendations on the steps necessary to ensure the participation of women on equal terms and conditions with men in the political, social, cultural and economic life of the country and to indicate the implications generally – including the estimated cost – of such recommendations.

The interim report was delivered in 1971, and recommended equal pay and the removal of the marriage bar. Its recommendations were not implemented immediately, but 1973 heralded the removal of the marriage bar in the civil service, and in 1974, the Anti-Discrimination (Pay) Act was brought in. Both of these concessions were less to do with the interim report, than with the government's desire to join the EEC, and the realisation that it would be obliged to comply with EEC directives. Galligan (1998) contends that administrations of a more socialist persuasion are more likely to espouse the women's movement. Therefore, another catalyst for these legislative changes may well have been the election of a Fine Gael/Labour coalition government in 1973. The Anti-Discrimination (Pay) Act was welcomed by women, but some employers and trade unions lobbied successfully for the postponement of its implementation on the grounds of inability to pay, and resultant losses of male jobs. However, women refused to accept this, and successfully lobbied the Commission in the EEC to direct the government to implement the pay legislation. In the final throes of the same government in 1977, the Employment Equality Act was enacted so that, according to Galligan (1998), Ireland would comply with an EEC directive.

While political advancement of the women's movement was taking place, activists mobilised to address some of the more contentious social issues concerning women. Many of the protagonists were journalists in leading media outlets, which helped bring the issues to the notice of the general public. In 1970, the Irish Women's Liberation Movement (IWLM) was formed, and according to Connolly (2003), its membership was made up of left-wing and Republican activists, as well as professionals, journalists, and university-educated women. While the IWLM disbanded after a couple of years, it left its mark, and famously staged the Contraceptive Train to Belfast in May 1971. This brought the issue of the lack of availability of contraception to the fore, with some of the central characters appearing on *The Late Late Show*. However, Connolly (2003) observes that this radical move caused a split in the IWLM because it alienated moderates who wanted gradual change, and inspired activists who wanted to push harder. This latter group continued to agitate for change, and in 1975, Irish Women United (IWU) was formed. Its core issue was the legalisation of contraception, and in 1976 it initiated the Contraceptive Action Programme (CAP). According to Galligan (1998: 142), the struggle for access to contraception cannot be underestimated in the context of the women's movement:

> The contraception controversy can be taken as a reflection of the changing nature of Irish society in the course of a generation. It represented a visible weakening of restrictive social norms and religious orthodoxy and it became a focus for liberal voices in parliament and public life. Significantly, it mirrored a silent revolution on the part of women, changing in a fundamental way the nature of women's relationship with society.

The issue did not go unnoticed by politicians, and due to the work done by CAP, Fianna Fáil committed to introducing legislation on contraception if it were elected in 1977. It did win the election but it took seventeen months in office before it published the Health (Family Planning) Bill in 1978. It was a cautious bill, limiting access to contraception to prescription, and it exempted chemists with ethical objections to contraception from dispensing it. Galligan (1998: 151) sums it up well when she describes the quest for contraception for married and unmarried adults alike as:

> A struggle for dominance between the views of liberals and conservatives and between secular and denominational forces … a conflict between the status quo and the forces of change around sexual matters and morality.

As already documented in Chapter 1, it is evident that by the mid-1960s, some of Guinness's ads reflected the mood in some quarters for greater gender equality. However, it was not until the 1970s that the women's movement gathered momentum, and this is clearly reflected in many of Guinness's ads during this period. Feminism was not the only factor driving the interest in appealing to women through advertising. McCoy (1991) notes that while women traditionally drink less than their male counterparts, by 1991 there was considerable convergence of gender drinking patterns. The downside of this is demonstrated by Walsh (1980) who reveals that with the exception of 1971, there was a significant jump in the death rate of females from cirrhosis of the liver per 100,000 population aged 15 and over. In 1970, the rate was 3.6, compared to 2.6 in 1961, and by 1977 it had climbed to 4.4. By comparison, in 1961 the rate for males was 4.3, in 1970 it was 6.1, and by 1977 it was 5.6. While it is not intended that these statistics be viewed in a positive light, they do reveal that by 1970, women were consuming more alcohol. This trend, allied with the legislative changes affecting women in the labour market, declining fertility rates, and the growth of jobs in the services sector, represented an opportunity for Guinness to grow its market by targeting a relatively untapped group of consumers. In light of greater competition in the drinks market, recruitment of new customers would have been a very important priority.

In 1970, a print ad specifically aimed at women was published. It reflected a stereotypical view of women's interests, and ran with the headline: 'Fashion Note.' Beneath an illustration of a glass (not pint) of Guinness in a Victoria goblet, the copy picked up on the fashion theme:

> A charming creation in traditional dark material featuring a creamy white collar. Its timeless elegance is never likely to date. Note the refreshing use of barley, hops and pedigree yeast. Available waisted or tulip line or with plain glass finish.

The ad concludes with: 'Goodness from the house of Guinness (marc well),' firmly positioning Guinness as a premium brand that might be compared with some of fashion's leading couture houses.

A more contemporary take on the fashion theme is executed in a 1972 print ad (see Figure 9). Beneath the simple headline 'Chicness' is an image of a young woman sitting in a pub, holding a glass of Guinness. She looks directly at the camera with an enigmatic, sensual gaze. She wears a very short, fashionable dress that just skims the tops of her thighs. Her style is cosmopolitan, and she appears confident. She represents the new generation of Irish women, and she would fit in just as well in a pub in London or Paris. Beneath her image is the tagline: 'There's more than goodness in Guinness.'

Figure 9: Chicness

This tagline is used in a number of print ads in 1970 that portray men and women as equals. One of these ads features a crowd of men and women gathered around a piano (see Figure 10). Everyone has a glass of Guinness and the women are participating fully in the fun. One of the women is young, and trendily clad in a contemporary dress of the type that might be seen on fashion-conscious young women in London, while the other woman and the men are dressed in the type of conservative attire that would have been prevalent in the 1960s. The ad conveys a sense of the old and the new, therefore giving it wide appeal.

Figure 10: Get togetherness

A popular way for food and drinks companies to appeal to a female audience is to emphasise the dietary benefits of their products. By the 1970s, Guinness was synonymous with the 'Guinness is good for you' moniker, and the health benefits were promoted frequently. However, just being 'good for you' might not hold sufficient appeal for women. One concern frequently cited by women when consuming beer is the calorific content. In a 1970s print ad, Guinness attempts to address this concern by addressing women directly. The headline is a rallying call: 'Free to women! The Guinness Diet … or how to reduce weight without being reduced to tears.' An illustration of a Guinness in a goblet style glass, adorned with a measuring tape, is at the centre of the ad. The copy is empathetic and upbeat: 'The Guinness Diet shows you how to lose weight … and enjoy it!' In order to add authenticity to the claims, and to form a tangible relationship with consumers, women are invited to send away for a free booklet that contains details of 'a seven-day diet, with complete menus for three meals every day.' Guinness attempts to take the drudgery out of dieting and reassures women: 'We think you'll enjoy The Guinness Diet. Because it shows how slimming can be a pleasure.'

In 1972, in another example of a print ad representing gender equality, a man and woman are depicted drinking Guinness at home as they put the finishing touches to the Christmas decorations. The woman is at the front of image, holding her drink while she works. The man is in the background, focused on pouring his Guinness. The positioning of the woman is important because it signifies the moves that are being made to achieve gender equality. There is no suggestion of a hierarchy in the ad, the man and woman are equal and they are enjoying the same drink. Like so many of Guinness's ads at that time, a take-out pack of Guinness is foregrounded, capitalising on the growth in drinking in the home.

In 1973, Guinness published a press ad that overtly acknowledges one of the changes, albeit a less important one, that came about as a result of the women's movement in the 1970s. Clearly aimed at both men, and women, the ad's headline is: 'His and Hers' (see Figure 11). It goes on to present a scenario that would resonate with women in the 1970s: 'There was a time, and not so very long ago, when no respectable woman would be caught dead wearing trousers. Or drinking a dark, elegant glass of Guinness.' While

Figure 11: His and Hers

the idea of women wearing trousers seems trivial today, their inclusion in a woman's wardrobe at the end of the 1960s and early 1970s was a radical departure, and symbolised freedom and change. The ad acknowledges this change when it states matter-of-factly: 'Trousers and Guinness were for men only.' Pairing these two stalwarts of Irish masculinity might have persuaded women who up until then would never have worn trousers but now did so with enthusiasm, to consider drinking Guinness. The ad puts it up to women when it says: 'And now that you're wearing trousers, isn't it time you had a Guinness.' This line might be taken as a signal of Guinness's solidarity with the women's movement, as it appears to imply that it believes women have more power, an implication inherent in wearing trousers.

A colour print ad from the same year that was published in *Woman's Choice* magazine has a conspiratorial tone to it. In the foreground of the image, three women, professional in appearance and attire, sit around a table, talking to one another. Two of them drink Guinness, while the third woman has a cup of what looks like coffee. Two men are relegated to the background of the image, but one of them appears to look longingly at the glass of Guinness in one of the women's hands. The headline is retaliatory: 'Men have been keeping a good thing to themselves for long enough.' The body copy goes further and asks:

> Why, of all the drinks in the pub, should Guinness, dark, mysterious Guinness, be the last preserve of male chauvinism? Is this a male bid to keep the best things in life to themselves?

The tone in these questions has a radical edge, but as if reaching out to the moderates in the Irish feminism movement, Guinness balances the ad by responding in a more conciliatory tone: 'No. It's simply a tradition. A tradition that's fast disappearing. Thank Guinness! Liberate a Guinness. And taste the good life.'

Again in 1973, a colour ad was published in the women's magazine, *Woman's Way* (see Figure 12). Four women gather in someone's home. Wearing contemporary, fashionable clothes, they sit on cushions at a low table, upon which there are two glasses of Guinness a bowl of fruit, and a bowl of snacks. On the floor, in the foreground of the image is a six-pack of Guinness, flanked by two unopened bottles. The women appear relaxed. The only copy in the ad reads: 'Afternoon tea. Get together with a Guinness.' For many women in the 1970s, the lifestyle represented in the ad is aspirational, but by removing men from a social occasion involving drink, Guinness broadens the types of scenarios when women might enjoy drink.

Figure 12: Afternoon tea

A number of TV ads between 1971 and 1974, depict women's growing confidence. Initially, 'Happy Couple' represents the Ireland of the 1960s. It is set in a crowded pub, and the camera zooms in on a middle-aged man and woman who appear to be drinking gin and tonic. The man has a worried expression on his face, and his wife warns him: 'Don't forget, we'll be with Mary's mother and father. For your son's sake don't talk about horses and don't go ordering pints for everyone.' His facial expression turns to despair, and he says (to himself): 'Cruelty to husbands, that's what it is!' His wife's monologue continues when all of a sudden, Mary and the couple's son arrive. She continues: 'Since meeting Mary, he's been a changed lad, I'm telling you.' Mary is a friendly, confident young woman, and greets her future father-in-law. She leans towards him, and when she sees the gin and tonic, she asks in a puzzled tone, 'What's that you're drinking?' Then she whispers in his ear 'Wouldn't you rather a nice pint of Guinness?' He admits that he would, and Mary retorts, 'Well, while you're there, will you get me one too?' He laughs conspiratorially, and smiles at his wife triumphantly. The ad concludes by showing Mary and the couple drinking Guinness. The mood has changed, and Mary's future father-in-law gives his seal of approval: 'Sure, the lad doesn't know how lucky he is.' The tagline 'Get together with a Guinness' appears on screen, emphasising the sociable aspect of Guinness. Mary's behaviour in the ad is in stark contrast to that of the woman in the 1965 ad, 'Young Man'. In that particular ad, the woman takes the lead from her boyfriend, and behaves in a very demure fashion.

Another ad in the series, 'Noisy Party' is set at a crowded house party. A young man makes his way towards two fashionably dressed young women. He carries a tray of drinks, which includes a pint of Guinness in a tankard glass. He gives a drink to one of the women and apologises to the other saying that 'they didn't have what you wanted.' She responds with a disappointed 'Aw', and the man almost seems to gloat as he hands the pint to another man at the table. Smiling, the 'disappointed' woman grabs the Guinness and says: 'Mmm, I'll have a taste of yours then.' He is crestfallen but she merely responds: 'Mmm, nice'. In the final scene, she says to the man who lost his pint to her: 'Didn't you get one for yourself then?' The woman's behaviour underlines the diminution of social mores, and the growing confidence of women to express themselves.

By 1977, the imagery in the print ads captures the growing confidence of Irish women, and the greater equality that exists between men and women. A series of print ads with the tagline 'What's a Guinness between friends?' portrays couples in informal, sometimes intimate poses. This is a noteworthy signifier of social change in Ireland. In most instances where women and men were portrayed together in the 1960s ads, there was a formality, and an assumption that any of the couples in the ads were married or engaged. Signs of change were palpable towards the end of that decade, mirroring the growing interest in gender equality that bubbled beneath the surface.

Figure 13: Cooling

In 1977, a series of print ads was published featuring couples drinking Guinness in a holiday setting. In one of the ads, the woman is seated in a relaxed pose, and wears a bikini that reveals an ample cleavage (see Figure 13). A man sits beside her, and he wears a swimsuit. In the background, the out-of-focus scene comprises other women wearing bikinis, seated on sun loungers, and at tables beneath sun umbrellas. Despite the couple's choice of drink, the setting seems foreign, possibly Spain, and acknowledges the growth in package holidays taken by the Irish. However, the striking difference between this ad and ones from the 1960s is the nature of the relationship between the couple. The 'What's a Guinness between friends?' headline implies that they are not married, and yet there is an intimacy between them that they display with ease in public, despite the fact that they are scantily clad. There is no suggestion of subservience by the woman, and the only indicator of gender difference is the size of the Guinness glasses. She drinks a half pint, and he drinks a pint.

Staying with the 'What's a Guinness between friends?' theme, Guinness continued to feature men and women in their ads in 1978. In instances where couples are featured, intimacy is conveyed, be it through a touch or sitting in a relaxed pose with arms around one another. Once again, the word 'friends' in the headline emphasises the societal shift in Ireland. That men and women can be friends and equals, and that couples can display their intimacy in public without being married represents significant change. A Christmas print ad portrays a convivial social setting where the women in the ad outnumber the men. A group made up of two women and a man is foregrounded. All are drinking Guinness, he a pint, and the women glasses. The smiling women appear confident.

Another such ad features a man and woman crouched on a riverbank. They are dressed in angling attire, and the woman holds a fishing rod in one hand, and a glass of Guinness in the other. The man holds a glass of Guinness, and nothing else. In front of them, two salmon are displayed on the grass. The contrast between this ad, and fishing themed ads in the 1960s is unambiguous. In the 1960s ads, the men are the anglers. In 1978, the woman's firm grip on the fishing rod communicates that she is just as involved in the pursuit as the man.

A print ad in the same series features a greyhound in the foreground. Behind him, a couple stand close together, smiling at one another fondly. The woman hugs the winning trophy in one arm, and a glass of Guinness in the other. The man holds a glass of Guinness in one hand, and his other arm is around the woman's waist. Again, even though a team effort is implied, the woman is portrayed as the victor, maybe even the team leader.

Despite Guinness embracing the women's movement in many of its ads in the 1970s, some ads still pandered to the more traditional status of women in Ireland. An example of this is evident in the 1970 press ad that features a traditional dresser stacked with flowers, delft, a Guinness bottle, and a glass of Guinness (see Figure 14). The headline 'Cupboard loveliness' suggests domestic bliss, and the copy in the ad speaks directly to the stay-at-home wife: 'When he comes home in the evening and you've got something special to tell him, or worse, to ask him, try a little cupboard love.' This sentence paints a picture of a household where the man is in charge, and the woman happily indulges his needs. In fairness

Figure 14: Cupboard loveliness

to Guinness, it is still very representative of the times because, as previously stated, in 1971 only 27 per cent of women worked outside the home. The ad appeals to the conservative consumer, and positions Guinness as a product that will sustain domestic bliss: 'And what could be lovelier than Guinness stowed away lovingly for times like these? So when you can't think how to begin … begin with Guinness because Guinness says so much so well.'

A 1974 poster follows a similar vein. Its objective is to promote the takeout pack of Guinness, but the main body copy reaches out once more to the stay-at-home wife: 'You're his better half. So you know what's best. And what could be better than Guinness? For when he comes home. For when he needs a bit of Goodness. And to say that you've thought of him – well a Guinness does that, too. Guinness says so much so well.'

Timelessness, continuity and heritage

Another advertising strategy that is often used by market leaders like Guinness when facing increased competition is to build a campaign around the product's history. It is an angle that younger, less-established companies cannot utilise. As discussed in Chapter 1, Guinness frequently used the 200-year anniversary and its long history to promote its beer between 1959 and 1969. In the 1970s, some ads drew openly on its long history. A print ad in 1970 with a musical theme features the Guinness harp, Arthur Guinness's signature, and the headline 'Symphonyning.' The ad is accompanied by copy that underlines Guinness's longevity, and prowess on the market: 'Performed 9,000,000 times daily (with glass accompaniment) by barmen all over the world, this symphony has won the hearts of the public since its first performance in 1759.' A print ad that was first published in the Irish Export Directory in 1971, features a bottle of Guinness and the headline: 'Guinness – famous all over the world for over 200 years.' A variation on the copy in this ad was published in 1972, bearing the headline: 'Over 200 years … goodness!' That same year, a print ad featuring the stamp used to celebrate Guinness's bi-centenary in 1959 harks back to themes used in the brewery's early ads in Ireland.

In 1972, an ad was created specifically for publication in *Castles, Houses and Gardens of Ireland*. Today, this is an online directory service, which as its name suggests promotes Irish castles, houses and gardens to interested parties. In the 1970s, it was a print publication, and the ad features a pint of Guinness in a tankard-style glass, complete with the Guinness logo, and a strapline: 'also part of our heritage.' Guinness positions itself as a brand with a heritage that can be compared to some of Ireland's oldest and most treasured buildings and amenities. A colour print ad in the same year reveals how the role of a sales person is still a job most associated with men in the 1970s. Below an appealing photograph of two pints of Guinness and a ploughman's lunch sitting on a bar, the copy that accompanies the headline, 'The Inn Drink,' paints the picture of a travelling salesman's lot:

> Next week, as usual, you'll have five problems. Monday, Tuesday, Wednesday, Thursday, Friday. And five lunchtimes. Consider the alternatives: There you'll be, far from wife and oven, confronted with the choice of boring directors' dining room or the nearest pub.

The copy nudges the reader towards the pub option because:

> We have a drink you might enjoy.
> It's not, perhaps, as subtle as Montrose, nor as expensive as Lafite, but it does have a dry, distinctive taste that goes down remarkably well with almost any pub food, from oysters to steak and kidney pudding.

This excerpt revives the message that Guinness promoted so vigorously in the UK from 1929 up until the 1960s, and to a lesser extent in Ireland in the 1960s, that is, that Guinness and food go together. Then follows copy that draws attention to the brand's heritage and popularity, when it identifies a drink that the reader might enjoy: 'It's called Guinness. We invented it in 1759 for drinking in pubs, where, currently, several million glasses are drunk every day.' In 1977, a witty print ad invites the reader to: 'Take up Irish history tonight.' Guinness is not mentioned by name but the content of the history lesson is made clear with the image of a head of Guinness stout in a glass with the Guinness harp. When a brand is able to omit its name in lieu of visual clues, it infers success, notoriety, and confidence on behalf of the owner.

As well as the print ads highlighted above, some TV ads in the 1970s underline the brand's longevity, but their main thrust is to reassure audiences that despite the immense change taking place in Ireland at that time, Guinness is a constant, something upon which the consumer could depend. The 1974–6 *Timelessness of Guinness* series of TV ads portrays the Guinness brand as being trustworthy and resilient. In the ad *Changing Taste*, the main actor transitions through a number of costume changes that bring him on a journey through time. At the start of the ad, he wears an eighteenth-century costume of jodhpurs, boots, top hat and tails, most likely dating back to 1759 when Guinness was founded. The accompanying voiceover says: 'Over the years, men's tastes in fashion have changed quite dramatically – from ruffles and laces to this.' Then the main character changes into a late nineteenth-century suit and hat, at which point the voiceover says: 'In fact, their tastes seem to change all the time, with one exception – Guinness.' The actor holds out a pint of Guinness and the voiceover states proudly that: 'The dark drink with its rich creamy head has remained consistently popular since the 1700s.' At this point, the man changes into a 1920s striped blazer and boater hat. The next change of clothes sees the actor in a contemporary 1970s three-piece suit, before he is transformed into a David Bowie-style space suit, an outfit that would have been seen as very futuristic and cutting edge for that time. The actor is not happy with this change and says: 'Just a minute, this is going too far,' upon which he reverts to the 1970s suit. The voiceover says: 'The unchanging quality of Guinness is very much to a man's taste.'

A second man in a contemporary suit joins the actor and they walk away from the camera, talking and each holding a pint of Guinness. The final frame of the ad is a still, featuring the Guinness harp and the text: 'Guinness – men's tastes haven't changed.' Reassurance is at the heart of the ad and while some changes cannot be avoided, preferences for Guinness can remain the same and will still be satisfied by the reliable, long-standing brand.

Cultural references from outside Ireland are evident in the execution style of the ad. Firstly, the BBC's children's cartoon series *Mr Benn* was very popular in the 1970s. The central premise behind his adventures was his costume changes that transported him into different eras. Secondly, the visual references to another BBC favourite from the 1970s, *The Morecambe and Wise Show*, are evident in the stark studio setting of the ad. The actor stands in an all-white studio, and, at the end of the ad, when he and the second man walk away from the camera, they reference the iconic manner in which Morecambe and Wise closed each show. Finally, when the actor dons the silver space suit, not only is the highly influential pop icon, David Bowie, being referenced, but so too is the decade's interest in space, and the accompanying imaginings about what space, and its inhabitants, might be like. The use of international cultural themes in ads aimed at Irish consumers underlines the expansion in the diversity of influences to which the Irish population was being exposed at that time.

Another TV ad in the series, *Holiday*, concentrates solely on the space theme, and using humour, plays on the frequently discussed fantasy in the 1970s of what it might be like to live on another planet. The TV series *Star Trek* was very popular in the 1970s, and made fantasies of living and travelling through space imaginable to the general public. Arks harnessed this theme in a humorous way to show viewers that even if their space fantasies were realised, Guinness would remain the same. The setting is a futuristic bar with clean lines, and the customers wear space age, silver costumes. The backing track is ultramodern, a sound achieved by synthesisers, which grew in status and popularity in 1970s popular culture. The dialogue between the two main characters in the ad is delivered in broad Dublin accents, and their exchange is awash with nostalgia.

CHARACTER 1: 'It's terrible the way they're changing everything.'
CHARACTER 2: 'At least there's one thing they haven't changed.'
As both men near the end of their pints of Guinness, Character 1 asks: 'What's that?'
CHARACTER 2: 'Guinness – do know my father, and his father, and his father before him, they all drank it.'
CHARACTER 1: 'What?'
CHARACTER 2: 'Guinness – and my great-grandfather lived to be 103.'
CHARACTER 1: 'Imagine that!'
CHARACTER 2: 'There's history in Guinness.'
In a wistful tone, Character 1 admits: 'I like a bit of history.'

While the ad is humorous, the exchange between the two men underlines the pace at which change is occurring in Ireland at that time, a rate that causes anxiety in some people. The caption at the end of the ad reassures: 'Guinness, it's got a great future.'

The TV ad 'Ye old Tavern' is set in an eighteenth-century tavern, populated with working-class men and women. The women are barmaids, not customers. The main interaction is between a young farmer and an older man. The older man is nostalgic about harvests past: 'Would I were that age again and a strapping lad. They were the good old days, when summer really was summer and winter … the harbour be frozen over. Aye, Guinness was Guinness in those days.' The ad picks up on an insight into the age-old obsession that Irish people have with weather, a phenomenon that symbolises change and uncertainty. The closing caption in this ad is a reassuring: 'Guinness, straight from the good old days.' Yet again, popular culture is referenced in the ad, this time in the tagline, which connects with fans of the long-running, BBC show, *The Good Old Days.*

A sense of identity

In the past, identity was largely determined within the confines of a nation's boundaries and was easily understood and interpreted. However, identity is not a static construct but evolves in response to new and changing influences. Ward (2009) acknowledges this and states that depending on the agenda favoured by key influencers like politicians and the media, particular elements of a nation's identity might be emphasised or downplayed. The evolution of Ireland's identity is testament to this. Perhaps the country's many upheavals can be attributed to its island status, a geographical reality that makes its people open to many influences, from economic and political to cultural and technological. However, equally it could be argued that in the past, this geographical isolation has served those with the ability to influence the shape of Ireland's identity very well.

Archbishop McQuaid's leadership of the Roman Catholic Church in Dublin brought with it a period of introspection and conservatism when the majority of the Irish population was aligned to conservative Catholic values, all of this at a time when secularism was on the rise in mainland Europe. In their article on national identity, Maguire and Tuck (2005: 88) build on the concept of *habitus* posited by Elias and describe it thus:

> At the social level, there reside a collection of personality characteristics which individuals share with other members of 'their' group. The social habitus of people forms a foundation from which more individual feelings can develop.

This definition provides some insight into the reasons why the 'managers' of national and brand identities might intervene to reinforce or accentuate certain personality characteristics shared by the Irish or by consumers who might purchase a particular brand. McCoy (1991) makes reference to Blaney's analysis of the Irish race's disposition to alcohol, which he refers to as the 'Irish Trait,' whereby Irish drinking is used to bond with people. The trait is a common theme in Guinness's advertising, and throughout the 1970s, several print and TV ads impart the convivial advice: 'Get together with a Guinness.' Friendship, and sociability come through in other print ads with headlines like 'Hospitality,' 'There's neighbourliness in Guinness,' 'There's cheerfulness in Guinness,' 'There's friendliness in Guinness,' and 'Have a Guinness tonight, just between friends.' In 1972, the Irish-language print ad goes a step further when it depicts Guinness as the consumer's friend:

> *Fíoras nach n-aithníotar ach ar éigin sé sin má sheasann tú fada go leor taobh le buidéal Guinness go gcasfar ort beagnach gach éinne atá ar aithne agat.* [One of the little known facts of life is that if you stand by a Guinness long enough, you will probably meet everyone you've ever known.]
>
> *Tharlódh seo toisc gur duine cáiliúil tú féin (nó ar an dtaobh eile de toisc an tóir atá ar Guinness).* [This may of course be because you're popular (on the other hand it may be because Guinness is popular).]

Just as the Irish State in the 1970s was still relatively young, so too was Guinness's experience of advertising to an Irish audience. Ireland and her people grappled with a new reality, one that positioned the nation in a customs union with her European neighbours. Meanwhile, Guinness continued to adapt the themes in its ads in an attempt to keep up with, and in some instances precipitate, the relentless change faced by consumers. Many iconic brands associated with Ireland have Irish values at their core but no longer promote them explicitly (Patterson 2009). For example, to focus on the provenance of the brand may be a waste of resources when its origin is firmly embedded in the mind of the consumer. Consumers are familiar with the Irish roots of brands like Guinness, so their 'stories' can be crafted around alternative themes. This is not to say that those themes should not have an Irish flavour; instead, they might fit in with aspects of identity that are important to the Irish consumer other than country of origin.

After nearly two decades of advertising in Ireland, Guinness marked the end of the 1970s and the start of the 1980s with two distinct series of TV ads. The ads in the 1977 series, 'You're at home with a Guinness', vacillate between the identity of an Ireland, before it opened its economic, social and cultural borders to outside influences, and that of the evolving Ireland. 'In the City' and 'In the Country' impart interesting takes on the migration of Irish people between rural and urban areas. As previously highlighted, the numbers employed in agriculture had fallen to 25.9 per cent of the labour force by 1971 (Kennedy and Giblin 1987), and they continued to decline between 1973 and 1986 (Nolan 1987). Increasing levels of employment in the manufacturing and services sectors forced workers to migrate from rural to urban centres. This is reflected very strongly in the TV ad 'In the City'. It is set on the busy streets of Dublin where the sounds of seagulls and traffic prevail. The voiceover is delivered in a strong rural accent, which accentuates the contents of his script. It assumes the air of a migrant's letter home, written in such a way that it might reassure the receiver of his happiness, while at the same time convincing the writer himself that he is content:

> Ask me what it is I like about the city. Is it the peace and quiet or the nice easy pace of life? The smiling faces? The cheery faces? (A driver gestures at a pedestrian who walks in front of him.) Or is it the fact that you occasionally come across a friendly sign? (At this point, the camera lens focuses on a Guinness sign outside a pub.)

> Wherever you go, you're at home with a Guinness. (A pint is poured and then two men drink pints from glass tankards. One man in particular smiles when a woman walks into the pub.) Ah well, even city life has its compensations.

The final line of the script has an air of resignation. In the 1970s, men and women from rural areas had little choice as to whether or not they should move to Dublin or other urban centres. Drinking Guinness in a pub filled with friendly people is the one past-time that transports him home and to happiness. It gives him a sense of place, and allows him to identify with the people around him. This sentiment is reinforced when the campaign tagline appears at the end of the ad: 'You're at home with a Guinness.'

In the 1970s, if cities were the places where people were most likely to find work, rural areas were destinations for city people looking to unwind. The TV ad, 'In the Country', accentuates this role reversal. It is set in a rural location, and features two men hiking through fields. Their shoes are ill suited to the terrain, a shortcoming that is underlined as they slide across the rocks in a fast-running stream. This time, the voiceover is recounted in a strong Dublin accent. The script and their actions accentuate their discomfort:

> Me and Joe, we're used to the city – right? With buses and traffic – right? And nice dry pavements. I'm watchin'. (This is a nervous warning to some cattle.) And who left all these hills lying around? Then we saw the sign that gave us the heart to go on. (They see a Guinness sign outside a pub.) Wherever you go, you're at home with a Guinness.

Once they have their pints, one of the men admits: 'the country's not such a bad place after all!'

The desire to feel at home, to achieve a sense of place is what unifies the men in the two ads. This is a recurring theme in Guinness's ads in the Irish market. The messages empathise with the migrants as they attempt to settle into a new environment, and cope with the challenges that might bring. Guinness is with them, no matter where they go and helps them make the transition.

'Island', the iconic, award-winning ad from the same series succeeds in taking the viewer to a part of 1970s Ireland that remains untouched by the changes sweeping across the country. The setting is a pub on a sparsely populated island off the west coast of Ireland. The visual imagery is evocative and timeless – the sea, stone walls, seagulls, and a whitewashed, thatched cottage, which turns out to be the pub. The scene juxtaposes the congestion and busyness of the ad 'In the City'. The interior of the pub is dark, and a turf fire burns. All of the customers are men, and none of them are young. They are deep in thought, as is a black dog lying on the floor. The only sound is that of a clock ticking, a sound that heightens the air of anticipation in the room. The ad alternates between this indoor setting, which is calm and frozen in time, and a more frantic outdoor setting, which features a *currach* carrying three men as they row towards the island. O'Brien (2009: 181) describes these two contrasting scenes as a 'series of cuts from the active rowing to the passive waiting, and all is done in silence.' The clock strikes 6.30 and the moment they have all been waiting for has arrived. A man enters the pub and utters the ad's only dialect: '*Tá siad ag teacht*' [They're coming]. At this point the stillness lifts and some customers rush to bring in a keg of Guinness from the *currach*. The Guinness is poured and the mood in the pub transforms. The clock's ticking is drowned out by the sound of chatter. The tagline at the end is in keeping with the tone of the ad: '*Bíonn tú sona sásta le Guinness*' [You're always happy with a Guinness] (see Figure 15).

Despite Guinness's willingness to acknowledge change, one of its most memorable, and critically acclaimed ads, portrays a way of life that faces extinction, but one that evokes memories (real or imagined) among Irish people. It is the Ireland that tourists want to experience, the place that emigrants think of as they start new lives in foreign countries, and the setting that migrants take comfort from as they move away from the country. The ad contradicts the gender equality message largely espoused by Guinness in the 1970s. As observed by O'Brien (2009: 182), 'Guinness is being associated with traditional, male, patriarchal, and rural consumer culture.' From a brand perspective, it celebrates one of the Guinness pint's most talked-about characteristics and that is the time it takes to pour the perfect pint. As suggested by the signifiers in the ad, it is a ritual that should never be rushed. Nothing in the demeanour of the men on the island suggests impatience. Guinness is worth the wait.

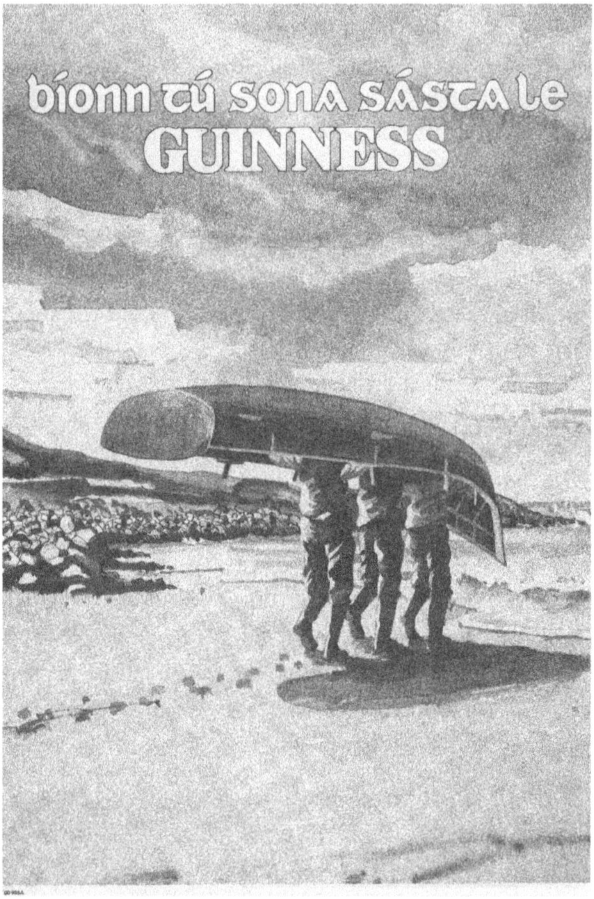

Figure 15: *Bíonn tú sona sásta le Guinness*

In contrast, the 'Have a Guinness Tonight' series of TV ads that marks the end of the 1970s and the beginning of the 1980s draws upon a very different cultural, and social backdrop to the one that inspired 'Island'. The ads exhibit Guinness's desire to reflect the changes in Irish society and highlight what might be interpreted as a newfound confidence. Young people, at ease in a global setting, populate the ads. This is a nod to what lies ahead for Guinness's advertising, whether intended or not. The colour production marks an obvious change since the 1960s but the visual signifiers have evolved significantly too. The settings and the clothes are cosmopolitan, and several scenes draw on a combination of Irish and international cultural references. In 'Fireworks', a group of young, energetic men and women, dressed in bright bomber jackets, is involved in erecting a stage for an outdoor concert. They wear the 'uniform' of young people from all over the world at that time, so until they encounter a street artist at College Green in Dublin, nothing in particular associates them with Ireland. The artist draws a chalk sketch of a bottle of Guinness and a glass on the pavement. From then on, the group embarks on a journey that takes in the Statue of Liberty and a dolphin-watching boat trip in foreign climes, all the time emphasising the ease with which this confident demographic travels across borders.

Conclusion

The 1970s continued to be a decade of prolific advertising output by Guinness. Change in Ireland was portrayed in more than twenty TV ads, and a wealth of print ads. Effective advertising is built on insights into the consumer's world, thus enabling the brand to connect with its target audience. Undoubtedly, Guinness endeavoured to forge connections with its Irish audiences by publishing and broadcasting highly relatable ads that were created around a wide variety of pertinent themes, ranging from the economy, friendship, leisure pursuits, migration, heritage, and gender equality.

From Guinness's perspective, the intent appears to have been to harness advertising so as to create an identity that would position the brand at the heart of Irish life. Like a live entity, it refused to stand still, but instead adapted its messages in response to changing consumer tastes, and mounting competition. Having to endure such challenges motivated the brand to empathise with its customers in a way that seemed to suggest that it understood what people were going through when facing change. This is particularly true of the 'You're at home with a Guinness' series of ads. The message is clear. When all else is changing, Guinness remains the same, a metaphor for a loyal friend. Change presented challenges and opportunities for Guinness too in the form of more competition, and expanding markets respectively. The ads suggest that it responded to this by promoting its product to female drinkers, and by attempting to steer younger drinkers away from competing drinks. At first glance, the broad-based, cosmopolitan tone of the 'Have a Guinness Tonight' series might appear to distance Guinness from its birthplace. However, the ads capture the transformation that Ireland experienced since the insular, inward-looking decades that followed Independence. By the late 1970s, increasing numbers of Irish people travelled abroad on holidays, laws discriminating against women were being dismantled, albeit slowly, and television programmes created a close affinity between the viewers, and British and North American cultures. These programmes informed Irish fashion trends and created lifestyle aspirations for younger audiences in particular. The soundtracks used in many of the ads were not of an Irish genre but from a young person's perspective, musical influences in the 1970s were just as likely to come from the UK and the United States, as they were to come from Galway. To young, Irish audiences watching the ads, the context fit seamlessly with their own lives and aspirations. Like Ireland, Guinness had moved on, and was poised to face even greater upheaval in the decades that followed.

CHAPTER 3

1980–1989: Economic hardship

Introduction

From the moment that the Irish government committed to economic policies shaped by T. K. Whitaker's seminal 'First Programme for Economic Expansion' in the late 1950s, Ireland embarked on a journey that would make it one of the most open economies in the world. Protectionism was cast aside and Irish society evolved, assuming a more cosmopolitan outlook. The launch of an Irish television station in the 1960s, and membership of the EEC in 1973, prised open Ireland's borders and exposed its people to more diverse influences and opportunities. This was not without its drawbacks, as evidenced by the turmoil that was visited on the country in the 1970s, when worldwide recession and oil crises made it clear that Ireland's fortunes were directly related to the international economy. Government policies aimed at insulating the Irish economy from the worst ravages of the global downturn simply delayed the pain and stored up worse problems for the State. Excessive borrowing to fund public spending hid the extent of Ireland's woes, and led to an unsustainable building boom and an expanding public sector. While unemployment was kept at bay in the short term, stability and prosperity came at a price, one that was borne in the 1980s when Ireland experienced one of the worst recessions in its short history.

Consequently, 1980s Ireland was an economically battered country, precipitating the exodus of thousands of young men and women. Those who remained lived in an increasingly open country, heavily influenced by European and American culture, society and economics. This chapter contends that one of Ireland's most famous brands, Guinness, embraced many of these stimuli, as evidenced in its advertising to its domestic audience.

Some might argue that this made Guinness seem less Irish but if that is true, does it also mean that an Irish person who is open to international influences is any less Irish? Like the Irish of the 1980s, Guinness looked beyond the confines of Ireland for inspiration. It used this outward-looking approach to set the narrative in ads aimed at Irish consumers. In many ways, its experience mirrored that of its Irish audience, thus enabling the brand to connect with the Irish consumer.

A tap that could not be turned off

According to the NESC (1991), 358,000 people emigrated from Ireland between 1981 and 1990. The UK attracted the lion's share of the emigrants, with around 68 per cent opting for the close proximity of Ireland's nearest neighbour. A not insignificant 14 per cent went to the United States, where immigration policies were selective but not off-putting. Emigrants were most likely attracted by the presence of previous generations of emigrants and a familiarity with its culture, borne from the ubiquitous American dramas seen on Irish television and cinema screens. Neil Jordan captures the impact of this when he recalls how on a trip to the US, he realised that the landscape he encountered there was more familiar to him than the typical Irish landscape. He put this down to the all-pervasive American culture evident in the media at that time (Hewson et al. 1988). Such familiarity may have eased the pain of emigration for the many thousands of Irish people who boarded the plane to America.

The profile of the Irish emigrant in the 1980s differed from that of previous generations, as illustrated in the NESC's (1991) analysis. More males than females emigrated, due to the greater displacement of male jobs during the recession. In the past, they would have found employment in agriculture, construction and factories, but according to the NESC (1986), there was an exceptionally hard recession in construction and agriculture between 1980 and 1985. This precipitated falls in employment of 27,000 and 40,000 respectively. Historically, proportionately more women emigrated, either because they could not find suitable employment, or they were excluded from the work place as a result of discriminatory employment legislation. However, by the 1980s, employment opportunities for women had improved, particularly in the burgeoning service sector, whereas according to Whelan et al. (1992), male unemployment reached 20 per cent by 1985, which was almost 3 per cent greater than the overall unemployment rate.

Another defining feature of emigration in the 1980s was that young people, between the ages of 15 and 34, left the country in disproportionately greater numbers than any other age cohort. Geographic location did not provide protection from the realities of economic hardship. Rural regions and Western counties in particular continued to be hardest hit by emigration but in the 1980s, mass departures from Dublin were commonplace. However, the most marked difference between the emigrants of the 1980s and previous decades was their social profile and educational background. Traditionally confined to the lower socio-economic groups, more professionals, employers and managers left Ireland in 1987 and 1988 than the skilled, semi-skilled and unskilled working class. Favourable tax reform in the UK in 1987 and 1988, positively impacting on high earners in particular, only strengthened its allure. More worrying for the future prosperity and development of the country, the NESC (1991) report highlights the marked increase in the numbers of graduates emigrating – in 1980, 8.4 per cent had emigrated by the spring following their graduation, and by 1988, this figure had more than tripled to 29.4 per cent. This is understandable when one considers that between 1980 and 1988, the proportion of graduates who secured work in Ireland fell from 80 to 62 per cent.

Such high levels of emigration proved to be a self-perpetuating prophecy. According to the NESC (1991), migration networks formed, thus reducing many of the problems facing would-be émigrés. New arrivals to foreign shores could call on an extensive network from amongst the Irish diaspora. Significantly, their exit was facilitated by the falling cost of air travel. At the vanguard of this travel revolution was Ryanair, which was established in 1985. The following year, it was granted permission by the authorities to challenge the British Airways and Aer Lingus duopoly on the Ireland/Britain routes. Passengers could fly between the two countries for £99 return, which was more than half the price offered by the two incumbents (Ryanair n.d.). Emigration was no longer a one-way ticket, but was made more palatable by the possibility of it being a seasonal foray in some instances. Even if permanent return could not be countenanced, the prospects of regular trips home for some emigrants, or visits from family and friends were made possible by cheaper, more accessible air travel between Ireland and the UK.

Despite soaring unemployment rates in the 1980s, which peaked at 17.7 per cent in 1987, it is estimated that inward migration was around 150,000 between 1981 and 1990 (NESC 1991). This was not always an economically fruitful decision, and the unemployment rate among this cohort was high (more than 30 per cent). However, it did mean that those returning brought back cultural influences from abroad. This would have an impact on values, cultural reference points and consumer tastes, all of which would come to the fore in the 1990s. As posited by Bourdieu (1984), an individual's tastes are learned and acquired from groups in different locations within the social class structure. Even emigrants, who clung together in their ethnic and social groups, were exposed to different aspects of their adopted country's culture. Therefore, many of them would have succumbed, in part to the influences of other cultures.

Against this backdrop of chronic unemployment and record levels of emigration, Ireland's GDP per head was only 62.4 per cent of the EC average (NESC 1989). This ensured that in the ranking tables, it was only ahead of Greece and Portugal. This lowly ranking and the lot of the Irish when compared to that of other EEC citizens, is contextualised in the report by exploring specific product categories. In 1984, there were only 20.8 private cars per 100 Irish residents, compared to 32.7 in the EC. In 1983, TV ownership lagged behind too, with 20.5 TVs per 100 Irish residents and 29.4 in the EC. The gap was even more pronounced when it came to telephone subscriptions that same year. Just 23.5 per 100 Irish residents had a subscription, compared with 57.2 per 100 residents in West Germany, 71.9 in Denmark, and 46.6 in the EC. Consequently, many Irish expatriates enjoyed higher standards of living than those they left behind and for those that returned the inequality must have seemed very pronounced.

In the midst of all the hardship imposed by the dire economic scenario, corruption, and the 'Troubles' in Northern Ireland, life continued for those who remained in Ireland. Looking at the situation from a more positive perspective, just over 80 per cent of the working population had jobs, and while income tax was high, workers had money to spend. Just like any other consumer economy where there is disposable income, advertising and its narratives provide an insight into the state of a nation at a particular point in time. In the main, Guinness reserved references to economic travails for print media. It may have kept messages of good housekeeping and economic woes away from TV because for many, it was a vehicle used to escape the realities of an economically broken Ireland.

So, in 1980, while TV was not used by Guinness to deliver practical, money-saving advice, print was. Such ads tended to be concise and helpful: 'Get a new slant on value,' alongside images of a pint of Guinness at various stages of consumption. In 1981, Guinness declares: 'There's far better value in a Guinness.' It does not reveal the identity of the brands against which it is comparing itself but nevertheless, it is a bold and confident statement of intent. In the same year, the product's attributes are extolled and linked to the economic virtues of buying Guinness: 'Creamier, smoother, longer laster. There's far better value in a Guinness'; 'Richer Cooler Fuller flavour. There's far better value in a Guinness'; and 'Richer Cooler Creamier Smoother Longer Laster Guinness. There's far better value in a Guinness' (see Figure 16).

Figure 16: There's far better value in a Guinness

Again, no specific reference is made to the products that Guinness is compared with in these adverts, but a brand with such heritage and success has the confidence to take this approach, while not expecting to be challenged. Rather than just focusing on price, value is linked to the product's attributes and consumers are advised to consider all aspects of their choice carefully. Cheap is not always good but if one takes into account everything that a product has to offer, it can seem better value. Guinness infers that its flagship product has the facility to sate the drinker due to its fulsome characteristics. Like a fine wine, it should not be rushed. Instead, it should be savoured and a drinker is fully justified taking longer to consume it than, say, a lager drinker takes to consume a pint of lager. In theory, this translates into financial savings for cash strapped consumers and makes Guinness more appealing to their rational side.

Severe weather at the start of 1982 brought the country to a halt and heralded the tough year that lay ahead. In an attempt to find some cause for optimism, a print ad cheers: 'The Blackout's over! Guinness. It's good to be back.' More than likely, this headline relates to the havoc that was visited by the severe snow in January, which brought the country to a standstill. Meanwhile, on the economic front, unemployment jumped from 14.5 per cent in 1981 to 19.9 per cent in 1982 (NESC 1991). Guinness empathised with Irish adults in print adverts that acknowledged the dire economic circumstances, made worse by an austere budget submission from the Fine Gael/Labour coalition government. It was enough to bring the government down, a collapse that was largely attributed to John Bruton's controversial proposal to levy VAT on children's shoes. In February, Fianna Fáil was elected but by November, Fine Gael and Labour were back in power again. Against this politically unstable backdrop, Guinness published print adverts that made reference to the crisis. In one, a pint and a tankard glass of Guinness are set against a newspaper bearing the headline: 'Gloomy Forecast for '82 – Year of the drop' (see Figure 17). Judging by the partially revealed masthead, the newspaper is *The Irish Times*, likely chosen for its reputation as a reliable commentator on economic matters. Guinness offers some solace: 'Take the smooth with the rough. Guinness. First and Lasts.' In another ad in the series, Guinness dares the reader to counter the ill effects of the budget: 'When the budget bites, bite black! Guinness. First and lasts.'

Figure 17: Take the smooth with the rough

For the remainder of the year, Guinness's advertising agency created succinct copy for print adverts that played on words without masking the fact that money, or lack of it, was top of people's minds: 'A valuable pint'; 'As long as your thirst'; 'Long on satisfaction'; 'Here's a good pint'; 'Get to the pint'; and 'Stick to the pint.' All of the ads sign off with the attention grabbing tagline: 'You can't beat a Guinness for good value.' The austere economic environment is captured in this series of adverts. Despite this, new competitors challenged Guinness's flagship brand at a time when consumers' spending power was in decline. Therefore, these ads indicate that Guinness reacted to this test by reminding consumers that a pint of stout was value for money.

The print ads explored above were designed to empathise with hard-pressed consumers, who were forced to make tough economic decisions on a daily basis. Using print ads that were published alongside stories of an ailing economy, Guinness resonated with the rational side of its audience. This left the job of emotional titillation to television, an arena where happy endings were possible. There were exceptions to this in 1983, when Guinness broadcast three TV ads that focus on value and conclude with the tagline, 'No beer comes near – for good value.' In keeping with the sombre atmosphere in the country at the time, these TV ads are not showy, nor do they suggest indulgence. Production values are minimal and the stories that they tell do not require the ad agency to travel abroad to exotic locations in order to shoot the ads. Instead, the message empathises with the cash-strapped target audience and offers them a product that will help them through straitened times.

Donning the rose-tinted glasses

Regardless of the themes and tone of the adverts explored in the previous section, advertising tends to be an optimistic pursuit and usually seeks out the positives in any scenario. In his critique of Irish advertising, Moran (1984) contends that most ads are aimed at people with money, therefore perpetuating an idealised view of society. He identifies a clear shift in the focus of alcohol advertising in the 1980s, from promoting the tangible pleasures of the drink, to eulogising the pleasures, which come to those who drink it. Even as far back as the late 1960s, Guinness was a forerunner at employing this narrative in some of its adverts and it is very evident in many of its TV ads in the 1980s, despite the prevailing economic situation.

The 1980/1 ad 'Racehorse' from the 'Have a Guinness tonight' series is a case in point. It seems determined to foreground many of the progressive lifestyle changes that have been visited on Irish people since the 1970s, with no reference to the negatives. The recession has not quite taken hold, and the positive associations between Guinness and successful people are heavily promoted. The ad opens with a shot of horses racing on a track, while a voiceover poses the question: 'What's a Guinness between friends?' The attention switches to an excited male punter in the crowd, pulling out his betting slip. The connection is clear between Guinness, happiness and good fortune. Then, the voiceover is replaced with an upbeat, contemporary song that would resonate equally well with an international audience, as there is no trace of Celtic tones. At that time, Irish viewers were undoubtedly watching the BBC's *Top of the Pops* chart music programme, or Vincent Hanley's *MT USA*, which broadcast all the latest music videos from around the world on RTÉ, as they were to listen to home-grown musicians. The lyrics in the advert leave the viewer in no doubt that the punter is a winner: 'It's when the horse you fancy strides ahead to win the day.' This first scene offers no suggestion of the new, cosmopolitan Irish person. Instead, it draws on horse racing, a sport long associated with both Guinness and the Irish.

Just as the viewer is settling into the comfort of familiar scenes, the ad entirely changes direction. The racecourse is abandoned and a front shot of Concorde taxiing before take-off fills the screen. The scene is accompanied by the lyrics: 'A trip in Concorde taking off to New York, USA.' Concorde commenced commercial flights in 1976 and from the start was synonymous with success and wealth. A more aspirational metaphor at that time would have been hard to find. Within seconds, the viewer is transported to an oil field in Algeria, where workers run over to a gushing oil well. Even though the ad was made a few years before emigration reached its peak, it captures the reality that already faced many Irish workers, a reality that had been there for decades. In order to find work, some had to travel abroad. However, these workers were not to be pitied. The singer trumpets their luck: 'It's when you get a lucky break and strike oil in Algeria.'

The celebratory mood contrasts sharply with another oil worker's melancholic frame of mind captured just a year later in the memorable Harp advert, which featured the infamous Sally O'Brien. In order to counter the growing demand among Irish consumers for imported beers, Guinness launched Harp Lager in 1960. At the time, it was brewed in Dundalk and it went on to become a market leader in Ireland. However, an influx of imported lagers in the 1970s, led by Heineken, put it under pressure. According to Felton and Devlin (1983: 202), the creative team behind the ad, it was created in order to defend the lager's number one position in the Irish market from two lagers in particular, Tenant's and Heineken. Essentially, they were charged with creating an ad that would combat Heineken's international appeal, while at the same time coming up with a narrative that would 'look at Harp Lager from *outside* Ireland.' Their solution was to produce an ad in which the overriding themes of nostalgia and homesickness were made all the more poignant by the narrator, a fictional Irishman who worked in an oilfield in the Middle East. The searing heat made him thirsty and he yearned for a pint of Harp. This desire conjured up images in his mind of his local pub and its customers, in particular a certain Sally O'Brien and 'the way she might look at you.' The ad's high profile and long-lasting appeal was due to the fact that it connected with a public who could relate to the feelings experienced by the lead character. When the allure of Sally O'Brien's enigmatic smile was added to the mix, it went on to become one of the most famous ads ever made and broadcast in Ireland.

The next scene in 'Racehorse' features an affluent couple at breakfast. The way in which the man and woman are presented reinforces Moran's (1984) contention that advertising at that time was aimed at consumers with a healthy disposable income. In fact, the pair could just as easily be in London or Boston as in Ireland. The table setting belongs to a middle-class couple, and includes a modern-day coffee pot with matching china cup, saucers and milk jug. Once again, happiness and luck prevail, as the woman fishes out a diamond necklace from her cereal. The ad's singer enthuses: 'Like finding it's your birthday with a diamond in your cereal.' As if to remind the viewer that the advert is for Guinness, the ad concludes with a crowded pub scene. The soundtrack cajoles the viewer and commends the virtues of Guinness as the singers croon: 'Creamy and smooth.' This is the advert's first direct reference to the drink's attributes, as opposed to the benefits that accrue from imbibing it. As if to foreground the amicable atmosphere, the final still is a close-up of the Guinness logo on a glass with the tagline 'Just between friends' beneath it (see Figure 18).

Figure 18: Have a Guinness tonight – just between friends

Rather than focusing on just one theme, Guinness presents a collage of scenarios in 'Racehorse' that fosters 'an association in the viewer's mind between the desirable activities which befall elegant people and the consumption of the advertised beverage' (Moran 1984: 85), in this case Guinness. There are fleeting references to the product itself, but the main message goes beyond its attributes. The advert makes sense of the cultural shift in Ireland. The storyline is set in an overtly consumer society, just like other Western economies. The style corroborates a view articulated by Rowley (1988: 91), who observes that the 'idea of personal happiness through love has been linked to consumerism, in the iconography of the happy couple who have responsibilities only to each other and their careers.' This suggests a modification to the way in which Irish people's lives and aspirations were represented, with the advertising industry taking the lead. Indeed, the ad 'Racehorse' might be viewed as a short montage that summarises these changes. It opens with a traditional representation of Irish life when it focuses on a day at the races, but the audience is swiftly given an insight into more contemporary, aspirational lifestyles. Such rhetoric contrasts sharply with Kiberd's (1984: 12) critique of Irish literature and its take on Irish society. He surmises that despite their socialist leanings, most pieces are wedded to the idea of Irish tradition. Consequently, he is quite scathing when he challenges that narrative:

> So one is forced to ask if all this talk of tradition has a basis in contemporary Irish reality. Do the families of suburban Dublin wake up sweating under the burden of Irish tradition? Do their children feel ravaged by crises of national identity as they reach for the multinational snap-crackle-and-pop? And the answer is clearly no. This obsession with tradition is a product of the conservative academic mind, endlessly rehearsing themes for an Irish-American audience. In their hearts, our scholars suspect that all this talk of tradition has a great deal more to do with tourism than with art, with peddling a national image than with understanding ourselves.

'Racehorse' is for a new generation of Irish consumers, one that has not yet been ravaged by the impending economic recession. Increasingly, the visual language of advertising in the 1980s reflected Irish society's predilection for the individual as opposed to the community. The individual did not literally mean one person, but encompasses couples, usually categorised as a unit. That unit was told that they could make it on their own and did not need to interact with the wider community. Famously, this ideology was pursued aggressively in Thatcher's Britain, where privatisation and the individual were given preferential treatment over the community when making policies. Such shifts in identity and societal orientation occupied the minds of many commentators in the 1980s. This was a time when the EEC was moving closer to greater cohesion, as a result of the forthcoming Single European Act, which would be ratified in 1992. Consequently, Brussels would have much greater power and influence over Ireland, but from a positive perspective, it had the potential to facilitate improvements in the fabric of Ireland's economic and social infrastructure. All of this change contributed to uncertainty in people's minds and Kearney (1988a: 115) asserts that in the 1980s Ireland faced an identity crisis:

> A national ideology begins to degenerate into rhetoric when it ceases to address the reality of people's experience … A yawning gap has emerged between the official expressions of the nation-state and the everyday experience of its citizens.

However, despite a growing disconnect between many Irish citizens and traditional cultural heritage in the 1980s, Kearney cautions against 'jettisoning' it. Rather, he views it as an opportunity to reinvent it in such a way that it meets the challenges of contemporary Ireland. In many ways, this is exactly what Guinness and its advertising agencies had been doing since 1959 in its ads. The signifiers in the advert 'Racehorse' suggest that Guinness was well aware of this crisis and accepted that traditional representations of identity no longer resonated with Irish people to the same extent. The advert imparts an idealised view of Irish identity but captures the growing influence of international cultural references on everyday life. It is not suggested here that images of Concorde and *chichi* breakfast *rendez-vous* represented reality for the vast majority of people in the 1980s. Concorde was unattainable for most people, but it symbolised the democratisation and perceived glamour of international travel. By the beginning of the 1980s, Budget Travel was a staple among many Irish holidaymakers and a return to emigration had started to take hold. Consequently, Guinness recognised that Irish people were just as comfortable imagining themselves in situations beyond Ireland's shores, as they were with their country of origin. The idealised narrative of an agricultural nation with comely maidens at the crossroads belonged to a bygone era. The 1980s was a decade when Irish people emigrated, or commuted to and from England where they often found work on major construction sites like the Channel Tunnel. They also headed to Norway to work on the oilrigs and to the Middle East to toil on the lucrative oil fields.

The advert's go-getting, upbeat tone may be seen as a panacea to what Gibbons (1988) describes as the austere, cultural climate that prevailed in Ireland at that time. He cites the divorce and abortion referenda, censorship, moving statues and the Kerry babies tragedies as contributing to the oppressive atmosphere. In 1981, the Pro-Life Amendment Campaign (PLAC) exerted considerable pressure on the main political parties and secured pre-election promises of a constitutional referendum, which if passed, would outlaw the possibility of introducing legalisation that would allow abortion in Ireland. While Fianna Fáil's Constitutional Amendment was carried in 1983 by 66.9 per cent to 33.1 per cent, it merely confused matters and did not eradicate uncertainty about the matter in the future. Meanwhile, the 1986 referendum to remove the ban on divorce was equally divisive and was rejected by the electorate.

These issues, when combined with the severe economic situation, did indeed create a very bleak environment in Ireland. However, he does not even mention the constant spectre of protest and violence, which emerged because of events in the North. The tone was set at the start of the decade when the hunger strike in the H-block cells at the Maze Prison claimed ten lives, thus elevating the dead to martyr status. Brown (2004: 326) describes the protests on Dublin's streets in the summer of 1981 as 'expressions of solidarity with the republican hunger strikers.' Despite the subsequent signing of the Anglo-Irish agreement in November 1985, the Northern Ireland conflict was rarely out of the news in the 1980s. It seemed that the historic agreement counted for little with the terrorists, a disdain that was obvious in November 1987 when a devastating bomb went off in Enniskillen. The unstable situation in the North merely added to Gibbons' list of 'bad news' stories that dominated the media in this most dreary of decades.

However, advertisers did not dwell on the fallout from these events, preferring instead to focus on the hopes and dreams of its audiences. The advert, 'Racehorse', offers consumers the possibility of what Packard (1957) refers to as, emotional security. As a remedy to the many challenges that face them, the Guinness brand is a signifier of hope and optimism. It is a catalyst that brings friends and lovers together, helping them forget any anxieties they might have. Most importantly, it is a familiar 'face' that leads by example – it has willingly embraced the new.

Figure 19: Big Wave

Living on an island

Due to Ireland's island status, the sea is a recurring theme in its storytelling. Unsurprisingly, the advertising industry is no stranger to creating adverts that incorporate the infinite manifestations of a marine nature. Apart from its physical proximity to the island of Ireland, the sea is a metaphor for many aspects of Irish life, including survival, work, leisure, tragedy, time and separation. It has the ability to evoke powerful and conflicting emotions. Guinness's 1977 advert, 'Island', as discussed in Chapter 2, is testament to this. 1981/2's 'Big Wave', part of the 'Move over to Guinness' series of TV ads, saw Guinness revisiting the sea and casting it in a leading role (see Figure 19). Its constant movement breathes life into the drink, and simulates draught Guinness as it is released into a waiting glass. However, unlike 'Island', the advert liberates the audience from Irish stereotypes. Rather than confining it to Ireland, the beach might just as easily be in California as in Cork. The not very Irish soundtrack, which was composed by Bill Whelan, is a vital ingredient and exuberantly launches the advert with a sliding guitar riff. In turn, this is joined by the soaring timbre of a saxophone. The visual language alternates between enhanced images of black and amber liquid, swirling freely towards infinity, and dramatic landscapes. Early on, the viewer is treated to the sight of an immense, curling wave crashing down. Another wave follows, this time ridden by a surfer. The waves are a visual representation of Guinness being poured, a point that is reinforced when the wave morphs into just that.

The camera zooms in on the seashore activity, where a woman in a white bikini settles on a rug. She has a cream Labrador pup beside her, perhaps signifying one of the colours in the Guinness palette, as might the woman's long, dark hair. Her complexion suggests that she might be oriental. In 1981, Ireland was still a very homogeneous society, so her presence raises the possibility that the advert might be set outside Ireland. The images alternate between the surfer, the shore and Guinness being poured in dramatic swirls. Meanwhile, the music pounds in time with the waves and finally the saxophone emits a climactic strain as the Guinness settles. All is calm and a voiceover says: 'Move over ... to Guinness.'

In this advert, it is obvious that horizons have broadened and the visual and aural signs speak in an expansive language. Towards the end of the 1980s, such an outward orientation was debated by Kearney (1988b: 7) when he cautioned that Ireland could 'no longer be contained within the frontiers of an island.' In order to pique the attention of its target audience in the 1980s, Guinness's advertising agency appears to have taken this insight into account by creating an ad containing imagery that might relate to a middle-class audience in any developed, Western society.

In 1986, the ad 'Logo' drew on a range of symbols that encapsulated many aspects of Ireland's identity, past and present. A soaring, sliding guitar riff accompanies the opening shot of two planes above the clouds. Their route is choreographed in such a way that they leave behind a trail of white smoke in their wake, which in turn transforms into the swirling pattern of a Guinness being poured. Part of the letter 'N' is transposed on the liquid, but despite being incomplete, its provenance is undeniable. It is rendered in Guinness's unique style, which means that even without the whole letter or the name, it triggers recognition. The planes connect Ireland to other countries and could just as easily be leaving as arriving.

However, if planes symbolise modernity and progress in Ireland, dolmens denote the past. Without warning, the viewer is jolted back in time with a nocturnal shot of a dolmen, shrouded in fog. There is an otherworldly air about it and this is accentuated by the sound of birds' wings flapping, as game birds take flight rising into the night sky. Again, the suggestion of a letter from the Guinness logo flies above the mix of cloud and swirling draught. Just two years before this advert was broadcast, Walker (1984: 215) observes a rise in the popularity of prehistoric structures, both in Ireland and abroad. According to him, Bank of Ireland and the Industrial Development Authority of Ireland (IDA) use images of prehistoric structures in their promotional material. He surmises that the 'Filofax generation' is drawn to these images because they 'confer an aura of permanence on the new information order.' In the 1980s, the Filofax became a metaphor for a new breed of confident, successful businessperson. It was as ubiquitous as the iPhone is in the twenty-first century. While change can be exhilarating, it makes some people fearful and causes them to hanker after what went before. By referring to a familiar prehistoric structure, Guinness reinforces its own longevity and might be considered the dolmen of the drinks industry because of its constant presence. The viewer does not have long to linger in the past, as two speedboats come into view. They leave the top of a letter 'S' in their wake, again rendered in the unmistakable style of the Guinness logo. The boats are contemporary and, as in 'Big Wave', water is a playground. Those aboard are affluent, thus portraying what Moran (1984) refers to as a very idealised society. They are far removed from the realities of 1986 when few people could have afforded a speedboat. They are much more aspirational than the Guinness adverts of the 1960s, which featured hardy fishermen toiling on their trawlers. Then, the water was a workplace and the adverts did not offer the viewer an escape from hardship or reality, save when the fisherman drank from a bottle of Guinness.

Figure 20: Carrick-a-Rede Bridge

Subsequent scenes in the 'Logo' advert depict other popular leisure pursuits, including a golfer in a bunker, a pub scene where a musician plays the saxophone and a couple standing on the famous Carrick-a-Rede Rope Bridge in Co. Antrim before it is transformed into the Guinness harp (see Figure 20). Again, the still of the bridge reminds viewers of Ireland's island status.

Throughout, the 'real' images are interspersed with Guinness's unique visual language and by the end of the advert, parts of most of the letters in its name have been utilised. With the benefit of hindsight, the constant movement of the water in 'Big Wave', and the planes in 'Logo', might symbolise the restless spirit of the Irish.

The boundaries come crashing down

As seen earlier in this chapter, the tide of emigration visited Irish shores in the 1980s in tsunami proportions. However, due to technological advances, it differed from previous episodes in that emigrants did not necessarily face permanent exile. Even if they were unable to return in person, it was easier for them to keep in touch with home as a result of a changing communications landscape. This encompassed major advances in mass media and telecommunications. In the late 1970s, Seán MacBride presided over an extensive piece of research that was compiled by the International Commission for the Study of Communication Problems. Published in 1980, it examined the implications of the burgeoning changes that were emerging in worldwide communications at that time, many of which would be directly relevant to Ireland in the 1980s and beyond. From the outset, it establishes that communication plays an integral role in spreading culture in individual countries, thus helping to preserve their heritage. It does not advocate that countries should retreat within their own boundaries in order to safeguard their cultural specificity. Rather, it acknowledges the importance of communication's role in: 'widening the individual's horizons, awakening his imagination and stimulating his aesthetic needs and creativity' (p. 14).

However, the authors of the report are in no way naïve about the ability, or lack thereof, of countries operating within the realities of the new communications world, to achieve a balance between preserving and invigorating their cultures. It foretells that while the inter-dependence of culture and communication between countries may offer smaller countries the opportunity to bring their cultures to a wider audience, it is very possible that they may be overpowered by outside influences. The report (p. 30) reminds the media of their responsibilities 'because they do not merely transmit and disseminate culture but also select or originate its content.' The implications of the report's findings are prescient, as they implied that Ireland was even more open to outside influences than in previous decades. The prospect of what the authors term 'cultural domination' are very real and the perils are clearly articulated with a sense of foreboding when it opines that:

> Cultural identity is endangered by the overpowering influence on and assimilation of some national cultures through these nations may well be the heirs to more ancient and richer cultures. Since diversity is among the most precious qualities of culture, the whole world is the poorer. (International Commission for the Study of Communication Problems 1980: 31)

Such a vista was one that Ireland's inward-looking, post-Independence governments nurtured up until the late 1950s. The paucity of communications technology aided their vision. However, an inward-oriented outlook was impossible to sustain with the arrival of television and the remarkable growth in travel to and from the island. Despite the establishment of an indigenous television network in 1961, by the 1980s, Ireland's TV screens were dominated by the BBC, a far richer and better resourced corporation than RTÉ could ever be. In addition, domination by British media was further strengthened by the availability of UTV and the new arrival, Channel 4. The ramifications of a British-led TV media landscape are reinforced by Bell (1985: 27), who concedes that due to the rising volume of trans-border data-flows controlled by transnational corporations, individual countries are less able to regulate the flow of information and entertainment. He argues, 'in so far as the integrity of nation states rests on a degree of cultural hegemony within their political boundaries, national sovereignty is potentially eroded.' The situation was compounded by the deregulatory stance that prevailed in the 1980s, as Europe prepared for the Single European Act. This would have far-reaching effects on many sectors, including broadcasting and communications.

In the 1980s, Irish authorities participated in European cable and satellite broadcasting projects. However, their mandate remained the pursuit of broadcast strategies aimed at preserving Ireland's culture and identity. According to Bell (1985), senior management in RTÉ was optimistic, surmising that digital satellite technology would enable the national broadcaster to extend its coverage across the UK and some European countries, including Spain and Portugal. This conforms to Kearney's (1988a: 127) assessment of the situation, as he refuses to view the communications revolution as a threat, seeing it rather as an opportunity to import cultures. As a *quid pro quo*, it would be easier for the Irish to export their culture to other parts of the world. He observes that:

> Post-modern culture crosses national boundaries. It is culture without frontiers. But in order to resist the domination of a centralised bureaucracy of communication, the post-modern task is to ensure that a culture without frontiers does not degenerate into a culture without differences.

Herein lay the challenge, namely, how to nurture, promote and sustain all that was good about Irish culture, without remaining wedded to the past and closed to new ideas. The International Commission for the Study of Communication Problems (1980: 160) refers to the homogenisation of different societies, ably assisted by the surge in levels of information and entertainment transfer: 'Life-styles, habits and manners, tastes and preferences, even beliefs and opinions tend to become uniform, to the detriment of social variety and human individuality.' This is just as likely to occur within countries as between countries, when urban ideals 'infiltrate' rural customs and traditions. However, Ireland's close proximity to the UK offers an example of inter-country cultural dominance, which due to the nature of the communications infrastructure, is logically driven by the UK. This may precipitate a lack of clarity about a nation's identity. According to Fennell (1986), nations should have a clear idea of where their own identity ends and others begin. The disintegration of boundaries between nations makes this tougher and dilutes identity. Irish identity in the 1980s is an example of this scenario, with emigration and a more deregulated communications landscape making their mark. Without realising it, many Irish people assimilated cultural reference points from other nations. Judging from many of its ads in the 1980s, Guinness understood the significance of the internationalisation of popular culture in Ireland.

The 1981 advert 'Move into the Smooth' contains references to the popular culture that had by then captured the imaginations of Irish people. Early on in the ad and in a nod to Irish culture, traditional indigenous pursuits are represented, such as a man on a trawler and the native game of rings. These are followed by two 'sports', which assumed widespread popularity in Ireland, primarily due to their coverage on the BBC. The first is snooker. The initial scene comprises various fruits, including red apples, arranged in triangles. This subsequently transforms into a triangle of red balls on a snooker table. Then a snooker player chalks his cue, strikes and snooker balls move in various directions. The accompanying voiceover urges the viewer to: 'Move into the smooth,' words that might be used to describe the technique of a skilled snooker player and the action used to pour a pint of Guinness.

In the 1970s and 1980s, the Northern Irish snooker player Alex Higgins, was highly successful on the professional circuit. He sparked great interest in the sport among Irish people. In 1972 he was crowned World Champion and then he won the title again in 1982. In 1985, another Irishman, Denis Taylor, emulated his achievements when he too became World Champion by beating the seemingly unstoppable Steve Davis in a final that gripped television viewers across the British Isles. Harris (2009) reports that a record-breaking 18.5 million viewers watched the drama unfold on BBC2. The popular one-frame, shootout programme on BBC television, *Pot Black* was very popular at that time among Irish TV viewers with access to the BBC. It supplemented the annual coverage of the World Championship tournament and showcased the habits of its stars. Unlike today's snooker players, it was the norm for competitors to smoke and drink while playing at that time, so it made sense for Guinness to exploit snooker's imagery and associate with the sport. The manner in which the ad is constructed conveys Guinness's certainty that its target audience was so familiar with snooker that it would not struggle to understand the visual references therein.

Darts is another television 'sport' that grew in popularity in the 1970s and 1980s in Ireland. While it is a quintessentially English game, it found its way into Irish sitting rooms, once more courtesy of the BBC. Champions like Jockey Wilson and Eric Bristow became household names, so when Guinness included an aerial view of a gardener tending a flowerbed designed in the likeness of a dartboard, many viewers could relate to it. Like snooker, darts and alcohol went hand in hand in the 1980s, whether it was on TV or in the local pub. The next scene in the ad features a man in a pub, lining up his dart before throwing it at the double 20. This part reassures the amateur that darts can be played in a social setting and what better way to enjoy the game than with a pint of Guinness?

Guinness's most high profile sport-related campaign of the 1980s ran in 1982/3. In a series of print ads, a number of very famous sports stars endorsed Guinness. All of them were Irish or declared for Ireland due to their ancestry and they participated at the very highest levels of their sports. 1982/3 were standout years for most of the featured sportsmen, so when Guinness ran the ads in 1983, they were of great interest to the public. Irish international football stars Kevin Moran, Frank Stapleton and Mark

Lawrenson were chosen to endorse Guinness. Not only did they represent Ireland on the pitch, Moran and Stapleton achieved FA Cup glory with Manchester United in 1983, so their stars were very much in the ascendancy.

One of the Stapleton ads contains images of the footballer in two contrasting settings. In the main image, he wears the green jersey and holds his hands aloft while standing in a packed stadium. In the other, he sips a pint of Guinness in a pub setting. The implication is that this is his reward after playing in an international match. The copy in the ad is written from his perspective and initially, he seeks to dispel any doubt in people's minds that his job is not full-time: 'Any spare time I *do* have is precious. So I usually spend it at home with my family or else my wife Christine and I head down to the local pub with a few pals, where a friendly game of darts and a nice creamy Guinness is the standing order.' These few lines say so much about Stapleton. He works hard, he appreciates his time off, he is a family man and when he goes to the pub, Guinness is a natural part of his routine. Despite his fame and success, the way in which he describes his life, equates it to that of any other workingman. His values and work ethic do not threaten the reputation of Guinness. His admiration knows no bounds and he equates the 'first taste of that lovely smooth head' with scoring a goal in an international match at Lansdowne Road. Later in the ad, he places the beverage in the same category as Manchester United, a football club that boasts a considerable fan-base in Ireland, when he muses:

> There's something very special about the pint of Guinness that's hard to pinpoint. I suppose it's like asking why Manchester United is different from other football clubs. There's a kind of charisma there that makes anything else seem like second best.

Manchester United won the FA Cup in the 1982/3 season, making it the leading football team in the England that year. By association, the implication is that Guinness is in a league of its own and is the best in its category. This is why, in Stapleton's opinion, there is no substitute for Guinness: 'First Division football, there's always another man willing to fill your jersey – but when it comes to pints, there's simply no substitute for Guinness.'

Professional cyclist Seán Kelly did very well on the European circuit and in 1982 and 1983, he was the overall winner of the Paris–Nice race. He featured in a number of print ads for Guinness. Like Stapleton, Kelly compares the taste of his first pint to one of his sporting highlights. However, Kelly's ad is pitched at the novice Guinness drinker, hence the comparison with his first days as an amateur cyclist in France. He addresses the long-standing challenges that someone faces when trying something new. In doing so, he captures the innate apprehension of someone about to sample their first sup of Guinness, a feeling that, he assures the audience, dissipates with trial:

> I remember having my first pint of Guinness. Even though I'd heard a lot about it, and was very keen to try it, I didn't know what to expect. But after my first taste, I knew I was on to a good thing.

His words address one of the most significant barriers that confront potential Guinness drinkers. By 1983, much had already been written about Guinness and compared to many of the new drinks, it was marked out as 'an acquired taste.' Everyone has to start somewhere and just as Kelly tentatively sampled his first Guinness, so too did he launch his cycling career. Tenacity in sport paid off and after a year in France, he signed with the Sem-Loire France team. In the ad, he explains that his new employers 'don't mind if I relax with a Guinness now and then – since it has less calories than most lagers.' Traditionally, Guinness aimed this message at women but on this occasion it charges Kelly with the task of spreading the good news to those, particularly men, who are interested in competitive sport. While he highlights the calorific benefits of Guinness, his espousal of the beverage might subliminally resurrect the 'Guinness for strength' moniker. Kelly was a much decorated sprint cyclist, a pursuit that calls for strength and power. In common with many professional sports people, he seems concerned with diet and enthuses about Guinness because 'it's pure and natural. I've always found most other drinks taste a bit synthetic.' Without naming them, he dismisses many of Guinness's competitors and reminds audiences that this is because the stout's provenance does not include additives and manmade ingredients. The main image in the ad shows a jubilant Kelly as he crosses the finish line on his bike. In a second photo, Kelly sips a pint of Guinness in a relaxed and convivial atmosphere. The overall narrative suggests that it is possible to enjoy a pint of Guinness from time to time while still managing to fulfil one's potential. The headline, which is presented as a quote by Kelly, fits with the sporting theme: 'A smoother pint from start to finish.' The closing tagline, 'Guinness. No beer comes near,' places Kelly and Guinness in the same elite category, way ahead of the competition.

The remaining Kelly ads are less wordy and instead they use sporting and cycling metaphors to convey messages that put Guinness ahead of its competitors. For example, in one of the ads the word Guinness, rendered in its unique lettering, constitutes what is usually the continuous white line marking in the middle of a road. Kelly wears the gold and black of Guinness and leads the peloton by some considerable distance. The headline compliments the visual components of the ad: 'Guinness is miles ahead of the rest.' To lend credibility to the statement, it is endorsed by Kelly's signature. In another ad, the head of a pint of Guinness represents the finish-line of a bike race. Kelly crosses the line first and this time the headline boasts: 'A better pint from start to finish.' A striking feature of the Kelly ads is the absence of a helmet. Protective headwear was not mandatory for professional cyclists until Andrei Kivilev died in 2003 having sustained catastrophic injuries in the Paris–Nice race.

A pithy black-and-white press ad for Guinness in 1983 features a cyclist's gloved hands on handlebars and a Guinness lorry transporting kegs (see Figure 21). The cyclist is unidentifiable, save for the text: 'You'll never find Sean Kelly behind anything else.' With the tagline 'No beer comes near,' Guinness and Sean Kelly are placed ahead of their competitors.

By 1983, Irish-American tennis player Matt Doyle was at the peak of his powers and was part of the first Irish team ever to compete in the World Group stages of the Davis Cup. The team played against the United States in the RDS in Dublin. Ireland was beaten, but in reality many spectators attended the contest in order to see the multiple grand slam champion John McEnroe. However, it raised the profile of California-born Matt Doyle, who soon became the number-one ranked tennis player in Ireland. Being the best in his sport made him an ideal ambassador for Guinness and in 1983, he featured in the 'No beer comes near' print campaign. An Irish audience could relate to his heritage. He was born in the United States, he spoke with an American accent but he had Irish roots and his name was very familiar. Many Irish people had American cousins with a heritage just like his, so it did not seem strange that he would want to represent Ireland in competitive sport. The ad followed the familiar template and started with a tennis-oriented headline that was endorsed by Doyle's signature: 'When a Guinness is served, it's always an ace.' Unlike Sean Kelly, he does not allude to the fact that some people struggle to acquire a taste for Guinness. Instead, he compares his sport to tennis in a very favourable way:

Figure 21: Handlebars

> At one time, I think tennis was a slightly exclusive pastime. People saw it as being tasteful and relaxing – not unlike a pint of Guinness. I can tell you first hand that the pint hasn't changed. It's still beautiful – lovely and smooth and creamy.

In his opinion, there is nothing difficult or challenging about Guinness. Like Kelly, he refers to the beer's quality, something he judges when in Ireland for three months each year: 'That's when I appreciate a nice pint of Guinness. European and American beers always seem a bit watery to me. Guinness is much more natural.' This might have been a reference to Heineken, which came from Europe. He went on to justify his preference by mentioning the favourable calorie count when compared to lagers. He and Kelly make it acceptable for men to take this into consideration and show that concerns about calories are not confined to women.

The national hunt jockey Tommy Carberry retired in 1982 but was a firm favourite with Irish punters, having achieved considerable success at home and abroad. Guinness capitalises on this with the 1983 poster ad, which mainly consists of imagery and a horse-related headline: 'It's a jump ahead of the rest,' a sentiment that is endorsed by Carberry's signature endorses the sentiment.

In 1989, Ray Houghton featured in a print ad for Guinness. That year, he scored the winning goal for Ireland against England in the European Championships and with that, the Scot of Irish origins achieved notoriety in Ireland. All of these sportsmen had much in common with many Irish people. They journeyed to other countries to find success, and even those who were the offspring of previous generations of Irish emigrants, donned the green jersey with pride. Leaving Ireland had not made these people feel or seem any less Irish and most onlookers could relate to their journeys.

In the 1987/8 'Switch over to cool Guinness' series of TV ads, Guinness experimented with a number of themes that personified the fluid state of Irish culture and the nation's appetite for outside influences. The advertising agency drew inspiration from the popularity of British television among Irish viewers. The ads comprise a series of puns that are reinforced by simple images, which anyone familiar with television programmes would understand. The ad 'Soap' takes advantage of the fact that soap operas, particularly those of British origin, were firm favourites in Ireland. Irish TV audiences enthusiastically added the BBC's *Eastenders*, which launched in 1985, to the likes of the long-running *Coronation Street* and *Emmerdale Farm*. However, some viewers may have felt that they were being bombarded by too many soap operas. This sentiment is captured in *Soap*: 'When you're tired of watching soap …'. The voiceover is accompanied by a simple, literal image of a piece of soap in a soap dish on a television screen, as if the centrepiece of a programme. The solution to the tedium is provided in the ad. A man changes the channel on the television, and the voiceover advises: 'Switch over to cool Guinness.' The simple imagery sees Guinness usurping the leading role in the TV programme, having supplanted the soap.

'Laughter' pays homage to the sitcom, which was a highly successful format on the BBC in the 1980s. For example, *Only Fools and Horses* drew millions of viewers every week across Ireland and the UK. Like so many programmes in the comedy genre, canned laughter was a common sound effect. This is conveyed literally in the ad. The format is the same as 'Soap' but this time, a can labelled 'Canned Laughter' takes centre stage. Its lid moves up and down to simulate a laughter motion. The ad concludes in much the same way as 'Soap', only this time as the man's hand presses a button on the TV to change the channel, the voiceover says, to the sound of canned laughter: 'Joking apart, isn't it time you … switched over to cool Guinness.'

The next ad in the series, 'Rhubarb' picks up on the fact that throughout the 1980s current affairs programmes grew in popularity. Productions like RTE's *Today Tonight* gained approval in the ratings, as Irish people attempted to make sense of the issues that impacted on their lives. Also, they watched current affairs programmes like *Panorama* and *Newsnight* on the BBC. However 'Rhubarb' intimates that a TV diet rich in current affairs programmes may have been overwhelming, especially for Irish viewers who were in the throes of coping with very challenging times. It foregrounds the colloquial term, rhubarb, in recognition of the fact that politicians often populate these programmes and of course, they are renowned for talking a lot of 'rhubarb.' This time, stalks of rhubarb star in the TV programme. To background murmerings of 'rhubarb, rhubarb,' the voiceover offers some hope to viewers: 'When you're fed up with current affairs … switch over to cool Guinness.'

In the 1980s, the production values of nature programmes benefitted from technological advances and David Attenborough's *The Living Planet: A Portrait of the Earth* enthralled television audiences. The ad 'Bird' picks up on this, although it is not very complimentary about the nature programme genre! The voiceover clearly implies that nature programmes might bore viewers when, against a soundtrack of birdsong, he empathises: 'If you tend to (pause) drop off during nature programmes … switch over to cool Guinness.'

This series of quirky ads demonstrates just how influential and ubiquitous British popular culture had become in Ireland by the 1980s. They are very simple and yet they capture Guinness's willingness to allow its advertising agency to draw on a diverse range of international cultural references when creating ads.

Dancing to a different tune

Music has always formed an integral part of Irish culture and identity and according to O'Connor (1991), it offers insights into Ireland's history, particularly in relation to emigration. Like its emigrants, Irish music ebbs and flows between home and abroad, particularly the United States, England, Canada and Australia. O'Connor (1991: 8) suggests that: 'The traditional music of Ireland was the only enduring cultural baggage, intangible as it was, that impoverished emigrants could take out of the country.' Building on this insight, she cites the journey as a recurring theme in Irish music and suggests that due to its forced, involuntary nature, it has connotations of enforced exile. Her interpretation of exile transcends physical departure from Irish shores, as she contends that those who remained during the Viking and Norman invasions and the English colonisation, were sentenced to an internal exile. Such experiences inspired artistic endeavours, including music and in the meantime, emigrants who returned to Ireland came back with a 'fuller suitcase' that included influences from abroad. Consequently, by the 1980s it was difficult to define what was meant by the term Irish music. Its exponents pursued a myriad of directions and counted country, rock, pop, folk and blues among the genres that inspired them. Consequently, O'Connor (1991) views the 1980s as a time in Irish popular music history when rock and traditional music merged as Irish artists adopted a more contemporary style while maintaining an Irish voice.

Did this imply that Ireland's music culture had all but disappeared by the 1980s, having surrendered its identity to more powerful musical influences from around the world? Vignoles (1984: 72) argues that: 'It's almost impossible for a country like Ireland to have an independent pop music culture, given Britain's size, its media's influence and its linguistic dominance.' However, Irish music as a category continued to exist, as Irish artists who were successful on the international stage were just as likely to be categorised according to their nationality as their music genre. On paper at least, this kept the Irish music category alive, but even this is something that puzzles Bono. He muses (Hewson et al. 1988) about the benign cultural backdrop against which he grew up. He contends that, at a surface level at least, there is nothing particularly Irish about his music and that it was influenced by the same things that might have influenced his contemporaries in Britain. However, he admits that U2's music does betray the nationality of the band because if one listens to the lyrics, honesty and passion permeate them in a way that he feels is lacking in the words of British musicians. He recalls how he was:

> Called a 'White Nigger' once by a black musician, and I took it as he meant it, as a compliment. The Irish, like the blacks, feel like outsiders. There's a feeling of being homeless, migrant, but I suppose that's what all art is – a search for identity. (Hewson et al. 1988: 190)

His words were spoken in 1988, when emigration rates were still very high. They articulate the struggles that often went through the minds of both those who left, as well as those who stayed behind in Ireland in the 1980s. They express the feelings of exile that haunted many Irish people, regardless of where they lived.

In 1982, Guinness launched a series of TV and print ads featuring musicians who had achieved success in both Ireland and abroad. Their careers mirrored the journeys on which many Irish people had embarked. The Chieftains featured in the first of the TV ads, in what was referred to as the 'No beer comes near' series. They had achieved what O'Connor (1991) describes as 'supergroup' status in the 1970s and this was underlined in 1982 when they performed at Slane Castle with American artists The J. Geils Band and George Thorogood and the Destroyers. The headline act was the British act, The Rolling Stones. Slane Castle hosted its first stadium style concert in 1981 with great aplomb, although that year was a much more Irish affair, headlined by Thin Lizzy. However, like The Chieftains, they too were internationally acclaimed and capable of drawing a large crowd. It would appear that this is an important determinant of success in Ireland for Irish artists. Vignoles (1984) contends that unless Irish bands make it in England or America, they are unlikely to court high levels of success in their home market, regardless of talent. In 1981, U2 were a mere support act at Slane because they had not yet made it on the international stage. Vignoles notes that in 1982, they attracted a crowd of around 3,000 to Punchestown but it was not until the following year, when they had achieved success abroad, that around 18,000 music lovers went to see them at the same venue.

In relation to the 'No beer comes near' series, it was important for Guinness to align the brand with artists that would appeal to its target audience, in the same way that the artists themselves would appeal to the record-buying and concert-going public. The Chieftains and the other musicians in the series fell into this category. The international popularity of The Chieftains is clear in the ad. It is largely set in New York, always a popular destination for Irish emigrants and it features live performances in front of very large audiences. The ad opens with an aerial shot of the head of a pint, which quickly morphs into a *bodhrán* being played. Strains of the music of The Chieftains can be heard in the background and the rhythm of the *bodhrán* creates an air of excitement. The voiceover links the ancient instrument, much loved by traditional Irish musicians, to the long-established drink when he says: 'The beat of the *bodhrán*, the cream of the head.' Attention turns to The Chieftains on stage, playing in front of a very large outdoor audience, possibly at Slane Castle in 1982. The implication is clear. This is a very popular band, capable of drawing large crowds.

The voiceover continues to link Guinness with the band: 'The cream of the head. The unmistakeable taste. The unmistakeable sound.' The success of both Guinness and The Chieftains is comparable. The word 'cream' is a metaphor for 'best' and 'Guinness' and at that time both are deemed the best in their category. As the ad progresses, the individual members of The Chieftains endorse Guinness. First up is a close-up of Paddy Maloney, eulogising about the famous drink: 'Guinness is a beautiful pint – smooth as you like it.' The camera pans to shots of an appreciative audience, beholden to The Chieftains and Guinness. The next shot takes in Derek Bell playing the harp, a subtle nod to the Guinness logo that forges yet another link between the two.

Suddenly, the band is transported across the Atlantic, where a yellow taxi is being loaded with the band's equipment, on what can only be a New York street. Their international success is evident. A woman wearing a New York Yankees jacket is served pints of Guinness at the bar. She might be Irish, living in New York, or she might be American. The point is that Guinness is equally at home in Ireland as it is in New York, but by being there, it brings a little bit of Irish culture to a place where Irish people feel at home. Like the Irish, Guinness travels, while still retaining its strong Irish identity.

Throughout the ad, there is a sense that being able to enjoy Guinness during their downtime makes them feel at home. This puts them on a similar footing with fellow Irish travellers, be they emigrants, holidaymakers, or business travellers. Another of the band's fiddle players, Seán Keane, stares into the lens of the camera and without flinching says: 'Guinness has a style and taste of its own and it comes naturally.' This statement says so much about the impression that Guinness wants to convey – it is a unique product and it is made of natural ingredients. The closing shot is given over to a solitary pint of Guinness, set on a stage. The pint has taken centre stage and like its co-stars, it is an international superstar.

Clannad was another one of Ireland's most successful groups in the 1970s and 1980s. Their Irish provenance was never in doubt, despite the fact that their music was a mix of Irish and international genres, including folk, jazz and classical. Technology was widely used in popular music at that time, with bands like Depeche Mode and Kraftwerk enjoying considerable success across Europe. Clannad embraced technology in their music, adding an otherworldliness to their sound. In doing so, they demonstrated a willingness to put a contemporary twist on their deeply rooted Irish sound. They utilised all that was positive about Irish identity, in that they drew on a deep well of Irish music influences, marrying them with contemporary techniques and genres to create their own unique sound. In 1982, they became the highest charting Irish artists in the British charts by reaching number five with the theme song from the Yorkshire Television production, *Harry's Game.*

In 1983, following on from this success, Guinness invited Clannad to feature in an ad in the 'No beer comes near' series. Like The Chieftains, they achieved considerable success outside of Ireland and therein lay their appeal to a wider audience. This status is conveyed from the start, with a shot of shimmering water and an illuminated bridge in Amsterdam. It is filmed at night and the narrative moves to a tram, winding its way through the city, before it stops at the world famous Concert Hall, Concertgebouw. The sign aloft the front of the building informs the viewer: 'Clannad on tour,' before going inside where Clannad are on stage. The camera focuses on the band's flautist, Pól Brennan. He introduces a song to the audience and his words create a link between the band's music and Guinness: 'This song is about a famous pint. It's called *Into the Dark*. We hope you like it.' The drink is so famous internationally that its name is not required in the introduction. The song selection is deliberate and is played throughout, adding an atmospheric and instantly recognisable backing track to the ad. Using visual triggers throughout, 'the Dark' referred to in the song signifies Guinness. Clannad performs on a circular stage, which perches on top of a giant pint of Guinness. The image is surreal, in keeping with Clannad's mystical sound. The harp is a vital ingredient in Clannad's sound and the instrument is centre stage. Like the harp in The Chieftains ad, it serves as a link to the harp in Guinness's logo.

Suddenly, the band is at the top of a cliff in Ireland, most likely in their home county of Donegal. Surrounded by megalithic stones, Pól and Ciarán sit at a picnic table, bedecked with sheets of music and a pint of Guinness. This reinforces the link between Guinness, music and creativity. The atmosphere is magical, remote and ethereal and although it is night-time, strong, unearthly shades of intense blue and green prevail. This particular scene appears to be influenced by David Mallet, who directed David Bowie's seminal and surreal music video for the global 1980 hit, 'Ashes to Ashes'.

Meanwhile, the accompanying voiceover in the ad tells the audience that Clannad are going to talk about their music, whereupon Pól is seen writing music for 'Into the Dark', seemingly taking inspiration from the setting in which he finds himself. He shares his thoughts with the viewer: 'You never know how good a song can be until you try it in front of a live audience. That's the real test.' The narrative returns to the concert hall in Amsterdam, where Pól plays the flute in front of an audience. Ciarán Brennan remarks: 'You never know how good a pint can be until you've had a pint of Guinness.' He advises people to try it before dismissing it, recognition of the fact that its notoriety can be a hindrance at times. Preconceived views of what Guinness tastes like might deter people from trying it in the first place. The camera follows Clannad where the band drinks Guinness, and the voiceover boasts: 'There's only one worthy of the name.' While these words refer to Guinness, they might just as easily relate to Clannad, a band that is unique in the music world, just as Guinness is unique in the world of alcohol. Ciarán Brennan holds his pint aloft, and having taken a long sip, he says: 'That's what I call a pint … beautiful.' The viewer sees a final shot of the band on stage. This time Clannad conclude their show, which prompts a relieved Pól to say: 'I think they like it.' While he is referring to the show, Guinness has the last word as a pint appears in the closing seconds of the ad, and the voiceover boasts: 'Guinness, no beer comes near.'

Another ad in the same series features the English singer, Elkie Brooks. She enjoyed stellar success in the UK and Ireland in the 1970s, with hits like 'Lilac Wine' and 'Pearl's a Singer'. Her star still shone brightly in the early years of the 1980s and in 1983 she fronted an ad for Guinness. Partnering The Chieftains was a more obvious choice for Guinness, not just because they are Irish but because, when the ad was made, the band members were men in their late thirties, representative of the typical Guinness drinker. Elkie Brooks was around the same age, but as a woman she symbolised a much smaller group of Guinness drinkers, namely females. She embodied independence and determination and she had made it in an industry dominated by men. Despite her success, she came across as a very natural, down-to-earth woman, someone to whom women and men could relate. By selecting an English woman and filming her in an Irish environment, Guinness capitalised on the fluid state of communications that had widened its target audience's horizons. Many Irish people at that time would have been just as familiar, if not more so, with music and entertainment that originated outside the State. This situation was copper-fastened when the global music channel, MTV was launched in 1983 (the same year the ad was made). Its remit was to deliver popular music from all over the world into the homes of young, Irish people, twenty-four hours a day, seven days a week. The democratisation of communications willingly tapped into a cohort that typically embraced change and, with that, music went global.

The soundtrack to the ad is Elkie Brooks' 1977 hit single, 'Pearl's a Singer'. The voiceover copy is succinct and the words are carefully chosen so as to encapsulate Elkie's and Guinness's overlapping characteristics:

> The natural style of Elkie Brooks.
> The natural taste of Guinness.
> Smooth
> Original
> The unique sound.
> The unique taste of Guinness.

The script is brought to life with images of Elkie on tour in Ireland. The viewer sees her in various scenes – disembarking from a private plane, performing 'Pearl's a Singer' at a concert, emerging from the Shelbourne Hotel (the most famous Irish hotel at that time) and shopping on Dublin's Grafton Street.

In one scene, Elkie sits at a table with friends (one of them wears a Guinness t-shirt), when a tray bearing the Guinness logo and goblet glasses of the beverage is placed on the table. The women have permed hairstyles, which were the height of fashion in the 1980s. This suggests that they keep up with trends and, by inference this most likely extends to their choice of beverage. Elkie smiles and says in her distinctly Mancunian accent: 'Two things come very naturally to me – singing the blues and sinking a Guinness.' In the final scene, she turns to the camera, smiles and licks Guinness from her lips. The male voiceover concludes: 'No beer comes near.' Throughout the ad, Elkie is presented as a very approachable, friendly person, despite her star status. She laughs and smiles and in many of the scenes, she is with male and female friends. Her clothes are predominantly black and white, perfectly aligned with the Guinness colours. Her demeanour exudes an air of friendliness and familiarity, and if Guinness was a person, it might exhibit similar traits.

The 'No Beer Comes Near' series was accompanied by a number of print ads that featured the stars of the ads discussed above, as well as some other popular artists. One of them was the international star, Mike Oldfield who enjoyed enormous success in the 1970s with the experimental album, 'Tubular Bells' and with the hit single, 'Moonlight Shadow' in 1983. In another ad, the popular Irish artist, Freddy White is shown, standing at a microphone stand playing his guitar. The Guinness name and logo are behind him and he is quoted as saying: 'Guinness is out on its own.' White enjoyed limited success on the international stage, but as a live performer and not in record sales. Many of his fans in Ireland would have associated seeing him in venues where alcohol was sold, so the link between him and Guinness made sense.

Mary Black features in a few of the print ads in 1983. Her star was rising around that time. O'Connor (1991) explains how she adapted her style from traditional and folk in her formative years, to a more rock-influenced sound in the 1980s. In addition to a successful solo career, she toured with the traditional band, De Danann, also in the 1980s. Her name held obvious attractions for Guinness, hence the headline in one of the ads, 'Black, smooth and natural.' In main body copy her strengths are compared to those of Guinness: 'If you were to describe Mary Black's music as pure, smooth and natural, then you would also have a pretty good description of her favourite drink, Guinness.' These words demonstrate that it was not just her name that appealed to Guinness. Like Elkie Brooks, she was a positive female role model, strong and successful in a male-dominated industry. The quote from Black in the second part of the ad offers an insight into the unique challenges facing women who worked in the music industry: 'And with less calories than most beers and lagers, Guinness is the perfect drink if you want to stay in top shape. So it's not just the Guinness that looks good.' Clearly aimed at women, the ad highlights one of the benefits of drinking Guinness, as opposed to other alcohol beverages.

In print ad featuring Black, she is given more space to express herself. She reminisces about her childhood: 'As far back as I can remember there was music in our family.' When she leaves her teenage years, she progresses to singing in pubs and clubs where she: 'developed a taste for a wide variety of musical styles – and a nice cool glass of Guinness.' Her next words are aimed at reassuring those who are deterred from trying Guinness because of its reputation as having a taste that takes time to grow on the drinker: 'Some drinks can take a long time to get used to but I seemed to take to Guinness the first time I tasted it.' She opens up about the challenges of touring, and strikes a chord with working mothers: 'I always miss my son Conor.' Her words conclude with an endorsement of Guinness's quality: 'Songs sound a bit different each time you sing them but Guinness is always the same – dark, creamy and lovely and smooth.'

The Chieftains, Clannad and Elkie Brooks all feature in this particular series of print ads. In the Clannad ads, Máire Brennan is the main focus, which positions Guinness as a drink that will appeal to women. She stares out of the poster, daring the viewer to make eye contact. Her bandmates stand behind her, leaving her to take centre stage. This position is reinforced by rays of sun, which are reminiscent of an on-stage spotlight that place even greater emphasis on Brennan.

In another ad, she is alone and pictured holding a glass of Guinness. She opens up about her life and, as with the Mary Black ads, she appeals directly to women. 'I'm often asked how it feels to be the only girl in an all-male band.' Later in the ad, she recalls how she first came across Guinness: 'When I was growing up in Donegal, more or less everyone drank Guinness. So I suppose I was bound to try it myself sooner or later.' Like Black, she admits to have been reticent about trying Guinness: 'I must say I was a bit cautious at first, not knowing what to expect. But it didn't take me long to lose my shyness!' Again, these words reassure potential Guinness drinkers, particularly women, that Guinness is a palatable drink. She continues enthusiastically: 'Guinness really is a smashing drink, lovely and creamy with a totally individual taste too.' Her next point addresses the main concern of women drinkers: 'An added bonus is that Guinness has fewer calories than many other drinks – which is all the more reason for liking it of course.'

The calorie count of a glass of Guinness is highlighted in some other print ads too. This focus continues in the spirit of some of Guinness's female oriented ads in the 1970s, which tapped into women's concerns with drink and weight gain. Not only do the print ads from 1983 state that there are ninety-four calories in a half pint of Guinness, but they tackle competitors head-on too by headlining the calorific composition of vodka and white lemonade and lagers as 104 and ninety-five to 180 calories respectively (see Figure 22). The blurred images of females socialising, without a male in sight, normalises their choice of drink and lends credibility to the claims about Guinness's calorie count. From a legal perspective, in the 1980s, advertisers were not permitted to name competitor brands specifically but it would have been relatively straightforward for consumers to deduce from the visual clues exactly which products and brands were under the spotlight.

Everything should be the same … or should it?

In the 1980s, discourse in the worlds of business and academia focused on globalisation and whether or not it would result in the widespread standardisation of marketing strategies. The debate was brought to the fore as far back as 1968 when Buzzell (1968) posed the question: 'Can you standardize multinational marketing?' In his pivotal article, he did not refer to globalisation, a term that was not part of the rhetoric at that time. Instead, he focused on multinational marketing and multinational corporations (MNCs). He considered the extent to which elements of strategy could be, or indeed should be standardised. At the time, this was quite a radical proposition because most MNCs favoured localised strategies. He described some of the benefits that might be reaped if standardised strategies were pursued. They included cost savings in areas like product design, packaging and advertising; consistency with customers, many of whom had grown more accustomed to foreign travel and borderless communications; improved planning and control in companies; and finally, the exploitation of good ideas, such as the roll-out of similar advertising concepts across markets. He presented a balanced case and conceded that as well as the benefits, there were barriers to standardisation. They included the existence of distinct cultures in different countries, dissimilar competitive environments and variations in the types of advertising media that were available across markets.

Figure 22: The long and the short of it

Importantly, the seeds were sown and the debate continued in the 1970s. Sorenson (1975) agreed with much of Buzzell's thesis. When he wrote his article, there was a more marked movement of people as a result of growing international tourism and the EEC's expansion. He contended that these factors would favour product standardisation across markets. In common with Buzzell, he was of the opinion that the increasing overflow of advertising media across borders helped create the conditions necessary for greater standardisation of marketing strategies. Irish consumers, particularly those living in the east of the country, were well acquainted with this phenomenon having watched ads aimed at a British market on Granada TV since 1956. With the arrival of Channel 4 in 1982 and the prevalence of print media from the UK, the overflow intensified. These media outlets were full of ads for British, European and international products and services, thereby familiarising Irish audiences with a vast array of brands.

Due to the open nature of Ireland's economy, business leaders, commentators and academics could not ignore the debate, especially when it reached new heights in 1983 with the publication of Theodore Levitt's provocative article, 'The globalization of markets'. In it, he asserted that consumers were rapidly becoming more homogenised and that given the opportunity, were predisposed to consuming the same products regardless of the country in which they lived. He advocated that technological advances would steer the world towards converging commonality in terms of communications, transport and travel. He argued strenuously that due to these changes, travel and communications would no longer remain the preserve of the few but would be open to the masses. It was not long before the de-regulation of Europe's airline industry and the arrival of Ryanair in 1985 would make the travel part of this prediction a reality for Irish people, thus awakening their latent tastes for new products. There were no half measures in Levitt's thesis and he surmised that for consumers, the lure of low-priced, homogenous products was too irresistible and had the capacity to extinguish demand for culturally sensitive products. He considered this an exciting prospect for consumers because they would have access to the same products, regardless of where in the world they lived. From a company's perspective, it offered the possibility of financial savings, which would arise from economies of scale in production.

Levitt's Orwellian conclusions invoked many responses and some railed against the vista of homogeneity, a world where individual cultural differences were ignored in the quest for the global standardisation of products. Boddewyn et al. (1986) refuted his claims, citing a lack of evidence for many of the views in his article. Their research led them to conclude that product standardisation was much more likely to occur in industrial product markets, whereas it was less common in many non-durable consumer products, such as food. They put this down to the existence of embedded national tastes and habits, varied national regulations and the diverse competitive structure of markets. Although an alcoholic beverage, Guinness is such a product and prides itself on its unique nature, perhaps protecting it somewhat from the vagaries of globalisation, for the time being at least. Quelch and Hoff (1986: 59) counselled that Levitt's all or nothing conclusions were too extreme and like other critics, conducted a more nuanced review of globalisation. It led them to conclude: 'the big issue today is not whether to go global but how to tailor the global concept to fit each business and how to make it work.' In their opinion, a 'one-size-fits-all' methodology was inadvisable and instead, he recommended a flexible approach.

Similarly, Douglas and Wind (1987) refuted Levitt's largely one-sided theory too, arguing that it was over-simplistic. Instead, they presented more balanced views on globalisation and took both sides into account. In its favour, they acknowledged the inevitable convergence of international markets, driven primarily by technology and the dismantling of barriers. Also, they were not opposed to the view that this facilitated the emergence of global market segments and the homogeneity of some consumer interests and tastes, the word 'some' being important. Significantly, they did not concur with Levitt's view that consumer tastes were homogeneous in all instances but that they were still often driven by nation-specific behaviour. They reasoned that Levitt ignored the fact that standardisation might only work in some product categories and with particular customer segments, for example, luxury branded products aimed at the wealthy for whom tastes were the same, regardless of nationality.

While the arguments about the possibilities of globalisation continued throughout the 1980s and beyond, Guinness experienced its impact at first hand. In the 1990s, it was subsumed into a global drinks corporation of the type envisaged by some of the academics at the forefront of the debate. Meanwhile, at the height of Ireland's recession in the 1980s, Guinness was the leader in the Irish beer market but nevertheless proactively sought out opportunities to keep competitors at bay in order to maintain that position. Just as predicted and recorded by commentators on multinational marketing and globalisation, their arrival in Ireland was facilitated by the reduction of international trade barriers, which would be dismantled further as a result of the Single European Act in 1992. In response to all of this change and debate about globalisation, the reconstruction of St James's Gate Brewery in Dublin was completed in 1988, paving the way for standardisation in production, if desired. It housed some of the most technically advanced equipment in the world, enabling it to produce high-quality, canned draught Guinness in large quantities (Guinness 1988). Its popularity is attributed to the fact that an innovative, patented, in-can system enabled drinkers to enjoy pub-standard draught Guinness in their own homes. In 1989, Guinness launched a number of simple, TV adverts, advising viewers that draught Guinness was now available in a can.

Despite their simplicity, the ads were a signal of intent from Guinness. In Levitt's version of the world economy, products are uniform and produced in cost efficient, technologically advanced factories. Therefore, unless the beverage was altered deliberately for export markets, someone in Germany consuming the 1989 version of Guinness draught from a can, would have had the same experience as a consumer in Ireland. Investment in a state-of-the-art brewing plant meant that Guinness drinkers around the world could replicate the taste experience of those living in Ireland. 'Wherever you're coming from, wherever you're going, canned draught Guinness – take it away.' This line of copy from one of the ads has many meanings. At its simplest, it speaks to the domestic Irish consumer who wants to purchase a few cans of pub-standard Guinness from an off-licence. However, it might resonate with visiting emigrants who want to bring the authentic taste of Guinness back to their adopted homes, where draught Guinness in pubs, if available, did not match the standards in Ireland at that time. Tourists who visited Ireland and enjoyed the experience of drinking Guinness in a pub might have wanted to relive the taste experience when they got home. In essence, the innovative breakthrough presented Guinness with the opportunity to explore the possibilities of pursuing a globalisation strategy of its own.

Meanwhile, Irish consumers' tastes had evolved for many of the same reasons cited by Levitt (1983), including their acquaintance with new products and experiences when travelling for work and leisure purposes, more product choice and greater exposure to international influences via more diverse media platforms. In 1986, Guinness launched Budweiser in Ireland (Guinness 1987), a move that captured the *zeitgeist*. Irish people did not have to visit the US to have been exposed to this all-American brand. Images of actors quaffing the lager were broadcast into their sitting rooms on a regular basis, making Budweiser as desirable as a pint of Guinness. Budweiser seemed to support Levitt's argument and was the ideal poster child for globalisation. The question is, did Guinness stout fit into this category?

In 1989, Guinness broadcast 'Journey', an ad that seems to question the merits of globalisation from a human perspective. It tells a bleak story in a surreal style and implores viewers to stop what they are doing and take stock. It has a cinematic style and opens with an aerial shot of a young man as he enters a warehouse filled with hexagonal boxes, all marked 'Same.' He removes his yellow overalls and defiantly, he flings them to the ground. This signifies his individuality and determination to think differently. He enters the main part of the building and joins a stream of people who walk in line, all wearing yellow boiler suits, similar to those worn by satirical, cult band Devo and carrying yellow bags, overprinted with 'Same.'

It is as if he has walked in on a re-enactment of Dutch graphic artist Escher's seminal work, 'Ascending and Descending' (1960). In an explanation of his graphic design Masterpiece, Escher (2000: 15) refers to its stairway as one that never ends and that it forms part of a daily ritual for a group of inhabitants, possibly monks. 'It would seem that when they get tired they are allowed to turn about and go downstairs instead of up. Yet both directions, though not without meaning, are equally useless.' The futility of the exercise is clear, which makes the actions of two dissenting individuals, who refuse to take part in it, all the more admirable. The headstrong, individualistic character in the Guinness ad might be compared to them although Escher does not hold out much hope for his rebels when he concedes that: 'They have no use for it all, but no doubt sooner or later they will be brought to see the error of their nonconformity.' The scenario bears a similarity to Levitt's extreme view of globalisation, where consumers and organisations alike surrender to homogeneity.

The facial expression of the ad's lead actor betrays his determination to escape from a world where everyone wears the same clothes, walks in the same direction and carries the same bags, which are aptly labelled 'Same.' The colour yellow and stencil-style lettering on the bags and boxes in the ad are reminiscent of the Yellow Pack own brand packaging of food retailer, Crazy Prices. Financially pressed, Irish shoppers were very familiar with the low price range in the 1980s, which represented a joyless, uniform way of consuming everyday products. Meanwhile, the lead actor makes his way to a box marked 'Imitations' and takes out a yellow and black LP sleeve titled, 'More of the same.' He removes the LP and flings it to one side. It disintegrates and a storm crashes into the room, causing objects to swirl around. He battles against the storm, making his way towards the exit, steps outside and stands facing a stormy sea. Up until this point, the soundtrack is a repetitive, uniform synthesised beat, but when the door to the outside world opens, the music changes and dramatic chants can be heard. Some of the workers make it outside but are pushed back inside, and he is alone. Perhaps they do not have the courage to break away from the crowd. At this point, the music switches to the sustained rock notes of a triumphant electric guitar and the main actor walks along a white line towards a dark, swirling horizon that simulates the settling motion of a Guinness. Now he is flanked by figures, and the white line lights up, and a gold Guinness logo and exploding harp appear against a pint. The shimmering image of people in a bar drinking Guinness are reflected in the pint, and to the relief of viewers, the voiceover reassures them: 'Guinness – you'll never look back.' Guinness stands out from the crowd in terms of taste and quality. The ad symbolises one man's victory over Levitt's stance on globalisation, where consumer tastes converge and everything is the same. It emboldens people to be different and step away from the inexorable march towards sameness. For Irish consumers, this means resisting the influx of mass-produced, indistinguishable drinks, in favour of Guinness.

Ironically, despite 'Journey's' message of disdain for sameness, its visual language bears a striking resemblance to Apple's ground-breaking ad, '1984', which launched Apple's Macintosh personal computer. '1984's' mostly black-and-white tale of conformity is interspersed with colour in the guise of a young woman who is determined to rescue the downtrodden masses from a world of conformity. Just as Guinness is the hero in 'Journey', Apple is the saviour in '1984'.

Conclusion

For many Irish people, the 1980s was memorable as a result of the hardship that was visited upon them. It was a decade when unemployment soared and a record number of young people left the country in search of work. Those fortunate enough to have jobs saw their incomes fall as a result of a series of austere budgets, which gave rise to punitive taxes. Even the forces of nature conspired against the nation and harsh winters made life difficult. All of this coincided with the acceleration of Ireland's internationalisation, which challenged its culture and identity. Rather than dwelling on the negatives, Guinness's advertising mainly sought to instil its messages with an air of optimism and positivity. However, rather than ignoring the decade's themes, trends and challenges, it used them to create relatable adverts with a cheerful hue. Even the recession-themed print ads in the early 1980s offered some relief to consumers with their promise of unbeatable value for money.

Guinness did not ignore the emotive issue of emigration but rather than focusing on the sombre side, it dealt with it through upbeat themes. Most notably, its ads showcased the successes enjoyed by Irish people working in other countries. Granted, they featured high-profile artists like the Chieftains, Mary Black and Clannad and successful sportspeople like Seán Kelly and Frank Stapleton. Their bonds with Ireland were evident in the deliberately crafted copy in the ads, which highlighted the ease with which they travelled across boundaries to ply their trades. Those left at home while their sons and daughters, brothers and sisters, aunts and uncles built new lives in the UK and the US, might have been reassured to know that despite their loved ones' commitments abroad, Ireland would always be home. First- and second-generation emigrés like Matt Doyle and Ray Houghton provided comfort too. They symbolised the possibility that even the children and grandchildren of emigrants were deeply connected to their Irish roots.

Many of the ads captured the extent of Ireland's internationalisation and its impact on Irish culture. A growing penchant for popular British sports like darts and snooker was referenced and the inclusion of international music artists like Elkie Brooks and Mike Oldfield sat comfortably with an audience well versed in non-indigenous music. Irish television viewers' familiarity with British programme formats was evident in some of the ads. Even Ireland's age-old relationship with the waterways was given an international twist. Swirling images of the sea were deployed to symbolise the movement in a pint of Guinness as it settles. However, the prominence given to surfers and bikini-clad, oriental women on the beach planted a seed of doubt in the viewer's mind as to whether or not this was an Irish beach. As if sensitive to the enormity of the changes facing Irish audiences, tropes that symbolised Ireland's ancient roots were interspersed with contemporary, imported images. Hauntingly beautiful images of dolmens sat alongside scenes of darts and snooker, reassuring viewers that internationalisation did not have to mean a total desertion of the past.

However, if one compares 'Racehorse', which was broadcast at the start of the decade, with 'Journey', which concluded the decade for Guinness, the change in tone was very apparent. In 'Racehorse', any references to international influences were presented positively. They depicted the types of aspirational lifestyles that could be within the reach of ordinary Irish people. Even if the viewers did not have the jobs to fund it, they could work abroad, just like the oil workers in the ad. In contrast, the narrative in 'Journey' was much more sombre, created for a battle-hardened audience that had been adversely affected by the harsh realities of globalisation. Where 'Racehorse' embraced international influences without interrogation, 'Journey' challenged globalisation and its implications for the individual. Without realising it at the time, it set down a marker for the next decade when both Ireland and Guinness were irrevocably transformed by global forces.

CHAPTER 4

1990–1999: A period of unprecedented change

Introduction

With the benefit of hindsight, the early years of the 1990s in Ireland provided many clues that the years that followed would prove a seminal period in the country's history. In many ways, it was a decade of two halves, both operating at different paces, whilst heading in the same upward trajectory. Its early years bore witness to a number of events that laid the foundation for unprecedented success, prosperity, and confidence. In the summer of 1990, for the first time ever the Irish soccer team participated in a World Cup tournament and its performances brought immense joy to the entire nation. Despite not advancing beyond the quarter-finals of the tournament, 500,000 proud fans turned out on the streets of Dublin to welcome the team back home. It is possible that its exploits were just one of the catalysts that helped change the mind-set of Irish people, for at the end of 1990 Mary Robinson was elected as Ireland's first female president. That this could happen in a country where, less than twenty years previously, women working in the public and banking sectors were forced to resign when they married, prompted many to believe that anything was possible. Peillon (2000: 140) argues that Mary Robinson was a symbol of the 'new' Ireland, a country ready to break with the old ways, and all of its failures.

> She represented an Ireland from which the gloom was seemingly lifting. And this modern Ireland did not reject the past or exclude tradition: all could celebrate this Ireland. Mary Robinson was the medium of this celebration; or rather, Ireland celebrated itself through its President.

Lack of confidence gave way, on the surface in any case, to a golden decade for Ireland. It was fuelled by economic performances that matched, and at times outstripped, the strongest economies in the world. International commentators extolled the virtues of the Celtic Tiger and its economic indicators. Negra (2010: 840) notes that the international press changed the discourse about Ireland and Irishness from one that foregrounded 'the values of idleness to the values of productivity.' In a few short years, Ireland's economic renaissance became a story of international import to journalists with respected publications, including *The Economist* and *The Financial Times*. The country's economic success had an impact on many facets of Irish life and Negra notes that journalists were just as likely to write about U2's commercial prowess, as they were to eulogise about their creativity. Being Irish was a distinct advantage for some artists who used it to achieve considerable success on the global stage during the Celtic Tiger years. While Coulter (2003: 3) hypothesises that they made it 'fashionable to be Irish,' it might be argued that some of them were fashionable because they were Irish. Therefore, it was, in effect, a symbiotic relationship.

One band that achieved long-lasting success was U2. The band conquered the notoriously difficult United States music fans in 1987 with the release of the 'Joshua Tree' album. In the course of the 1990s, they brought things to another level in vast stadia around the world, with their spectacular, multimedia extravaganzas. Smyth (2014: 80) is of the opinion that: 'U2 anticipated the Celtic Tiger, and in some senses provided a language with which to begin to approach and articulate the new moral and socio-economic dispensation.' Their music mirrored the interconnectedness of the world, and resonated with global audiences. Many of the issues and cultural references facing music fans were shared across the globe, something that did not go unnoticed by U2. Fagan (2003: 117) captures this when he suggests that the Irish artists who succeeded on the global stage in the 1990s looked outward for their reference points. With their mix of local constituents, their art is created for a global cultural market. Consequently, he likens them to 'local cultural keys turning global locks.' An example of this is *Riverdance*. When it first came to the attention of a worldwide audience in 1994 as that year's interval 'filler' at the Eurovision Song Contest in Dublin's Point Theatre, few people could have predicted that it would go on to tour the world for more than twenty years (and still counting). It symbolises the moment when the slow, steady recovery in the broken Irish economy moved into top gear and took off. It was as if the Irish were making their presence known to the world, determined to share the joys of their unique style of dancing with as many people as possible. Scahill (2009: 71) suggests: 'In its centering of hybridity, Riverdance both constructs and reflects an image of Irish culture that is postmodern in texture, embracing the ancient and the modern, the local and the global.'

However, Negra (2010: 838) is more critical of some of the Celtic Tiger's international success stories, namely Boyzone and The Corrs. Taking the latter band as an example, she bemoans the fact that they stand for: 'the standardization of the symbolic economy of Irishness in a neo-liberal marketplace.' Just as the Irish landscape in the 1990s was populated by multi-national firms and global retail brands, so too did the output and image of many successful Irish pop groups become a mirror image of those that originated in major international music markets. In their pomp, the Corrs were a metaphor for the Celtic Tiger Ireland, whose young people had more in common with their counterparts in other countries than with a culture that pervaded in Ireland in previous decades.

Such turbulence in Ireland's cultural, economic and social landscapes presented many challenges and opportunities for advertisers. It required their advertising agencies to be agile and alert to the changes that were occurring. This chapter examines the evolution of Guinness's advertising during the Celtic Tiger years. It contends that between 1990 and 1994, the creative styles were largely inward-looking, until it had its '*Riverdance* moment' when one of its most memorable ads, 'Anticipation', was broadcast. It will be argued that while Guinness and its agencies did not always demonstrate an understanding of its target audience, in many instances their insights into the psyche of Ireland's rapidly changing adult population enabled them to create advertising that captured the nation's transition. Consequently, some of the ads perfectly illustrate the extent of the change that occurred in Irish society during the Celtic Tiger period.

The Celtic Tiger: A 'tail' of two halves

In an attempt to unearth the source of the constraints that held Ireland back in previous decades, O'Donnell (1993) argues that, up until the 1990s, Irish identity was not defined by a common national language. Instead, he hypothesises that Catholicism, a strong attachment to land ownership, and mass emigration were key defining features. In a very short period of time, two of these would be recast, one of them forever. Without doubt, a key driver for change was the economic boom that took off in the early years of the decade, gathered pace, and kept going until the early years of the new millennium. By 1994, it had gained a strong foothold, so much so that it was on the radar of international observers and commentators. The most famous of these was the Morgan Stanley economist, Kevin Gardiner, who is credited with coining the term 'Celtic Tiger' (Gardiner 1994). According to O'Hearn (1998), Gardiner defended the label when he cited the growth in Irish exports, a stable, strong exchange rate and economic growth rates, which exceeded the European average.

The seeds of recovery had been sown from 1987 on, when the government undertook to repair the country's finances, although it did not seem that way to many people living in Ireland in the 1980s. The dramatic improvements in the Irish economy were evident when one examines the GDP statistics between 1960 and 1999. According to Bradley's (2000) analysis of the figures provided by *European Economy* in 1998, the relative GDP per head of population in Ireland was 60.8 (out of 100) in 1960; 58.9 in 1973; 63.7 in 1986; and 111 in 1999. This data underlines the immense success of the economic boom, and to put it in perspective, comparable figures in 1999 in Europe's wealthiest economies, Belgium and Germany were 112.5 and 109.1 respectively. According to Fitzgerald (1999), the remarkable turnaround in the economy can be attributed to a number of factors, in particular the inflow of EU structural funds and the considerable growth in foreign direct investment (FDI). Bradley (2000: 14) believes that the FDI inflows 'hastened the de-coupling of the Irish economy from its almost total dependence on the United Kingdom.' While this is very true from an economic perspective, changes in the marketing communications industry and in Guinness's corporate structure brought the Guinness brand in Ireland closer to the UK.

Consumer spending took off in the 1990s, as evidenced by the steep increase in the number of private cars on the road. According to Delamere (2000), there were just 348,000 licensed private cars in Ireland in1968. By 1996, there were 1 million and by 1998, an additional 200,000 cars were licensed. New car sales had never been as strong and while the 109,000 new cars sold in 1996 signified unprecedented levels, this figure was surpassed in 1998 when 139,000 new cars were licensed. Another economic indicator that became synonymous with the Celtic Tiger was the housing boom that took off in 1994. According to Fahey and Duffy (2007), there were three main drivers behind this. They were the annual growth in population of 1.3 per cent in the second half of the decade, the increase in real disposable incomes and falling mortgage interest rates. These conspired to trigger a rise in property prices. The average price of a new house in Dublin more than doubled between 1993 and 1998, rising from £59,000 to £124,200 (McMahon 2000). The national increase was not quite as dramatic but nonetheless, it was significant, going from £55,000 to £97,800. The upturn had a positive impact on employment levels in construction and McMahon states that there were 149,000 people working in the sector by 1999.

In an analysis of male and female employment between 1990 and 2000, Hearn (2003) observes that total employment in the Irish economy rose by more than half a million, which translated into a negligible unemployment rate of just 4 per cent. O'Connell and Russell (2007) explain the relevance of this from a societal perspective. They contrast the fortunes of Ireland in the 1980s when surplus labour resulted in mass unemployment and emigration, to the 1990s when near full employment led to labour shortages and inward migration. However, this does not capture the structural changes that occurred, in particular those relating to gender differences. According to Kennedy (2003), women's participation in the labour force rose significantly in the 1990s. The number of females working in Ireland more than doubled between 1971 and 1996, and rose to 488,000 in that period. Between 1991 and 1996, the number grew by 102,000, which was significant because in just five years the increase equalled that of the previous twenty years. Kennedy goes on to report that the growth in female participation in the labour force was even more spectacular between 1996 and 2000, when it rose by another 128,000. Meanwhile, the number of males at work rose too but at a lower rate. Between 1991 and 1997, an additional 78,300 men joined the labour force (Treacy and O'Connell 2000). However, it was the particularly strong growth in the number of females in the workforce that had far-reaching societal implications. For example, by 1997 the percentage of women involved in full-time 'home duties' had fallen significantly to 41 per cent from 62 per cent in 1971 (Treacy and O'Connell). The full force of the legislative changes that were ratified in the 1970s had taken effect, which allowed women to keep their jobs in the public sector when they married.

However, other structural changes in the economy conspired to attract women into the labour force. The most pertinent of these was the sharp increase in employment opportunities for women in the burgeoning services sector. In common with employment patterns in other industrialised economies, Ireland's economic development resulted in sectoral recalibration. Hence, jobs in the male dominated areas of agriculture and industry declined, while prospects in the services sector became far more commonplace and favourable for women. Madden (2000) reports that the number of people working in agriculture in 1971 was 273,000. By 1996, this had plummeted to 134,000. In the same period, employment in industry rose from 323,000 to 354,000 but as a percentage of all those working, its importance declined and fell from 31 per cent to 27 per cent. In its place, the services sector was the outstanding performer and the numbers working in it between 1971 and 1996 almost doubled, from 459,000 to 819,000. This meant that by 1996, 63 per cent of the labour force was employed in the services sector. It encompasses areas like finance, real estate, education, healthcare, hospitality, advertising, and social work, all of which provided improved prospects for women and third-level graduates when compared to the types of employment opportunities in previous decades. Meanwhile, changing employment patterns and higher levels of exchequer funding helped transform the Irish education system. In 1970, there were just 18,600 full-time third-level students. By 1998, this had reached 112,200, 56 per cent of whom were female (Redmond and Heanue). Unlike previous generations, these graduates were not forced to emigrate and it is clear from many of the Guinness ads in the second half of the 1990s that they targeted this well-educated, affluent segment of young adults.

Another reason behind the transformation of the Irish economy in the 1990s was the dramatic turnaround in migration patterns. Record levels of emigration were a feature of the previous decade, and as previously stated in the 1980s section, many of the emigrants had a third-level qualification. According to Fitzgerald (2000), those emigrants are more likely to return to Ireland than those without a third-level qualification. He illustrates the point by stating that in 1991 more than 25 per cent of all people living in Ireland with a third-level education had lived abroad for at least a year. Like all returning emigrants, they brought back a wealth of experience from other cultures and, due to their qualifications, were more likely to take up well-paid jobs in the growing economy. This made them an attractive target for many advertisers, including Guinness. The phenomenon of returning emigrants was not new for Ireland. In the 1960s and 1970s, some emigrants returned, taking advantage of the improving economy. However, the immigration of the 1990s was very different to anything the country had ever experienced before because between 1996 and 2000, 40 to 50 per cent of immigrants were not born in Ireland, and most of them had a third-level education (Fitzgerald 2000; Hughes et al. 2007). The reason why there was so much immigration in the 1990s can be attributed to the employment opportunities that were available at the time. Suddenly, a new cohort of well-educated, affluent consumers was open to Irish companies, which posed considerable challenges and opportunities in terms of the types of products they might purchase, and the communications strategies that would be most effective in targeting them. Brown (2004: 386) captures the impact of this economic transformation on the Irish psyche when he proclaims that: 'A sense of success, nationally and internationally, gave the country a confidence that its problems would be overcome. An inveterate fatalism about the nation's role in the world was replaced by a spirit of enterprise and expectation.' This signalled a seismic turnaround from the lost decade of the 1980s, when confidence was at an all-time low. It can be likened to a perfect storm, the confluence of just the right mix of political, cultural, economic and legislative transformation.

Of course, the Celtic Tiger economy was not without its problems, and not everyone gained. The record-breaking economic data hid a growing inequality in Irish society. According to O'Hearn (1998), the nature of work changed from the late 1980s onwards, due to the greater incidence of peripheral jobs. These tended to be relatively low paid, part-time and without long-term security. Women and young people inclined towards this type of employment. Greater female participation in the labour force did not signal the end of inequity. According to McMahon (2000), female earnings in 1998 were only 66 per cent of their male counterparts. Another source of inequality was geographic. While enforced emigration took a backseat during the 1990s, national migration continued. By 1996, more than half of all Irish people, or 1.9 million lived in Leinster. Between 1946 and 1996, its population rose from 1.3 million to 1.9 million, while over the same period, the populations in Connacht and Ulster declined (Redmond and Heanue 2000). This was not a new phenomenon but according to O'Hearn, became even more pronounced in the 1990s because the boom was fuelled by inward investment. The multinational corporations (MNCs) that arrived were concentrated in urban areas, leaving rural western counties like Mayo, Roscommon, Leitrim and Cavan marginalised. He blames the paucity of infrastructure in large pockets of the country on this mismatch, thus making it difficult to convince MNCs that such regions would be able to cater for their needs. The inward investment was accompanied by the development of the construction sector, particularly in the Leinster region.

The ensuing exodus from rural Ireland into the country's capital is captured in the 1999 Guinness ad, 'Leaving Home'. Its soundtrack is intense and edgy, reminiscent of Born Slippy's 'Underworld', which featured in the seminal movie of the 1990s, 'Trainspotting'. In the opening shot of the ad, a coach is bound for Dublin. The commentary of a GAA hurling match is on the radio, which belongs to the main protagonist in the ad, a young male passenger. His thoughts form the voiceover, and provide an insight into what it might have been like for a young person living in one of the more marginalised parts of Ireland during the Celtic Tiger years.

> No more small town. No more small minds.
> No more tick-ankled girls. (The camera swoops on a middle-aged, hippy couple, kissing passionately.)
> No more nice job, nice car, nice tie. (Close-up of two middle-aged women, deep in conversation.)
> No more nice! No more Mr O'Brien. No more 'what time do you call this?' (Shot of middle-aged man in a sports jacket looking back disapprovingly at him. He seems to invoke the spirit of the aforementioned Mr O'Brien.)

> No more cosy grey, sat in front of the telly, nowhere to go to, same old, same old life. New job, new town (shot of Dublin's quays), new start.

He holds up his radio and the commentator extols the virtues of what he has witnessed: 'Hurling at its best. Crushing defeat for the home team.' The main actor flails at the air in exasperation and disappointment. Copy appears on the screen: 'Some things you can't leave behind.' This accentuates the tribal nature of inter-county hurling and reminds the main character and viewers that a move to another place does not sunder the deep links one feels for home. It is a discrete reference to Guinness's sponsorship of GAA hurling, which commenced in 1995.

In the closing scene of 'Leaving Home', the ad relocates to a pub, where a man drinks from a pint of Guinness and slams down his glass before the closing text urges viewers to: 'Live life to the power of Guinness.' As well as promoting Guinness, it is a plea to all disenchanted people, urging them to turn their lives around and do something meaningful. A strong economy would have enabled many people to explore their possibilities, provided they were willing to relocate if necessary.

Specific ads promoted the partnership between Guinness and hurling too, and soon after the agreement was reached, the 'Nobody said it was going to be easy' TV and print campaign was launched. Copy in these

Figure 23: This man can level whole counties

print ads states confidently that: 'This man can level whole counties in one second flat' and 'This man can reach speeds of 100mph' (see Figure 23). They emphasise the physicality of the game and in doing so, the ads draw associations between Guinness and strength.

The Celtic Tiger and the marketing communications sector

The years preceding the boom of the Celtic Tiger were quite unremarkable in terms of advertising activity in Ireland. In 1990, advertising expenditure per capita was approximately $140 in Ireland, while in the United Kingdom it was around $200 (Daniels 1995). To put this into context, the Association of Advertisers in Ireland (AAI) reveals that total spend by advertisers across the various media rose from IR£208 million in 1990 to a mere IR£284 million in 1994 (cited in Meenaghan 1995). However, despite the upward trajectory, Meenaghan categorises Ireland as an 'under-advertised' economy at that stage in its development when compared to many other countries, including the UK, where advertising spend as a percentage of GDP was almost twice that of Ireland at that time. The years that followed marked the start of record levels of growth in advertising spend, so much so that its upward flight can be likened to an economic barometer that replicated the highs and lows of the extraordinary changes in the Celtic Tiger's economic climate. According to figures compiled by IAPI/BASE (<http://www.medialive.ie>) in 1995, advertisers placed €344 million worth of ads with magazines, newspapers, TV, radio, cinema, and outdoor media outlets. By 2007, at the peak of the Celtic Tiger, this figure had increased more than fivefold to a record breaking €1.822 billion. Under-investment in advertising in the early years of the 1990s seems to imply that Ireland was at a lower level of advertising literacy than other English speaking countries like the United Kingdom and the United States.

Many factors provided the impetus for transformation in the advertising sector, both in Ireland and abroad. Due to the economy's open nature, any changes on an international level were felt in Ireland. Obviously, the strengthening Irish economy in the 1990s gave companies the confidence and finances required to invest in advertising. This was a boon to advertising agencies and media outlets. However, a number of other factors were involved, and most of these stemmed from abroad. The most significant of those is what Daniels (1995) and Leslie (1995) call the transnationalisation of the advertising industry. Multinational corporations (MNCs) precipitated this because they wanted to coordinate their advertising activity at an international level. Rather than employing the services of an agency in each market, many preferred to work with one or a few agencies in total. Leslie (1995) illustrates this point with IBM, which replaced forty agencies around the world with just one in 1994. However, due to disparities in terms of culture, social norms and legislation, agencies with local knowledge were still required in order to ensure that the execution of the campaigns was authentic and would resonate with local audiences. Importantly, Daniels (1995: 276) emphasises the impact of regulation on the ability of MNCs to standardise advertising and proposes that:

> Global strategies have been necessitated by the close links between the leading agencies and the significant players; the transnational manufacturing and service enterprises. But there is a tension between local and global advertising campaigns, which to a degree arises from the volatile regulatory environment that guides the conduct of advertising at the national level while trade liberalisation offers more flexible opportunities at the international level.

In the 1990s, the European Union started its quest to harmonise the advertising legal framework across member states. However, this has proved to be a slow process because of the prevalence of different legal systems in individual countries. In addition, self-regulation is commonplace in many countries, and Ireland is no different. The Advertising Standards Authority for Ireland (ASAI) is the self-regulatory body established and financed by the advertising industry. Despite its source of funding, it operates successfully as an independent body, and aims to promote 'the highest standards of marketing communications, that is, advertising, promotional marketing and direct marketing … Members of ASAI are required to abide by the Code and not to publish an advertisement or conduct a promotion which contravenes Code rules' (ASAI.ie).

Up until June 1995, Guinness's ads were regulated by the third edition of the ASAI's *Code of Advertising Standards for Ireland*. Significantly, it stipulated that anyone shown drinking, must appear to be more than 25 years of age. Nor could ads suggest or infer that alcohol makes the drinker appealing to the opposite sex. Excusing or encouraging over-indulgence were not permitted. These regulations remained in place until the fourth edition of the Code was published in June 1995, in which the requirements for social responsibility were more stringent. Section 6.4 (b) of the code stipulated that ads: 'shouldn't feature real or fictitious characters who are likely to appeal particularly to people under 18 in a way that would encourage them to drink' (ASAI 1995: 48). In the latter part of the 1990s, Guinness introduced a number of fictitious characters to its advertising, but they were nearly always aged in their mid- to late twenties or more. It is debateable whether or not the main character in 'Leaving Home' was over 25, but at no stage in the ad was he shown drinking alcohol. It did not elicit any complaints and did not become an issue for Guinness. However, contemporary music featured in many of their ads in the second half of the decade and this might have provided Guinness with a way of appealing to a younger age group without contravening the Code.

The revised Code attempted to safeguard against the social consequences of drinking alcohol. It prohibited the encouragement of excess and/or solitary drinking, as well as the purchasing of large rounds. Also banned was the portrayal of 'activities or locations where drinking alcohol would be unsafe or unwise' (ASAI 1995: 49). In this iteration of the Code, consideration was given to the distress that might arise from the advertising of alcohol. It stipulated that ads should not cause fear or distress. The exception to this was when the ad's intent was to deter people from drinking alcohol in a harmful way.

Van Raaij (1997: 268) hypothesises: 'If a brand is a market leader in several markets with the same competitors, a more standardized strategy is possible. If the market structures differ between markets, standardisation is less feasible.' The ASAI codes brought an added layer of complexity and had to be given due consideration by advertisers. In the second half of the

1990s, Guinness stout in Ireland faced many of the same competitors as it did in other markets. Significantly, around that time, while the ads were not completely standardised in Ireland and the United Kingdom, some of them had at their heart the same proposition and concept, while the execution was different (Van Raaij 1997). This is evident in the 'Black and White', and 'Live Life to the Power of Guinness' campaigns, which are discussed later in the chapter.

The 1980s and 1990s witnessed a concerted move towards the consolidation of marketing communications agencies across the globe. Due to its dependence on MNCs, the impact on the Irish advertising industry was particularly substantial.

Daniels (1997) identifies three strategies that international agencies deploy when entering new countries:

1. The establishment of a new office, typically staffed by executives from the founding agency, and some locals.
2. The acquisition of a full or partial interest in an existing agency.
3. The formation of a network of local agencies.

The first approach was not that common in Ireland, as it is quite risky and requires a significant investment. The second two were much more commonplace. Bell, which held the Guinness account for a brief period in 1996, was a subsidiary of Ogilvy and Mather in the United Kingdom and is an example of the second approach identified above. Since then, the Bell name has disappeared and Ogilvy and Mather Ireland Group is a network of local agencies, thus giving the group expertise across a number of key areas. They include advertising, public relations (PR), and digital. The group is overseen by Ogilvy and Mather Worldwide, which is owned by WPP, a global leader in advertising and marketing services. Similarly, Irish International BBDO (now known as BBDO Dublin), which took over the Guinness account in 2001, is part of BBDO Worldwide. In turn, it is owned by the global marketing communications giant Omnicom. Being part of such networks means that if an MNC awards an advertising contract to the parent organisation, the business comes the way of the local agency too. Therefore, these agencies, which are now in the majority, tend to list both domestic and international companies as their clients, thereby giving them a much greater mix of business. For example, BBDO Dublin works with Guinness, Mars, and Barry's Tea.

Oram (1986) recounts how the process of consolidation and international networking started in Ireland as far back as 1979, when the international agency Saatchi and Saatchi took a controlling interest in Dublin-based agency, O'Kennedy Brindley. This typified the way in which an international player might gain a foothold in a local market, and so the pace of mergers and acquisitions continued apace in the 1980s and 1990s. Exact figures for the number of agencies in Ireland under international ownership in the 1990s are difficult to ascertain. The Institute of Advertising Practitioners in Ireland (IAPI) does not keep an archive about members, but it is known that by 2005, thirty-five of the forty main advertising agencies in Ireland were owned by international conglomerates (Neary 2005). By then, the four largest global agency networks were WPP, Publicis, Omnicom and Interpublic and they accounted for 60 per cent of all global advertising billings (Datamonitor 2005).

At the same time, a number of media outlets were launched, thus affording advertisers greater choice when placing their ads, a change that resulted in improved targeting opportunities. The seeds of the expansion in the media landscape were sown in 1988, a year that marked the start of the enactment of a number of broadcasting acts by the Independent Radio and TV Commission (IRTC), subsequently renamed the Broadcasting Authority of Ireland (bai.ie). These acts paved the way for the rapid growth in licences granted to local radio stations in the 1990s, all driven by a commercial imperative and funded primarily by advertising. Similarly, the television landscape was redrawn and in 1996, TG4 commenced broadcasting, soon to be followed with the launch of TV3 in 1998. At the same time, the provision of television services through cable and satellite afforded viewers and advertisers alike more choice. Meanwhile, the profile of advertisers changed in the early years of the Celtic Tiger as globalisation took hold. Some well-known Irish brands were taken over by their more powerful global counterparts, and in many instances, names changed and were consigned to history. Other brand names remained intact but their new owners determined their advertising strategies from then on. For example, in 1996

Unilever acquired Lyons Tea but the brand name remained because of its popularity among Irish consumers. Conversely, Quinnsworth's 1997 acquisition by Tesco resulted in extinction for the Irish brand name. Of course, Guinness was not immune to such change in the 1990s, a decade that heralded the formation of Diageo.

The globalisation debate has formed the backdrop to much discussion in the world of advertising since the 1990s. In their quest to deliver efficiencies, brand managers in global giants like Diageo are constantly under pressure to focus on the similarities between consumers across each of their markets so that they can commission the creation of standard advertisements that resonate across cultures. For national advertising agencies, Fanning's (1999) prediction that globalisation will serve as a rallying call for the preservation of national identity, is a more palatable option. This view concedes that standardisation is inevitable with regard to some aspects of a campaign but if this can be confined to the underlying strategy, local agencies might be given the autonomy to execute it in such a way that the ads will resonate with local audiences. Therefore, it is preferable that advertising campaigns based on national insights be created for each individual market. A willingness to do this results in brands paying homage to variations in national culture and identity and takes into consideration the ways that people communicate with each other through language, visual images and music (Lawes 2002). This scenario contrasts starkly with the spectre of standardisation across all aspects of a campaign, from strategy formulation to creative execution. In all likelihood, this would condemn the Irish advertising industry to operate in a regional backwater that merely provides Irish voiceovers for advertisements that have been created in advertising hotspots like London and New York. Having interviewed many senior executives in the Irish advertising industry, O'Boyle (2011: 44) cautions:

> However, irrespective of their views on consolidation, all of my informants displayed a pragmatic (even resigned) acceptance of the power asymmetries and in general felt that Irish agencies could not develop proprietary attitudes towards brands and campaigns, or suffer from 'not invented here syndrome' as one account planner put it.

Until Dublin becomes a centre of excellence for the advertising industry, it will remain challenging for its agencies to take the lead on the strategic and creative direction of global brands. As evidenced in an analysis of Guinness's ads from 1996 onwards, the parents of local agencies are extremely influential when it comes to the strategic direction of brands' advertising strategies.

1990–1994: Easy as she goes for Guinness's advertising

Guinness's advertising in the early 1990s was quite conservative, concentrating on its visual brand identity (logo, name, colours, visual triggers) and its Irish provenance. To all intents and purposes, there is little evidence of the changes wrought by the fledgling years of the economic turnaround. However, based on the creative approach in Guinness's ads during this period, it would appear that advertising literacy had evolved, because Irish consumers were watching more TV, thus seeing and hearing more advertising. This, allied with the fact that returning emigrants had been exposed to cutting edge ads whilst abroad, meant that advertisers could move away from overtly product-led campaigns and build more subtle communications platforms.

Guinness commenced the decade with the 'Logo Identities' television campaign, which consisted of a series of simple, low budget ads that foregrounded the Guinness logotype. The first in the series, 'Only One', starts with a black background, before a countdown commences, from ten to one in gold Guinness lettering. A deep, smooth male voice says at the end, as the Guinness logo appears: 'When you get right down to it (*pause*), there's only one.' The soundtrack is fast, reminiscent of the theme music that accompanies the long-running and popular ITV quiz show, *Countdown*, which would have been viewed by many Irish people at the time.

The second ad in the series, 'Waiting', is even simpler, consisting of a black background and the Guinness logo. A clock ticks impatiently, getting louder and louder, before the voiceover asks, in a slightly exasperated tone: 'What are you waiting for?' Silence ensues and the viewer is afforded the time to contemplate having a drink of Guinness.

The 'After Dark' execution of the 'Logo Identities' communications platform opens with a black background and the word 'dark' rendered in Guinness-style lettering. In the background, the murmur of people chatting in a convivial pub setting is audible and the voiceover poses the question: 'What comes naturally after dark? (clink of glasses) What else?' The Guinness logo appears.

The final ad in the series, 'Commercial Break', commences with the word 'Commercial' in Guinness lettering on a black background. The silence is interrupted by the voiceover's silky tones: 'Now that you've watched a commercial ….' The voiceover stalls and the word 'commercial' literally splits after the letters COMM. The two parts of the word slide left and right out of the ad and the sound of people socialising in a pub comes into earshot before the Guinness logo appears. 'Why not enjoy one?'

Each ad is based on the assumption that the audience is familiar with the visual components of the Guinness brand identity – gold lettering, logotype, harp, black. They are aimed at loyal customers and do not incorporate any cultural references, with the exception perhaps of the *Countdown*-type music. The influx of immigrants from other countries has not yet started and the Irish population was still homogenous at that time.

Another series of TV ads, 'Draw your own conclusions', ran between 1990 and 1992. Visually, they were much more complex than the 'Logo Identities' series, but judging by the visual triggers in the ads, they too were aimed at an audience that was already familiar with the Guinness brand. They relied heavily on metaphors and symbols to express its personality. Surreal, dreamlike images were created with increasingly sophisticated post-production techniques. They tease the viewers, inviting them to pinpoint the brand behind the ad. The first ad, 'Sea', revisits a popular metaphor in the Guinness advertising repertoire, selected for its ability to mimic the constant movement of a pint of stout as it settles. In 'Sea', there are two main actors, a man and a woman. They do not feature together but the images suggest that they are on intimate terms. The contemporary Irish music is haunting and sensual and fits perfectly with the fleeting images that flow throughout the ad. Waves of Guinness and the sea merge at intervals to shroud the man's eyes and nose, or the woman's face. The sandy shoreline symbolises the head of the pint, and functions as a backdrop for the black, shadowy silhouette of the woman. In the closing frames of the ad, the shoreline metamorphoses into the flesh of the woman's neck. Wet hair flanks one of her shoulders and beads of water glisten on her skin, imitating the condensation on the glass of a chilled pint of Guinness. Draped across her shoulders, is a black shawl. It is the final piece in the puzzle and creates the illusion of a pint of Guinness. The tagline invites the viewer to: 'Draw your own conclusions.'

Another ad in the series, 'Coin', features the same music and similar ephemeral images of a man, woman and the sea. At one point a coin's presence alternates with discs of sunlight dancing on the water's surface. Later in the ad, it pirouettes through the water and creates ripples and waves that resemble a pint of Guinness as it settles. This time, the man and woman appear together. In one frame, a shimmering profile of the man moves towards the woman with his lips pursed as if to kiss her. She awaits his kiss before the coin drops into the water that shrouds their heads, or is it a pint? In any case, the moment of intimacy is interrupted but is reignited again when a bare, male arm comes into view. The arm rests against the wet strands of the woman's hair that fall down around her shoulders. The fleeting nature of the images throughout the ad invites audiences to do as the tagline at the end suggests: 'Draw your own conclusions.'

'Skier' takes to the ski slopes, and opens with the image of a pint of Guinness swirling in front of a man's face. He stares into middle space, before turning towards the camera. A transparent visor veils his face and frames a male skier as he glides down the slope of the man's nose. Then a female skier's head emerges. All the time white snow swirls and a grimace on the face of the male skier suggests that his endeavours have taken great effort. Dramatically, snow cascades downhill, clearing to reveal the blurred silhouettes of two semi-naked figures pulling away from one another. Does the avalanche signify the climax of their union? Dazzling light erupts, before a blurred, black head and torso shimmers against the white of the snow. What might be two pints of Guinness tilt sideways, in opposite directions to form a crude, harp-shaped, light-filled illusion. Based on what has gone before, the viewer might just as easily conclude that the two pints represent the lovers separating from a post-coital embrace. The drops of condensation on the pints might be beads of perspiration on the skin of the two lovers. Once more, we are urged to draw our own conclusions.

Neither the Guinness name nor the harp figures in the ads. This is testament to the fact that the brand and its iconography were engrained in the minds of Irish consumers. The imagery in the 'Draw your own conclusions' ads spoke a language that audiences could understand. Years of investing in advertising meant that Guinness could 'test' the consumer's knowledge of the brand. Like the instantly identifiable Labrador puppy in the Andrex ads, black and gold/cream metaphors were sufficient to garner recognition among TV viewers in Ireland.

Between 1992 and 1993, Guinness broadcast a number of very evocative ads, in that they strove to arouse memories from childhood and time spent with friends and family. There were two such series, 'Refresh your memory' and 'Seasonal sounds'. The central premise of the six ads in the 'Refresh your memory' series is nature. Each ad opens with the same image of what seems to be a pint settling, accompanied by the hushed tone of a male voiceover, who implores with the viewer to: 'Listen.' While the ads are for Guinness Draught, the sound effects at the beginning suggest that the pint originated in a can. The emphasis is on the swirling head and in each rendition, it transforms into a backdrop for various images from nature. Guinness pervades the mood at all times and as seen in other ads in previous decades, it is positioned as an important part of people's memories, memories that are shared by many. Following on from the initial 'Listen,' subtitles accompany each scene's transition to really focus the viewer's mind on remembering the sights, sounds, and smells of bygone times. By not employing a musical soundtrack, the sounds of nature and Guinness being poured, are amplified and take centre stage. Between them, the six ads remind viewers of the beauty of nature and the way in which it touches them at all stages of their lives, from childhood to adulthood.

Over the course of the ads, a wide array of scenes transports the viewer to another place and time. These include trees swaying in the breeze; a stone skimming across the water's surface; the sound of birdsong; the grasshopper's staccato chatter that accompanies long, summer days; an industrious bee harvesting pollen from a flower; a fisherman's hook and fly landing in a river; the gentle, whirring wheels of a bicycle gliding by, conjuring up images of, as the subtitle suggests, 'a change of pace'; sheaves of barley; the Cliffs of Moher, accompanied by the pounding of waves and the cry of gulls; the Poulnabrone Dolmen in the Burren, a relic of ancient times. As already stated, in the early 1990s, the vast majority of people living in Ireland had been born in Ireland. Rich or poor, they would have experienced the delights of these simple, yet redolent, sights and sounds. Each ad concludes with the image of a frothing head of Guinness in a glass with the Guinness logo and the text: 'The pull of the pint ….' The voiceover says: 'Cool Guinness,' and as if to emphasise the word cool, the surface of the glass is covered in condensation. The campaign's tagline, 'Refresh your Memory' is shown on the final screenshot.

In 1993, the 'Seasonal Sounds' campaign complemented the 'Refresh your memory' series. The execution style was similar from the start and once again, images and sounds of nature were the key signifiers in the four ads. Each ad relates to one of the four seasons and concludes with the moving head of a pint of Guinness, the sound of the liquid as it is poured from a can, and the line: 'And the pull of the pint.' Then the Guinness logo appears on the black background, complete with droplets of condensation. A man states simply but emphatically: 'Guinness' and a tagline, tailored for each ad, concludes. 'As Autumn leaves, turn to …,' '… as Darkness settles,' and 'Reawaken your senses,' for the ads aptly named 'Autumn', 'Winter' and 'Spring' respectively. Despite the availability of chilled Guinness, the summer season does not feature in this campaign. Instead, the 'Autumn' and 'Winter' ads meld the contradictory hardship and beauty of both seasons, with the comforting powers of Guinness. The 'Spring' ad is all about new beginnings, and has echoes of the 'Refresh your memory' campaign with its closing tagline: 'Reawaken your senses.' This is to encourage viewers to rediscover nature and to reawaken the taste buds with a Guinness.

A Christmas ad completes the series and utilises the same format as the other three. The images and complementary sounds include: a black sky, liberally sprinkled with stars as sleigh bells chime and a rendition of the lyric 'We wish you a merry Christmas' rings out; the glow of coloured lights; the convivial murmur of friends socialising, as a choir sings a festive carols; a plane preparing to land and a voice announcing the arrival of 'Flight 157', followed by someone shouting: 'Welcome home.' The closing tagline, 'Complements the season' firmly positions Guinness at the heart of social gatherings. Due to the large number of Irish nationals living abroad, Christmas is one of the busiest periods at Ireland's ports and airports. According to the Central Statistics Office (CSOa), 980,000 people travelled to Ireland to visit friends and relatives in 1993. There is no way of knowing how many of those arrived over the Christmas period, but it can be assumed that a significant proportion made the trip for that purpose. After the high levels of emigration in the 1980s, most people would have been able to relate to the sentiment that was captured in the ad.

This brings to the fore the marked increase in travel to and from Ireland in the early years of the Celtic Tiger period. According to Delamere (2000), cross-channel air travel doubled between 1984 and 1988 following the liberalisation of air travel in Europe. Much of this activity resulted from the high levels of emigration to the United Kingdom during that period. Between 1988 and 1998 it more than doubled again to 6,083,000 passengers. Almost 67 per cent of these travelled between Dublin and London. The scale of the increase in air traffic is evident when one considers that in 1949, a mere 213,000 passengers flew into and out of Ireland but that by 1998, this had reached 10,787,000. Ferry travel grew in popularity too and Delemere reports that by 1998, 2,421,000 people left Ireland by ferry and 2,434,000 arrived by ferry. While economic migrants into and out of Ireland accounted for some of the increases in air and sea travel, the growing attractiveness of Ireland as a tourist destination is evident from the statistics. In 1990, just over 3 million tourists visited Ireland and by 1998, this reached 5.7 million. Just as Guinness made overt references to the propensity of Irish people to leave the island in some of its 1980s ads, the emotive aspect of their return to be with family and friends features in its 1993 Christmas ad.

In the main, 'Refresh your memory' and 'Seasonal Sounds' position Guinness alongside nature and the seasons. They attempt to remind audiences that the brand is as much a part of people's lives as nature and the changing seasons. They hark back to the ads that foregrounded the stout's pure and natural ingredients, and like the brand itself, the ads are timeless.

A hangover from the 1980s

In the midst of the aforementioned ads, Guinness broadcast the ad, 'I believe', that features the bitter/sweet musings of a Guinness drinker from Dublin. It is shot in black and white and the actor Stanley stands on Dublin's Sandymount Strand, which is clearly identifiable due to the presence of the Poolbeg chimneys in the background. The screen is mostly black and forms a frame around another screen from which Townsend delivers his monologue. Throughout the ad, the camera remains fixed on the actor's head and shoulders, as the image magnifies and the black frame becomes smaller and smaller until his image fills the screen. His skin tone assumes a more sepia tone as his image magnifies, suggestive of the colour in a pint's creamy head. Townsend is rugged, windswept and a little scruffy and he speaks with a strong Dublin accent. He conveys the air of a man who spends many evenings in the pub, pontificating about life. He probably thinks of himself as a philosopher. He has strong opinions and lurches from one topic to another:

> I believe (pause) I'm paranoid.
> I believe W. Shakespeare is up there with W. Axl Rose (a bleep almost obscures 'Rose').
> And that everyone should have more of a chance than what I had (pause). That wouldn't be hard.
> I believe me da will never work again – ah go on, give him a job.
> I believe (rubs the side of his face) Irish liberals are a bunch of racists.
> And that Grafton Street *should* belong to the Northsiders.
> I believe, you know who, are a bunch of gurriers.
> And nothin', *nothin'* ever came close to Sgt Pepper.
> I believe Elvis is still alive, livin' with Lord Lucan (a bleep almost obscures 'Lucan') and ridin' Shergar.
> I believe in Brendan Behan – bacon, egg, sausage, beans and chips and a large pot of tea.
> I believe the DART should run to Tallaght; in flushing toilets; washing your hands and leavin' the seat down.
> I believe road repairs should be legalised (nodding) but I'd settle for a pint of Guinness (nods and smiles wryly).
> I believe.

In many ways, the timbre of the script and Townsend's delivery are more in keeping with the pessimism of the 1980s. At times he injects self-pitying emotion into his rhetoric, particularly when he alludes briefly to his less than ideal upbringing and the current plight of his unemployed father. Despite improvements in the Irish economy in the early 1990s, unemployment remained stubbornly high in the first few years of the decade. In 1993, it stood at 15.7 per cent (CSOb), which meant that, for some people, talk of a recovering economy was meaningless. It would have been particularly challenging for older workers to find work, which Townsend concedes when he pleads with someone to give his father a job. The sentiment is reminiscent of the storylines in the popular BBC dramas from the 1980s and 1990s, *Boys from the Blackstuff* and *Aufwiedersehen Pet.* Both series bring male unemployment to the fore, focusing on the particular challenges faced by men in their late thirties and older, when they lose their jobs. Townsend evokes the infamous *Boys from the Blackstuff* catchphrase, 'Gizza job' when he exclaims: 'Ah go on, give him a job.'

The cultural references in the ad are varied and take the viewer around the world and back and forth in time. Shakespeare, Elvis and the Beatles are familiar to everyone and even though they are from the past, their notoriety is timeless. On the other hand, in 1993, Axl Rose's band Guns 'n' Roses was at the height of its popularity on the international stage, adding a contemporary flavour to the script. His musings include in-jokes that need no explanation: 'Livin' with Lord Lucan and ridin' Shergar,' probably draws on the lyrics in Christy Moore's 1980s hit, 'Lisdoonvarna' – 'Shergar was ridden by Lord Lucan.'

Like Guinness, the ad is at times quite Dublin-oriented and reminds viewers of its heritage. Brendan Behan is one of Dublin's favourite sons and was known to imbibe pints of Guinness. However, his fame transcends county and country borders, unlike some of the other Dublin reference points in the ad. While viewers would have related easily to the global and national artists mentioned in the ad, some of Townsend's statements are quite parochial. Dubliners would have understood Townsend's assertion that 'Grafton Street should belong to the Northsiders,' whereas viewers from outside Dublin would not necessarily be aware of the friendly rivalry between residents north and south of the River Liffey. His subsequent labelling of 'you know who' as 'a bunch of gurriers' employs turns of phrases that are in the national vernacular. Nonetheless, the derogatory tag 'gurrier' is more commonly associated with Dublin.

Meanwhile, the Dublin Area Rapid Transit (DART) trains first ran in 1984, so any mention of them would have been instantly recognised by Dublin viewers. Still, it only serves those living along the coastline in Dublin and a small part of the Wicklow coast, as well as a limited number city centre residents. In 1993, it was not only the envy of the rest of Ireland, but of many Dubliners too. Therefore, his belief that it 'should run to Tallaght' picks up on this sentiment, making it a relatable statement to many. Conversations about the state of the roads have been commonplace in pubs all over Ireland for many decades, so his reference to road repairs would not have gone unnoticed by the entire adult Irish populace. Overall, Townsend's strong Dublin accent and his colloquial ponderings reinforce Guinness's enduring links with the city.

The actor's monologue mimics the ebbs and flows of the typical pub philosopher. He emphasises his certainty about matters by commencing each statement with the words, 'I believe,' thus invoking the opening words of the Apostle's Creed. CSOc (n.d.) reports that in the 1991 census, almost 95 per cent of the Irish population categorised themselves as Roman Catholic or Protestant. The Apostle's Creed is recited at all Christian services, so the words 'I believe' would have resonated with an Irish audience. Constructing the ad copy around such a ubiquitous duo of words in a country like Ireland may have been a deliberate attempt to strengthen Guinness's standing as a pivotal part of Irish life and culture. When he concedes at the end of the ad that he would 'settle for a pint of Guinness,' he does not start the admission with 'I believe.' Instead, he concludes with the words and they serve as an Amen, a full stop. When all is said and done, all he really wants is a pint of Guinness. Perhaps it is the one thing in life that truly makes sense to him.

The religious undercurrents are evident throughout the ad, and Townsend's recital has echoes of the Rosary, which lurches from one topic to another. This separates the Guinness brand from others because in the words of Sheffield (2006: 54), the stout is 'imbued with an image of the sacred by the meaning advertising gives' it. The ad was broadcast at a juncture in Ireland's social history when the Roman Catholic Church was relinquishing its hold over its congregation. Bourdieu is referenced by Inglis (2008: 79) when he analyses the changed habitus:

> Bourdieu's concepts enable us to understand how the dominant Catholic habitus of self-denial was gradually transformed into a culture of self-realization and indulgence through a decline in the dominant position of the Catholic Church and the religious field and their replacement by the media and the market.

Townsend's character has found his replacement. Guinness is the sacrament, his confessor and his religion. His belief in the brand is beyond question.

The backing track is a blues riff, taken from a music genre that is associated with the working class, inspired by adversity. According to Wyman and Havers (2001: 10): 'The Blues isn't just a style of music: it's an attitude of mind … Blues is life and life is the Blues. Inspired by suffering and despair, the Blues are rooted in courage and the will to survive.' The actor in the ad has not had an easy life and while the opening words of each line may borrow from the Apostle's Creed, they might also draw inspiration from the American Blues legend, Robert Johnson. One of his best known compositions, 'I believe I'll dust my broom', features the words too.

There's no time like Guinness time

Frequently, advertising is employed by organisations to solve problems, transform positives into negatives, and ultimately change consumer preferences. According to Conniffe and McCoy (1993), beer consumption per head of population aged 15 and over had more or less stabilised at 5.66 litres by 1991. It reached a peak of 6.01 in 1979, and dropped to 5.06 in 1987, most likely due to the worsening economic conditions. In contrast, while wine and cider consumption was low, and stood at 0.77 litres and 0.34 litres respectively in 1991, both were on an upward trajectory, especially when compared to negligible levels in the 1960s. By 1991, the consumption of spirits did not show any signs of growing, having fallen from a high of 3.23 litres per head in 1979 to 2.35 litres per head. Therefore, while consumption of spirits and beer remained flat or in decline, other categories were in the ascendency, which explains why the statistics show that Irish consumers were spending more, not less on alcohol. McCormack and Meany (2000) confirm the trend and reveal that in 1994/5, urban dwellers in Ireland allocated a higher percentage of their weekly household expenditure to the purchase of alcohol than in previous years. In 1951–2 it stood at just 1.1 per cent, 3.7 per cent in 1965–6, 4.8 per cent in 1980 and 5.5 per cent in 1994–5.

Guinness acknowledged the changing landscape in its 1996 Annual Report when it conceded that consumers' tastes in Ireland were expanding and diversifying. At the time, there was a revival in cider, largely driven by the Bulmers, 'Nothing added but time', campaign. It repositioned the beleaguered brand successfully and helped shake off its image as an illicit beverage enjoyed by underage drinkers. In response, Guinness launched its own cider brand, Hudson Blue. This was a necessary concession because Guinness and other stout brands differ from most other alcoholic drinks, with the exception of cocktails, in that they take time to pour and settle. Increasingly, this was an inconvenience that many young drinkers were not prepared to endure and it was fast becoming a disadvantage for Guinness. The challenge was to create an advertising campaign that would transform this hindrance into an appealing attribute. In 1994 and 1995, Arks created a series of ads with the objective of achieving just that. The communications platform at the heart of the ads is, 'There's no time like Guinness time'. The underlying premise is that Guinness time begins, even before a settled pint is served and that rather than seeing this as a hindrance, it should be viewed as something positive.

The early ads in the series are very simple and not particularly memorable. In 'There's no time like Guinness time' letters in Guinness style and colour enter the screen and form the line: 'There's no time.' They arrive in time to the rhythm of a brass band, playing in a staccato style. Message delivered, the letters disperse around the screen and reassemble to spell: 'There's no time like Guinness time.'

'Polaroid' opens with the magnified sound of a photograph being dispensed from a Polaroid instant camera. The undeveloped photograph sits against a black background. As it develops, a moving, settling pint of Guinness appears and the genial sounds of people talking in a social setting grow louder. A male voiceover says: 'There's no time (pause) like Guinness time.'

However, it was 'Anticipation' that really captured the imagination of audiences in Ireland and the United Kingdom, elevating it to cult status. It was the brainchild of Dublin agency, Arks and initially it was created for the Irish market. Nevertheless, it was broadcast to the British market as well, which was a major coup for Arks. While many ads created and produced in other countries make it onto Irish screens, it is uncommon that ads made in Ireland would be aired in Britain.

The ad features the actor, Joe McKinney, who plays the part of a customer. He orders his pint, and then waits for the barman, played by Gordon Winter, to pour it. Winter is in control, like a conductor in charge of an orchestra. He will decide when the pint is ready and he is not prepared to take any shortcuts. Nothing, not even the antics of McKinney, faze him, as he takes pride in his vital role as a master craftsman. Meanwhile, McKinney realises that he must wait for the maestro to complete his task before he gets his pint, so rather than idling, he uses the time to dance. He leaps across the screen in an ungainly fashion. At times, his moves are balletic without the grace. Despite his inelegant style, he dances to the rhythm of the music. In many ways, he emulates Rowan Atkinson's hapless character, Mr Bean, who moved awkwardly and seemingly lacked coordination. He was a staple of Irish and British television screens from 1990 to 1995, which coincided with the release of 'Anticipation'. Frequently, McKinney pauses to check up on the progress of his pint, willing it to settle. His facial expressions reveal that his desire is growing. Winter refuses to be rushed and appears to enjoy his customer's anticipation. As the pint settles, he teases McKinney and places it in his line of vision, which tantalises him even more. In a scene reminiscent of a young child pleading with a parent, McKinney's facial expression begs with Winter for his waiting to be over. Winter is having none of it and knows that the end result will be worth it.

When at last McKinney holds his pint, he stares at it, realising that it was indeed worth the wait. He smiles adoringly at it before closing his eyes and pursing his lips as if to kiss a lover. Such is his devotion to the ritual behind the wait, that it might be likened to a religious experience. In his description of the waiting ritual, O'Brien (2014: 218) captures its significance:

> Before ever a drop of Guinness touches the lips of the consumer, the ritualistic pouring and the need to wait for the drink to settle, during the 19.5 seconds of 'Guinness Time', the commodity has already been made magical or special through the chip of messianic time that is created by this process.

In light of the Catholic Church's loosening grip on Irish society, this description assumes greater significance as the baton passes from one religion to another.

The soundtrack is called 'Guaglione' and was recorded by the late Cuban bandleader, Pérez Prado. As a result of the ad, it became instantly recognisable and proved so popular with the public, that it reached number one in the Irish music charts and number two in the UK charts. Thereafter it was synonymous with Guinness, as were McKinney's eccentric, off-beat dance moves. The whole premise of the ad is simple, but therein lies its charm. Viewers could relate to McKinney, who has the appearance of an ordinary young man. He dresses just like someone's brother, friend or boyfriend and his dancing style is awkward and clumsy. His character does not intimidate viewers. Rather, young men can relate to him and it is easy for them to envision socialising with someone just like him on a Saturday night. The intention is to imbue the Guinness brand with a feeling of accessibility, thus endearing it to a young demographic.

While the ad itself garnered huge attention and became part of the cultural fabric of the 1990s, it might be argued that it was not a total success. The purpose of advertising is to achieve a specific objective. 'Anticipation' was supposed to persuade young people to drink Guinness by convincing them that it was a drink worth waiting for. Linehan (1997) reports that despite the ad's popularity, it did not result in higher sales of Guinness. Of course, it would be unfair to declare the ad a failure just because the stout's sales remained flat. The economic and social context in which it was broadcast should be taken into account. By 1994, Irish society and the economy had set out on a journey, which would consign many sureties to the scrapheap. It could no longer be assumed that young drinkers would gravitate towards Guinness as they had in the past, when there were so many other options available to them.

'Anticipation' was the stand-out ad in the series and it overshadowed the others in terms of the attention that it received. It is a very simple ad, but so too were the early ads in the series. The subsequent ads in the series, 'Chains and Settle' were rich in imagery and special effects. However, none of them achieved the notoriety of 'Anticipation', which possibly came along at the right time, just when Irish people were beginning to enjoy themselves again. As previously stated, by 1994 urban households allocated a higher percentage of their weekly expenditure to alcohol than before. In addition, McCormack and Meany (2000) report that just over a quarter of this cohort's weekly expenditure in the same period went on services. This implies that after the bleak years of the 1980s, people spent more on socialising outside the home and enjoying themselves. According to Murphy (2014), Ireland's restaurant scene had already started its renaissance in the mid-1980s, with the emergence of casual dining establishments in Dublin. Middle-class diners frequented them and while palettes remained quite conservative, Murphy is in little doubt that they paved the way for the food and drink culture of the Celtic Tiger. He illustrates the impact of this on employment levels in Irish hotels, guesthouses, restaurants and licensed premises when he cites the CERT Employment Survey of 2000. Between 1996 and 2000, the numbers working in those sectors rose by almost 40,000 to just over 184,140. Growing interest in food and drink among the Irish was in part influenced by the democratisation of travel.

Delamere (2000) states that the numbers of Irish people travelling abroad on holidays grew from around 2 million in 1993 to 3.33 million in 1998. This exposed holidaymakers to new influences, while suggesting that they wanted to enjoy life more. For many Irish people in the 1990s, another way of disposing of their newfound prosperity was shopping. Taking inflation into account, Madden (2000) estimates that there was a real increase in the volume of retail sales of 310 per cent between 1951 and 1996. This activity was supported by the transformation of the retail landscape in the 1990s and into the new millennium. The Square in Tallaght, Dublin, opened in 1990 and Corcoran (2000) views its arrival as a model for the shopping malls that followed in quick succession throughout the Celtic Tiger years. In retrospect, McKinney's performance in 'Anticipation' is a metaphor for the new breed of Irishman that emerged during the Celtic Tiger years, someone who took advantage of the economic upswing in all aspects of his life, from work to recreation. McKinney's unpolished and seemingly un-choreographed performance is authentic and relatable to a wide audience, ensuring that it connected with anyone who watched.

New names, new beginnings

The 1990s proved a significant decade for Guinness in terms of structure and ownership. Yenne (2007: 201) quotes the Guinness chairman, Tony Greener who described 1996 as 'a landmark year for Guinness,' largely due to the company's record earnings. This laid the foundations for 1997 when Guinness PLC merged with Grand Metropolitan PLC to become the largest wine, beer and spirits multinational company in the world. More change was to follow, as the wine and spirits operations of both companies merged to form a division called United Distillers & Vintners. Yenne explains that this merger was made possible by adding the Grand Metropolitan brands to the United Distillers component of Guinness PLC to form Guinness UDV. Guinness Brewing Worldwide remained a separate division. As well as the Guinness brand, the new entity owned a disparate range of well-known international brands, including Gordon's Gin, Hennessy Cognac, and Smirnoff Vodka. On 30 October 1997, Diageo was introduced to the world, born of the previous merger between Guinness and Grand Metropolitan. The name is based on the Latin word for 'day' and the Greek word for 'world' or 'earth' (Yenne 2007; Muzellec and Lambkin 2007). The words were chosen to 'suggest that every day, everywhere, people celebrate with Diageo brands' (Yenne 2007: 203).

From an Irish perspective, the formation of the new global entities in 1997 challenged one of the country's oldest and most loved cultural icons. Muzellec and Lambkin (2007: 323) summed up the conundrum in which Guinness found itself:

> The rebranding corresponded to a change in the brand architecture and marked the transformation from a situation where Guinness Stout and the St James Gate Brewery were quintessentially Irish to a situation where the group producing Guinness became a global multi-brand company.

The authors highlight just some of the ways in which Guinness had woven itself into Irish life, from the way in which it pioneered humane, high-quality work conditions in the 1800s, to its contribution to the community through sponsorship and engagement. However, they were particularly concerned with potential challenges that faced Guinness as a result of being part of a bigger family, Diageo, with which it did not share a name. When Guinness PLC owned the Guinness stout brand, any interactions between the parent company and the public had the potential to rub off positively (and sometimes negatively) on the brand. Muzellec and Lambkin (2008: 284) caution that it can be risky for a company to adopt 'a contrived corporate name disconnected from the company's heritage and brand portfolio.' However, the global giant's diverse portfolio of international brands necessitated a strong brand architecture that would unite the collection without compromising the strengths of each individual brand. Like nations, corporations and brands have identities that give them personalities and direction. Byrne (1995) stresses that statements of corporate identity should articulate where it is that the organisation wants to be or, as Kiriakidou and Millward (2000: 51) posit, it forces organisations and brands to ask the question 'Who are we?' They define corporate identity as:

> The tangible representation of the organizational identity, the expression as manifest in the behavior and communication of the organization. Therefore, efforts to manage corporate identity should reflect the organizational identity of the company (members' beliefs about its existing character).

This definition easily transfers to the concept of brand identity if the word 'corporate' is replaced by 'brand' and provides an insight into the complexities of being able to successfully navigate a brand towards success and longevity, something that Guinness had achieved. Wally Ollins (1989: 7) passionately believed that a brand's identity must be 'visible, tangible and all-embracing', because it can articulate a brand's *raison d'être* to its various audiences, including staff and consumers. If this is achieved, audiences will understand and relate to the brand more easily. Melewar and Saunders (2000: 539) view this as an imperative if a brand is to be successful and they argue that corporate visual identity can enhance reputation and goodwill, thus persuading customers to 'buy the company.'

In several instances, consumers have too much choice when it comes to making purchase decisions. Many products and services are similar so their main points of difference are found in the expression of their personalities and values. In support of this, Balmer (2001) puts the success of effective management down to the ability of the brand to communicate, differentiate and enhance. The expression of identity is achieved through a combination of names, symbols, logos, colours and communications like advertising and sponsorship, but it should always be remembered that these elements merely identify a brand. Upshaw (1997: 9) delves much deeper than this and likens a brand's identity to its core meaning or, as he puts it, 'its strategic DNA,' a key component of which is a brand's personality. Therefore, custodians of the brand must be adept at bringing emotion to their brand (emotion that enables the brand to connect with the target audience) if it is to enjoy longevity and success. Fanning (1999) refers to this important task as storytelling, which entails emphasising various aspects of the brand, maintaining core values and telling the brand's story in such a way that it will capture and hold the attention of the intended audience. He goes on to state that brand survival depends on whether or not it can capture the high ground when it comes to values and being relevant to the target audience.

Upshaw (1997) identifies a number of transferable truths that can be found in all successful brands. Three of these truths are particularly interesting in the context of Guinness's communications. They are that successful brand managers should understand their customers' lives (this understanding enables them to construct brand stories that will resonate and generate real interest); successful brands provide stability in turbulent times (this makes sense because in times of uncertainty, consumers turn to those that they can trust and derive comfort from); and very importantly, brands with strong personalities create compelling reasons for preference. In order to achieve these 'transferable truths,' it helps if brand managers understand the key associations that consumers have with their brand and the way in which their lifestyles fit with it (Waters 1997).

With globalisation gathering pace and mergers such as the one that resulted in the formation of Diageo becoming more commonplace, the marketing communications industry in Ireland experienced unprecedented change in the 1990s too. For a brand like Guinness, that was so ubiquitous in Ireland and such an integral part of its culture, the challenge from 1997 onwards would be to give top billing to Guinness when communicating with consumers. According to Muzellec and Lambkin (2008), this was the approach adopted by Diageo from the start, primarily using the new name for communications with all stakeholders apart from consumers. Therefore, the ads in the 1990s solely promoted Guinness with no mention of Diageo.

In 1996, the reality of globalisation and its impact on marketing communications strategies was felt in the marketing department at St James's Gate in Dublin. Guinness had worked with Dublin-based advertising agency Arks since 1970. Before that, the London agency SH Benson created Ireland-specific ads from 1959. Therefore, up to this point Guinness Ireland had a track record of working with its advertising agencies for long periods of time. However, that changed in 1996 when Bell Advertising, the Irish subsidiary of London agency, Ogilvy and Mather, was appointed on a short-term basis with the possibility of making it a long-term arrangement. Based on previous appointments, Bell and Ogilvy and Mather might have expected to work with Guinness for many years. However, despite pitching to extend the relationship on a longer term footing towards the end of 1996, London agency Howell Henry Chaldecott Lury and Partners (HHCL) won the contract for the Irish and British business. Before that appointment, Bell had the remit to create local ads, working with a communication platform devised by Ogilvy and Mather in London. The platform in question was 'Black and White' and the central premise was that each ad should present scenarios in which things were not always as they seemed.

In addition, the ads were to be shot in black and white and had to feature an appropriate music track from popular culture. UK audiences were entertained by the ad 'Bicycle', which brought to life the obscure tagline, 'A woman needs a man like a fish needs a bicycle', by famously featuring a fish on a bicycle in the closing scene of the ad.

Music formed an integral part of many Guinness ads from the 1970s onwards, an acknowledgement of its ability to 'provoke and emote in an often profound and visceral manner' (Arning and Gordon 2006: 3). They argue that music has the potential to be very effective because of its impact on implicit memory. Without realising it, someone can internalise the music and the more emotional the music, the more it lends itself to implicit learning. From the perspective of an advertiser like Guinness, if this occurs, brand recall is more likely to be triggered when someone hears the music in another context. In a crowded marketplace, this can prove vital. Ware and Branthwaite (1997) identify a number of benefits associated with using music in advertising, including its ability to draw attention to the ad, create mood and express personality and, most importantly, it can attract specific groups of consumers. Also, their research found that ads with music are considered more enjoyable than ads without music. If the lyrics of the music in the ad include the name of the brand, their research informed them that it is even more memorable.

As previously discussed, Guinness used this strategy frequently in the 1970s and 1980s, but many of the ads in the 1990s heralded a departure from this approach by featuring well known original tracks from various genres and decades. Ads that evoke an emotional response have a stronger likelihood of being remembered, and the right music has the potential to do just that (Ware and Branthwaite 1997; Binet et al. 2013). 'Anticipation' is testament to this and the track used in the ad will always be associated with Guinness. However, on the downside, music can distract audiences from the key message and does not always aid in the understanding of ads (Ware and Branthwaite 1997). They advise that one way to minimise the likelihood of this occurring is to ensure that the track used relates in some way to the brand. From 1996 onwards, Guinness relied heavily on the use of music in its ads, which featured the hits of some very well-known international artists. As will be seen in the analysis, the tracks usually complement the narrative and pace of the ads, but it is not always apparent that they related to the Guinness brand values.

Just two TV ads in the 'Black and White' series were made for the Irish market, 'Life' and 'Monogamy'. Both ads were stylishly shot in black and white. 'Life' features the classic 1920s track, 'Old Man River', performed by the American Civil Rights activist, Paul Robeson. His deep bass voice tells of the struggles of African Americans in the twentieth century and sets the tone for the travails enacted in the ad.

The main protagonist stumbles from one setback to another. The beginning of the ad places him in a rundown bookies shop watching a race on which he has placed a bet. We see the spectrum of his emotions during the race – anticipation, hope, realism and resignation when his horse fails to reward him. On leaving the bookies, he walks past the derelict gasometer in Dublin's Ringsend, its state of decay accentuating his despair and despondency. When he reaches his car, a parking ticket and a puncture await him. His body language exudes frustration. Leaving his car behind, he walks through the Dublin streets and during his journey, a female traffic warden passes behind him. Her inclusion in the ad is ironic, as in all likelihood she inflicted the pain of a parking ticket on him. Finally, he is home but water cascades through the ceiling. The audience wonders what further misfortune could possibly befall the man. He looks out a window, just in time to see a man discarding a battered stainless steel sink on the pavement, adjacent to a boarded-up building, complete with philosophical graffiti: 'Life is a hereditary disease.' He cannot even gain solace from his surroundings, so at this stage an air of foreboding accompanies him and the audience as he stands in a room and inhales deeply, as if bracing himself for the next challenge. A woman enters the room. She smiles and has an air of serenity about her. She places her arm around him and when he looks up, we see genuine hope in his eyes for the first time. He strokes her clearly pregnant belly while gazing into her eyes. At first, there is a hint of disbelief in his eyes, as if he cannot believe that this kind and tolerant woman is carrying his child.

The tagline: 'Not everything in black and white makes sense' is on screen, and seems applicable to this great anomaly and all that has gone before. Unlike 'Monogamy', where promiscuity and sexual liberation are foregrounded, the sexual relationship between the man and the woman in 'Life' is most likely monogamous. Her white clothing, allied with her aura, exude purity and serenity, perhaps prompting the viewer to draw comparisons between her and the Virgin Mary. Surely, she must be a saint to forgive her partner for his transgressions and to find happiness in less than perfect circumstances. Like his bad luck, her stoicism and tolerance do not make sense, an anomaly that lends further meaning to the tagline. There is no hint of eroticism in their interactions at that moment and their bond makes sense to him, unlike the other events in his depressing day.

The excerpt used from Robeson's recording is from the final verse of the song and the lyrics work in tandem with the pessimism that accompanies him up until the final scene:

> Ah gits weary
> An' sick of tryin'
> Ah'm tired of livin'
> An' skeered of dyin'
> But ol' man river
> He jes' keeps rollin' along.

The last two lines of the verse reassure the audience that despite the ups and downs, life continues and that Guinness will be there for them, as it has been for more than 200 years. It is a constant, like a river, and is one of the few things in black and white that makes sense.

Let's talk about sex

Since Independence, the Roman Catholic Church in Ireland took centre stage in everyday life and its influence left its mark on the legislative and moral codes by which people were governed. However, the 1990s was the decade when its grip was irrevocably loosened. Brown (2004: 367) captures the demise succinctly:

> An individualistic morality, which took cognizance of specific circumstances, began to replace obedience to authority and its absolutes even among devout believers (in the matter of contraception it was obvious that many of the faithful had for years simply disregarded church teaching in that area of their lives), especially as revelations began to emerge that distinguished churchmen scarcely practised what they preached.

Bishop Eamonn Casey's fall from grace in 1992 was just one of the many high-profile stories involving the Catholic Church that hastened the institution's demise. Ferriter (2005) reminds readers of two other incidents that undermined its credibility when it came to providing moral guidance. The first involved a Dublin priest who died in a gay sauna in 1994 while two priests, also clients of the establishment, administered his last rites. The incident followed the death of 'celebrity' priest, Father Michael Cleary (also known as 'The Singing Priest') when the media exposed that he had enjoyed a double life. Unknown to his followers and parishioners, he had lived with his housekeeper Phyllis Hamilton and fathered two sons with her.

While none of these incidences were criminal in civil society, unlike many of the subsequent scandals, which would unfold throughout the decade, they damaged the moral authority of the Church irrevocably. According to Ferriter, thirty-one Catholic priests and brothers were convicted of child sexual abuse between 1991 and 1998 in Ireland. Fittingly, the decade's revelations came to a head in 1999 when the government issued an unequivocal apology to victims of clerical and institutional abuse. In May of that year, they backed this up with the establishment of a commission into the abuse of industrial and reformatory schools. Consequently, many Catholics felt that they could ignore the Church's teachings without feeling guilty. This is apparent in the seismic change in attitudes among Irish people to sex before marriage. Fahey and Layte (2007) summarised the results of a number of surveys, which explored these attitudes. They found that in 1973, 71 per cent of those surveyed believed that sex before marriage was always wrong. By 1994, this figure had fallen significantly to 32 per cent, and by 2005, it had plummeted to a negligible 6 per cent. This change in attitude is evident from the rise in births to unmarried mothers, which increased from just 1,600 in 1921 to more than 15,000 in 1998 (Kennedy 2001). A sharp decline in marriage rates is indicative of changing attitudes, and according to Redmond and Heanue (2000), by 1994 it had fallen sharply to 4.5 per 1,000 of the population from a peak of 7.4 per 1,000 in 1973. They go on to emphasise the implications of this variation when they report that by 1996, there were 32,000 cohabiting couples in Ireland, while the number of lone parents was 129,000. This means that by 1996, almost 25 per cent of the population lived a lifestyle that was in direct contravention of the Roman Catholic Church's moral code. However, it should be noted that a number of widowed spouses accounted for some of the lone parent units.

Dissatisfaction with the Church was evident from a 1998 survey of Irish Catholics. Cosgrave (1998) disseminates the findings, which reveal a dramatic and steady decline in Mass attendance. In 1973, 91 per cent of Irish Catholics attended Mass every week, in 1983 it was 87 per cent, in 1994 it was 77 per cent, but just four years later, in 1998, only 60 per cent admitted to attending Mass once a week. However, the survey uncovered a significant difference between urban Catholics in 1998, where just 48 per cent attended Mass once a week, compared with 77 per cent of their rural counterparts. Tumbling numbers were not confined to Mass attendance. Redmond and Heanue's analysis of the 1996 census reveals that only 6,500 classified their occupation as Clergy and that half of them were aged 55 or over. When compared to the 1946 figure of 18,300, the extent of the drop is very stark. Meanwhile, according to Ferriter (2005), only forty-four priests were ordained in 1998, down from 412 in 1965. Zachary's (1999: 132) insightful account of the Church's demise contends that:

> Rather than showing a positive commitment to secularism, the Irish display a growing disaffection from Catholicism, not because of any concern that the privileged position of the church makes a full commitment to diversity in Ireland impossible, but because a series of scandals have battered its reputation.

The inability of the clerics to lead by example rendered their admonishments and preaching null and void, thus making it easier for Catholics to ignore the rules. Zachary captured the Church's newfound impotence when he observed that in the main, the Irish population accepted the extramarital relationship of its then Taoiseach, Bertie Ahern.

Such travails contrasted with the reforms, which occurred in the Protestant Church. In 1990, that Church's hierarchy ratified the ordination of women priests. Following the majority 'Yes' vote in the 1995 divorce referendum, the Protestant Church agreed to permit divorcees to remarry in the Church. No such allowance was sanctioned in the Roman Catholic Church, which further distanced them from their congregation. In 1997, the then president, Mary McAleese received Communion in the Protestant cathedral, St Patrick's, which was seen by many as an act of defiance. As reported in *The Irish Independent* (1997), the Bishop of Killaloe, Dr Willie Walsh, struck a conciliatory note when he conceded that: 'Many Catholics sometimes receive the Eucharist in churches of the Protestant faith. I have no doubt they do so with the best of intentions and according to their own conscience.' However, he concluded with an unequivocable reminder to Irish Catholics: 'The new Catholic catechism and the directory on ecumenism says: "It is not permissible for a Roman Catholic to receive Communion in churches of the Protestant tradition."' There is little doubt that McAleese's transgression (in the eyes of the Catholic hierarchy) was yet another setback for the beleaguered Church. O'Leary (2000: 146) argues that it can be seen 'as a challenge to traditional Catholicism, within an increasingly questioning and pluralist Irish society.'

The time was right for the State to distance itself from the Bishops and, in response to public opinion and the influence of Europe, legislators reformed some of the State's more conservative laws throughout the 1990s. In 1993, homosexuality was decriminalised. In the same year, the Health (Family Planning Amendment) Act was passed, thereby legalising 'artificial' contraception. At the end of 1995, the Divorce Referendum was passed, paving the way for divorce being available in Ireland from 1996.

Irish advertisers adopted the 'sex sells' adage long before the more sexually liberal1990s. As analysed in Chapter 2, Guinness incorporated women into their ads on a regular basis, and in some instances they appeared in scenarios that were deemed progressive in Ireland in the 1960s and 1970s. Sexual undertones might have been evident, but they were exactly that, undertones, and the conservative audiences at that time did not consider them offensive. In the 1990s, Guinness deployed overtly sexual imagery to promote the brand in some of its ads, satisfied that the more sexually liberated Irish audience would be comfortable with the change in direction. In her 1991 article, Stern employs Snitow's term, 'two pornographies,' to highlight the fact that one uses hard-core imagery and is more likely to arouse men, while the other is soft-core, which is more appealing to women. Obviously, no advertiser intentionally deploys hard-core images in its campaigns but soft-core images became more commonplace in advertising in the latter part of the twentieth century. Stern (1991: 385) categorises soft-core imagery as erotica, which 'depicts sensual images of shared sexual joy.' The concept of *shared sexual joy* is very important because advertising often stands accused of depicting a more pornographic understanding of the male/female relationship, albeit it in a way that is suitable for prime-time viewing. Stern (1991: 384) contends that the domination of women is implicit in pornography, and that: 'the participants in the exchange are either male conquerors (sadists) or female victims (masochists).'

The second of the two ads in the 'Black and White' series, 'Monogamy', revisits a theme used in the 1966 ad 'Party'. Like 'Party', 'Monogamy' is set at a house party, but the later ad is much more sexually charged. The moral code in Ireland had changed significantly in the intervening period and even though 'Party' depicted what can be assumed to be a cohort of sophisticated, educated women, they were not portrayed as sexual predators. Coulter (2003: 2) grasps the significance of this metamorphosis when he consigns historical stereotypes of the Irish to the past. He argues that these were uncomplimentary and racist because they regarded the Irish as: 'feckless, inebriated and violent.' Having seen an ad in a renowned popular music magazine while travelling in the United States in 2001, he was struck by the featured couple's cosmopolitan and sexually confident appearance, visibly free of the conservative shackles that had confined Ireland's young people for so long. The young male in the ad sported a tattoo on his back that proudly stated: 'Irish.' Taking his lead from the ad, Coulter concludes: 'To be Irish is to be young, fun, fashionable and, above all perhaps, belligerently sexual. Irishness has, in other words, become shorthand for "cool."'

Even though he came to this realisation in 2001, it had been a reality for much of the second half of the 1990s. For instance, *Riverdance* in 1994 gave international audiences of millions a different take on Irishness. The dancers were not demure and constrained. Rather, they were sexy and unbridled. They exhibited the characteristics contained in Coulter's description of the new Irish persona, as captured so succinctly in the quote above. Similarly,

'Monogamy' moved with the times and the ad tells a story of love, lust, betrayal, and disappointment. At the start of the ad, an aerial shot shows a car pulling up outside a house. A beautiful, confident woman takes the hand of a young, attractive man who awaits her arrival. They enter the party, both smiling and surveying the scene. Having removed their coats, they move further into the house, where attractive young people are dancing, drinking and generally enjoying themselves. Despite arriving with a beautiful woman, the man returns the flirtatious stares of other women as soon as she leaves his side.

At this point, the viewer assumes that the ad is taking the path most often travelled in ads and movies, that is that the man is anything but monogamous, while his partner is destined to be a victim of his philandering. The man is particularly drawn to a woman wearing a crop top (very fashionable at that time due to the popularity of pop stars like the Spice Girls). She is beautiful and confident, and interacts with him in a very flirtatious manner. Her crop top bears the phrase, 'Monogamy is unnatural' and she makes sure that he reads it before heading up the staircase, willing and daring him to follow her. He succumbs but momentarily falters at the top of the stairs when he sees an open door. Viewers expect the inevitable conclusion to the interaction and the formation of the ad thus far conforms to Stern's (1991: 388) finding that many ads reinforce an 'orgasmic sexual structure.' The ad recounts a story and excites the viewer by using sounds and images that build towards the climax. However, in this particular ad, the viewer is brought to a particular point and it finishes in an anti-climactic manner for the man. He goes into the bedroom and is taken aback by what he sees. A couple is engaged in deep and intimate conversation whilst sitting on the bed, the place where he expected to have sex with the woman in the crop top. Meanwhile, the woman whose tee-shirt derides monogamy, seems angry and distraught upon seeing her partner with another woman and runs from the bedroom, leaving him stunned. The couple on the bed are oblivious to the interruption but unbeknownst to them, they have had the last laugh. They are the ones who have turned their backs on monogamy. She is the woman who arrived at the party with the man who was prepared to have sex with another woman. The ad concludes with the tagline: 'Not everything in black and white makes sense,' followed by a settled pint of chilled Guinness on a black background.

Dusty Springfields's sensual 1960s hit single, 'The look of love', written and composed by Burt Bacharach, is the soulful soundtrack to the ad. The ad's story of love and lust is played out to the first two verses of the classic track, with the actions and expressions fitting each word:

> The look of love is in your eyes
> A look your smile can't disguise
> The look of love
> It's saying so much more than words could ever say
> And what my heart has heard, well, it takes my breath away.
> I can hardly wait to hold you, feel my arms around you
> How long I have waited, waited just to love you
> Now that I have found you.

The association between the Guinness brand and the song's lyrics is subtle. They might be construed to compare the excitement of newfound love, yet to be consummated, but keenly anticipated, with the discovery or rediscovery of a new product, in this case Guinness. The ad is aimed at a young, promiscuous (in terms of drinking habits) audience, who considers Guinness as a drink for older, more mature men. Many of them have not discovered Guinness for themselves and this ad places the brand in a relevant, contemporary, urban setting, complete with a lifestyle to which they aspire or already enjoy.

While the 1960s music and black-and-white tones are evocative of that decade, the clothes, hair and social mores on display clearly belong to a much more contemporary setting. No attempt is made to hide the sexual attraction between the main protagonists in the ad. Moreover, the innocence and formality of the 1960s is gone. However, despite protestations from both men and women that they are liberal and indifferent about monogamy, reality is different and it is this twist at the end that gives meaning to the campaign's tagline.

In 1999, the ad 'Oysters' was broadcast. It resurrects a decades-old tradition of using oysters to promote Guinness, a duo that was enjoyed as far back as the 1800s. On 21 November 1837, Benjamin Disraeli, future prime minister of the United Kingdom, wrote to his sister Sarah, telling her how he had celebrated the opening of Queen Victoria's first Parliament:

> There was a division on the Address in Queen Victoria's first Parliament, 509 to 20. I then left the House at ten o'clock, none of us having dined ... I supped at the Carlton, with a large party, off oysters and Guinness, and got to bed at half-past twelve o'clock. Thus ended the most remarkable day hitherto of my life. (Yenne 2007: 33)

High praise indeed from a future leader, who saw fit to name check Guinness, as opposed to a generic beer or stout. Furthermore, Disraeli's specific reference to Guinness is significant for a couple of reasons. Firstly, he positioned it alongside events that contributed to, in his words: 'The most remarkable day hitherto of my life.' Such positive affirmation for a brand and its ability to make people happy cannot be underestimated when it comes to building loyalty. In a contemporary context, such a testimonial might have been shared with a wider circle through advertising or public relations, thus having a positive effect on the Guinness brand.

One hundred years after the letter was sent, this is exactly what Guinness did when they published an ad in *Time* magazine (see Figure 24). Secondly, his statement singled out a gastronomic pairing between Guinness and oysters that would stand the test of time. References to Guinness and oysters were made in some of the earliest examples of its advertising in the United Kingdom. The campaigns were spearheaded by the advertising agency SH Benson, who employed the services of the illustrator J. Gilroy. Consequently, his iconic work became synonymous with many of the beautifully executed illustrations that featured in Guinness's ads.

BBC Good Food (n.d.) ranks oysters alongside caviar, *foie gras*, and champagne as one of the world's luxury foods, an accolade that helps explain why they merit their very own festival. The Galway International Oyster and Seafood Festival began as a modest affair in 1954. According to Galway Oyster Festival's website (n.d.), only thirty-four guests attended the inaugural festival, but by 2012, this number had risen to 22,000. It has become a major attraction for many domestic and international tourists. Guinness is its longest standing sponsor, a relationship that has been celebrated and highlighted through its advertising since the 1960s. In 1995, it published a colour poster, which advertised Guinness and Cuan Oysters from Co. Down. It extols the wonders of the duo, and presents an appetising image of what it might look like.

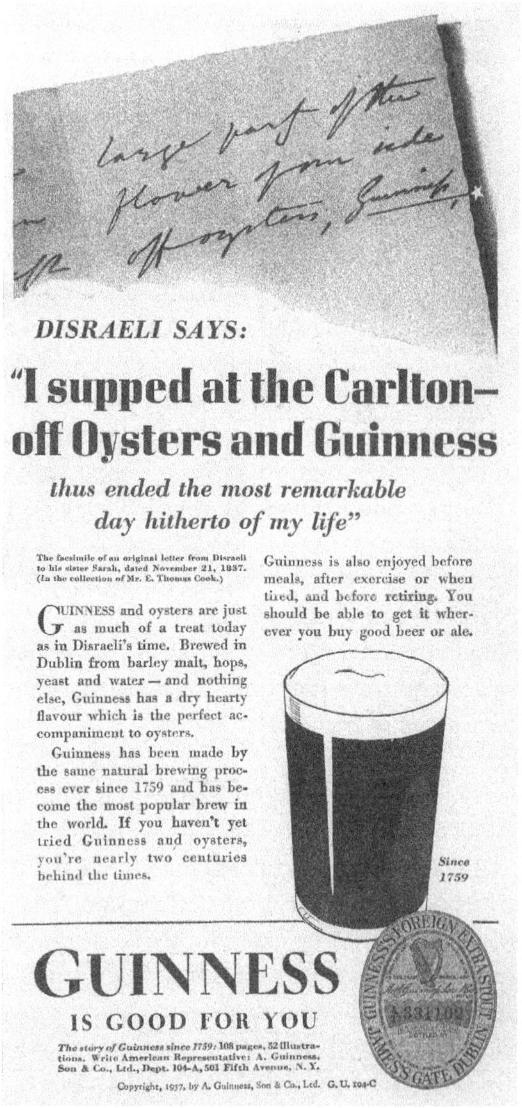

Figure 24: Disraeli says: I supped at the Carlton

In one 1995 poster ad, which was installed in pubs, Guinness used oysters to encourage customers to buy more bottles of its Extra Stout. These adverts reinforced the idea that Guinness and oysters are well matched from a culinary perspective, as demonstrated by copy in this 1966 press ad which declares: 'Guinness and oysters go swimmingly together.' As if to leave the reader in no doubt, it signs off with a tempting refrain: 'Guinness and Galway oysters. Delicious!' Meanwhile, evidence of Guinness's involvement with oysters from other regions can be found in ads published in the City Press Reports of the Colchester Oyster Feasts in 1961 and 1962.

Fast-forward to the 'Oysters' ad from 1999, one of the 'Live Life to the Power of Guinness' series. The ad was created by the London agency HHCL for an Irish audience and it contains overtly sexual themes. Clearly, it is targeted at a young, affluent, sexually liberated Irish audience that had found its feet in the Celtic Tiger economy. The ad motivated Linehan (1999) to write an article about it for *The Irish Times* and in it, the Guinness Brand Director, Kenny Jamieson explained what they were trying to achieve:

> The strategy is a dual one. Guinness has a huge amount of existing drinkers, but its profile in the marketplace is older than we'd like it to be. Every year, there's 30,000 or 40,000 new potential customers entering the beer market, and it's important that we keep them aware of us. But even older drinkers don't want the product to be seen as fuddy-duddy.

The creative execution in the ad bears no resemblance whatsoever to what had gone before in Guinness's oyster-related ads. Instead, the oyster's age-old reputation as an aphrodisiac is unashamedly foregrounded throughout the ad, a method that was by no means new. According to Buvelot (2017), it was a popular theme among seventeenth-century Dutch artists, such as is found in Frans Van Mieris's 'The Oyster Meal' (1661) in which a man presents a dish of oysters to a luxuriously dressed woman. In Gerard Borch's, 'Gentleman Encouraging a Lady to Drink' (1658–9), a man woos a woman with drink and oysters. In a staunch defence of the Guinness ad's plot, Jamieson stated boldly: 'I don't know about sexy. It's certainly sensual, and that will appeal to younger drinkers. But, in terms of older drinkers, there's a recognition that there's a historical link between Guinness and oysters' (Linehan 1999).

Shot in black and white, the ad features an attractive, sexually intimate young couple. In the opening shot, he is scuba diving. When he returns to his beautiful girlfriend with a cache of oysters, he sensuously feeds them to her while she is draped across some rocks. She helps him to remove his wet suit and there is a sense of urgency about her actions. The camera lingers provocatively on her toned, bare skin, which is dusted with sand and scantily clad in a black bikini. The flesh of the oyster unashamedly takes centre stage, functioning as a metaphor for the female genitalia. He feeds her fresh oyster flesh from the shell, which she hungrily devours. Once more, the imagery conveyed is a metaphor, this time for oral sex. The sea's movement, which alternates with images of the couple, simulates a sexual rhythm and one that is about to reach a climax. Then, the camera cuts away from the scene abruptly, affording them some privacy, and switches to a close-up of a woman drinking from a pint of Guinness. She licks her lips, while her expression suggests that the taste of the drink has conjured up an intimate memory.

The ad's backing track is the 1996 release, 'Pleasant Smell', which was a hit for the UK band, 12 Rounds. The lead singer, Claudia Sarne moans the lyrics in rasping tones and when married with the visual imagery, she intensifies the ad's aura of intense sexual pleasure:

> Ooh you're such a good boy bringing in my tea
> Scratching at my blood shoots me with sympathy.

Apart from this verse, two short excerpts from the track are included towards the end of the sea scene: 'Dream on' and a final, climactic: 'Come,' as the camera closes in on the woman licking her lips after drinking her Guinness. The ad concludes with a female voiceover's whispering instruction: 'Live life to the power of Guinness.' The fact that the voiceover at the end is that of a woman adds strength to the ad and reinforces the idea of sexual equality. The ad seems to straddle Snitow's 'two pornographies.' In my opinion, it leans more towards the soft-core category because it portrays shared sexual joy. Some might argue that the woman is objectified, but it appears that she is an equal partner, confident enough to lead proceedings at times.

Overtly sexual to the end, it is perhaps surprising that the ad does not feature in the ASAI's archive of complaints. Targeted media scheduling might explain why because it previewed in cinemas and was probably screened during age appropriate movies. Cinema is a much more contained media platform than television. However, by 1999 the growth in the number of commercial television channels and the ensuing programme choice facilitated better targeting, thus minimising the possibility of offending and alienating older, more conservative viewers.

What is the point of the Big Pint?

HHCL's first campaign, which was broadcast in Ireland towards the end of 1996, comprised a series of ads under the moniker, 'Big Pint'. Fourteen ads were created between then and 1998. The first nine ads, all produced in 1996, were based on humour. In retrospect, they convey a lack of understanding by HHCL of the Irish psyche or Guinness's deep association with Irish culture. With the exception of the dubiously named 'Chinaman' ad, there was nothing overtly Irish about the first ads in the series. However, two versions of the aforementioned ad were produced, one with English subtitles and the other with Irish subtitles. The lead actor is seemingly Chinese and his script is a comedic take on a Confucius-like philosopher who attempts to solve, according to the subtitles, 'The Big Conundrum,' or '*An Cheist Mór*.' A pint of settled Guinness shuffles across a petal-strewn stone surface, before an old, bearded Chinese man comes into view. He bears a puzzled expression. The camera pans out to reveal a Chinese garden, complete with a stone table at which the man is seated. The Guinness continues to move on the table and heads in the man's direction. He says:

> *Guinness … chun an tart a mhúcadh.* [Guinness … thirst quenching.]
> *Blas a théann go smior.* [Chunky full-on flavour.]

The Chinese man proffers a thumbs-up sign and sounds happy when he pronounces:

> *Blas iontach mór.* [Big taste sensation.]
> *Aitheanta ar fud na cruinne …* [Universally known as …]
> *An Pionta Mór.* [The Big Pint.]
> *Conas a dtógfá deoch chomh mór seo?* [So how does such a sizeable beverage fit into the human hand?]

He reaches for the pint and it evades him. Up until that point, calm Chinese music plays in the background. Suddenly, the zen-like atmosphere is shattered when the music switches to raucous rock. What follows is a high-paced collage of random images, all featuring a pint of Guinness. Just as suddenly, the pint sits on a workbench, surrounded by tools, before retiring to a mountain setting where it rests on a table, seemingly within reach of a woman's hand. These scenes signify the taming of the Big Pint, all challengers succeeding. Now, the pint of Guinness sits on a pedestal, elevated to a revered status. Will the Chinese man be buoyed by the success of the others? Perhaps telepathy will get the job done. He holds his arms above his head, maybe taunted by a fleeting image of a woman's hand picking up a pint. He circles the pedestal like a hunter and moves towards the pint. The scene is interrupted by the image of a hand holding another pint aloft against the backdrop of a bookie's board of favourites.

The energetic, rock music segues back into the calm, zen soundtrack. The Chinese man offers more words of wisdom: '*B'fhéidir nach bhfuil freagra le fáil*' [Don't try to ponder the imponderable]. He holds up his left hand, as if to surrender, and then while levitating, he advises: '*Is féidir and dá thrá a fhreastail*' [Have your cake and eat it too]. He floats above the pint, perhaps in the hope of confusing his prey: '*Beir greim daingean ar do phíonta id do láimhin beag*' [Stick the Big Pint in your small hand]. Clearly, his plan has failed because the pint has relocated to the safety of a birdcage.

The ad's narrative aims to make Guinness more approachable. Often perceived as a challenging drink that takes time for the uninitiated to master, the Chinese man's over-complicated approach to the pint seems totally unnecessary and redundant when contrasted with the others. The ad concludes with a black screen, over which gold lettering spells out: 'AN

PIONTA MÓR. NÁ TABHAIR AON AIRD AIR ACH ÓL É. THE BIG PINT. DON'T PONDER IT, DRINK IT.' As if to emphasise the point, the tagline is rendered in capital letters. It shouts at the viewer and cannot be ignored. Unlike most other Guinness ads, its logo is not shown alongside the closing tagline. Instead, black and gold letters combine to signify the brand. The tagline is a statement of intent by Guinness. Its name is already synonymous with the word 'pint' and in some ways it is a generic term, which many people use when ordering a pint of beer, rendering the word Guinness redundant. Also, the word 'big' might be taken literally, thus implying value. Allied with many of the images in the ad, it might just as easily imply that it is in vogue. It's the latest 'big thing.' Despite its exclusion from the closing screen, the Guinness logo is present throughout the ad, as it is emblazoned on the pint glasses.

The next two ads in the series, 'Red Indian' and 'Indian', are similar in style, but the narratives revolve around two new characters, which are caricatures, regularly seen in movies. They are known for philosophising and as in the previous ad, the subject of their musings is how best to tackle a pint of Guinness. A familiar face from Guinness's past is included in the collage of images in the 'Red Indian' ad, the toucan. He brings J. Gilroy's iconic character to life again and reintroduces him to a new generation of Guinness drinkers. In 1994, he featured in a series of poster ads at the time of the World Cup, which was used in an outdoor campaign so younger drinkers would have been familiar with the iconic bird (see Figure 25).

The 'Big Pint' ads are aimed at a young audience, used to absorbing rapidly moving images. The collage sequences are reminiscent of the multimedia shows popularised by many high profile music acts when on tour. For example, U2's 1992 to 1993 Zoo TV tour was staged in cavernous stadia and arenas around the world and one of the main talking points was the use of video images to help bring their performances to life. Since then, it is a technique that continues to be an integral ingredient in live performances, music videos, and nightclubs.

The London agency's seeming lack of familiarity with the Irish audience is evident in the next sequence of ads in the series. The fictional character Albert Dunwoody makes his debut in 'Train'. He wears an oversized, bright yellow three-piece suit and stands in a rural setting, holding a pint of

Guinness in his left hand. He smiles and says: 'Guinness is a big pint with a big thirst-quenching flavour.' In keeping with the first three ads in the series, he poses a philosophical question: 'So, how does it fit in the confines of a human hand? Well I, Albert Dunwoody know how.' He seems very pleased with himself. 'First … .' A train travels behind him and drowns out his voice. Throughout his monologue, he makes exaggerated hand and arm gestures. Just as his explanation draws to a close, the train disappears and his voice is audible again. However, it is too late to hear an answer that makes any sense. Instead, all the audience hears is a meaningless conclusion to his theory: '… then it slips neatly in.' He smiles, visibly suppressing a fully formed laugh. The ad closes with the tag line: 'THE BIG PINT. DON'T PONDER IT. DRINK IT.' Dunwoody says in the background: 'Simple.'

Figure 25: Guinness – where in the world would you be without it?

The agency perseveres with his character in two more ads, 'Bush' and 'Christmas Interference'. The former, 'Bush', features a lone bush flanked by a human figure, situated in a vast expanse of grassland. Dunwoody appears with a pint in his hand, this time clad in red and once again, he asks: 'How does the Big Pint fit in the human hand? Well I, Albert Dunwoody am privy to the answer.' Suddenly, the bush is beside him. 'I shall now explain as nothing is going to stop me.' At this juncture, two men pop up from behind the bush. Dunwoody attempts to impart his explanation but is interrupted when two men in silver space suits tackle him to the ground. He drops his pint and they place a sack over his head. He shouts: 'Aliens. Help! Help!' They lead him away and the ad nears its nears its conclusion with the now familiar tagline: 'The Big Pint. Don't ponder it. Drink it.'

'Christmas Interference' introduces viewers to Dunwoody's family in the customary setting of a Christmas dinner. He turns to the camera and picks up a pint of Guinness with both hands. This time, it prompts him to ask: 'How does such a big pint fit into the human hand?' As before, it is a rhetorical question because he prides himself on having the answer: 'Only I, Albert Dunwoody have the solution and nothing can stop me from now revealing the answer. What happens is …'. His answer is obliterated by very bad interference, which only clears in time to hear him say: '… then it slips neatly in.' The closing tagline takes on a seasonal feel: 'HAVE AN XTRA LARGE XMAS FROM THE BIG PINT.'

The main problems evident in the Dunwoody ads are his demeanour and faux-Irish accent. They present a caricature of an Irishman that has been created by an outsider. He comes across as gormless and from the Guinness brand's perspective, he lacks authenticity. Since 1959, so many of its ads succeeded in demonstrating empathy and familiarity with Irish consumers. 'Monogamy', which was broadcast in the same year as 'Train', was much more realistic and in tune with the cultural shift in the identity of young, Irish adults. Even though that ad was most likely set in Dublin, its cast and audience could just as easily have been at a house party in a cosmopolitan city like London or Paris. The creators of the Dunwoody character overlooked the fact that young Irish people in the 1990s were willing participants in global village life. Guinness brought these same liberated young people to the party in 'Monogamy', capturing the *zeitgeist*, just like they had done in many of their previous ads. However, that is not to say that 'Monogamy' should be categorised as a great ad for Guinness because while it understood young consumers, it did not demonstrate an understanding of the brand's values. Meanwhile, the Dunwoody ads do not understand the audience or the brand. They are a throwback to the stage-*oirish* representation of what it means to be Irish and, in my opinion, did little to enhance the Guinness brand.

Three subsequent ads in the series did not reinstate Guinness's reputation as a brand that understood its Irish audience. 'Hand Exercises' is a mildly amusing ad that might be construed as negative for the stout's cause. It opens to the sound of repetitive creaking emanating from behind a half-open door, which opens to reveal a man in bed. He is alone and he is not doing what the sound suggests. Instead, he holds a hand exerciser in his right hand. A pint of Guinness, lamp and alarm clock sit on his bedside locker. He leans over to pick up the pint with his right hand and inhales deeply, as if lifting weights. The ad is over in just ten seconds, concluding with the tagline: 'BUILD UP TO THE BIG PINT.'

The ad is clearly directed at males and while it is meant to be humorous, it reaffirms many consumers' reasons for not drinking Guinness. That reason is the heaviness of the beverage and when compared to cider, which was very popular in 1996, this ad may not have helped its cause. In contrast, the various ads in the 'There's no time like Guinness time' series attempted to turn one of the stout's negative characteristics into a positive.

'Tree (Day)' and 'Tree (Night)' (1996) were designed to work in tandem. The *Day* version contains absolutely no branding, so ideally they would have bookended a commercial break. 'Day' opens with a shot of a tree's bark. The sound of slow, rhythmic banging and birdsong accompanies the image. The camera pans downwards to focus on a man banging his head against the bark. The audience is left wondering, who is behind the ad? There is nothing funny about the short ad and it makes for uncomfortable viewing. It may raise the question as to why someone who may be on the autistic spectrum, is being portrayed as a figure of fun.

The provenance of the ad is revealed in the sequel, 'Tree (Night)', which is the same as 'Tree (Day)', but for the fact that it is dark and the happy birdsong has been replaced by the atmospheric hooting of an owl. Guinness's involvement in the ads is disclosed in the final shot. The implication is that overthinking the mysteries of a pint of Guinness is likely to lead to insanity. However, this does not make the ad any more palatable and rather than pondering the Big Pint, the audience is left contemplating the direction that Guinness's advertising has taken.

While the early ads in the 'Big Pint' series attempt to deploy a comedic approach, 'Water Tower' marks a significant change in style. It is an epic, emotive tale of twin brothers living in different parts of the world. One of them is a farm worker who lives in an arid, expansive space in California. The other occupies the overcast, busy environs of Dublin city. The contrast is immense – the twin in California toils in the heat, as his brother arrives in the Stag's Head pub to socialise after a day's work. The farm worker repairs a fence and hurts his thumb with a hammer. Simultaneously, back in the bar, his twin flexes his thumb. He gazes at his pint of Guinness as it settles, but there's a rumbling sound and the camera returns to the fence in California. A nearby water tower collapses, expelling a surge of water. The farm worker regards the scene helplessly and is carried along by the force of the water. His twin sips his Guinness and deep in thought, he rubs his thumb again. The farm worker surfaces, and is clearly winded, but it is reassuring to know that he is unharmed. The blurred image of a pint of Guinness sits on a pedestal, complete with a red dot on the lower part of the glass. In the right hand corner of the screen, the ad signs off with a newly designed logo that comprises an illustration of a pint, which is encircled by the words: 'The Big Pint.' This is a new departure for Guinness because the longstanding logo comprising its name and harp is not visible in the ad at any point. Even though the pints in the ad are in Guinness glasses, the name is not shown in its entirety and the trademark harp is absent. Guinness seems confident that the intended audience has reached the final stage of advertising literacy, and is capable of interpreting the clues laid as to its identity.

The soundtrack, 'What does your soul look like (part 4)', by DJ Shadow, is a 1996 release and appeals to a younger audience. Its rhythm synchronises with the ebb and flow of the drama as it unfolds. Visually, the ad has impact and a cinematic quality that captivates the viewer. According to Green (1997), the ad was broadcast on RTÉ One, RTÉ Network 2 (now known as RTÉ 2), UTV and Channel 4, which would have reached a broad audience, in particular young adults.

Two more ads with telepathic twins were produced, 'Drummer Boy' in 1997, and 'Black Market' in 1998. The narrative in each ad is similar to 'Water Tower', with one twin in Dublin and the other in Africa and South America respectively. The central concept in all three ads complements Guinness's attempt to foreground the power that it believes is contained in the 'Big Pint,' setting it apart from other beers. They are in marked contrast to the first nine ads in the series and are testament to the fact that in a short period of time, HHCL unearthed deeper insights into the minds of Irish audiences, in particular young people. The use of twins enables Guinness to tell two stories in each ad. In each case, one tale plays out in a Dublin city centre setting and suggests that the home-based twin has a successful career, a likely scenario in the thriving economy. Each ad places the other twin in a faraway setting but there is no sense of sadness or regret about their predicament. In the Celtic Tiger economy, emigration was not forced on young people and its partakers did not exude an air of despair or longing. Instead, they left Ireland willingly and considered it an exciting and positive choice. However, even though the agency appears to have understood the young, Irish consumers better, it is clear that its understanding of the Guinness brand is not as good. In many ways, this campaign contributed to problems that would become evident at the start of the noughties.

Live life to the power of Guinness

In 2000, Steve Langan, Marketing Director of Guinness in the UK, explained the concept behind the 'Live Life to the Power of Guinness' communications platform when he said: 'All the ads focus on the release of different emotions which drinking Guinness evokes' (Garrett 2000). 'Horses', features a man and woman on horseback in a dense wood. They do not wear helmets, an omission which suggests freedom and daring, tinged with danger. He chases her and they dodge branches but still gallop at a frenetic speed. When they emerge from the woods, they slow down and circle one another. Their clothes provide subtle clues as to the provenance of the ad – he wears a tan jacket and black gloves, while she is clad mainly in white, offset with black gloves and a black scarf around her neck. An obvious chemistry smoulders between them and they communicate with their eyes. They touch hands, a motion that appears to signal their next move, one that they have planned in advance. There is no going back. They gallop across a wide, open space until they reach the edge of the Cliffs of Moher. They are going so fast that it is impossible to stop and in unison, they leap forward. The camera freezes and viewers are reminded of the iconic conclusion to the 1991 movie, 'Thelma and Louise', in which the two leading actresses are filmed and freeze-framed as they drive over the edge of a cliff in their car, forever frozen in time and offering hope to the viewer that they had a plan which will ensure their survival.

The story switches to a close-up shot of a young man with long hair drinking Guinness. A female voiceover counsels in an urgent whisper, in keeping with the scene that the audience has just witnessed: 'Live life to the power of Guinness,' which also comes into view as the tagline on the final frame of the ad. The soundtrack is Patty Smith's 'Land', taken from her critically acclaimed 1975 album, 'Horses'. The urgent, edgy rhythm of the track perfectly suits the drama that unfolds, as does the artist's anti-establishment reputation.

It is not surprising that the ad elicited complaints to the Advertising Standards Association for Ireland (ASAI) from the public. The case report (ASAI 1999) summarises the nature of the complaints:

> The complainants objected that the commercial, in which a couple appeared to ride horses off a cliff, showed behaviour which is harmful to riders and horses and could be seen as glorifying suicide.

When the ad was first broadcast, different versions were made for the Republic of Ireland and Northern Ireland markets. The modification was subtle but in the light of the complaints received by the ASAI, it was significant. In the Northern Irish version, the riders head towards the cliffs but before they close in on the edge, the camera cuts to the man drinking Guinness. Also, cinema and TV versions of the ad were made for the Republic of Ireland market and in the cinema version, there is a stone wall with a small piece of land on the other side before the cliff's edge, the implication being that the couple's intention is to clear the wall as opposed to jumping off the edge of the cliff. However, it is very unlikely that any rider, let alone amateur riders, would have the skills required to clear the wall and then stop the horse's acceleration before heading for certain death. In their defence, Guinness's response is summarised by the ASAI (1999):

> The advertisers said that it was not their intention to make a film about reckless behaviour or suicide. They considered that they had captured the emotion of a vigorous ride through a forest where the dramatic expanse of the County Clare scenery was part of the freedom and exhilaration. The end sequence showed the couple approaching a wall at the edge of the cliff and actually slowing down to clear the wall with land on the other side. It did not show a jump off the cliff. The position message was also strongly reiterated in the end line which encouraged people to 'Live life to the Power of Guinness'. They believed the film was suitable for airing despite the seriousness of the complaints received. They had, however, amended the end sequence to show more clearly that at the end the riders jumped onto land. They explained that the horses involved had been accompanied by their owner/trainers and a vet who assessed the horses daily and produced a final report certifying that they remained healthy and free from disease or injury.

Having taken the advertiser's defence and the complainants' concerns into consideration, the ASAI (1999) upheld the complaint:

> The Complaints Committee considered that consumers would assume, on a normal viewing, that the commercial depicted riders jumping over the cliff and decided that the commercial breached the Code in that respect. They were pleased to note that the advertisers had altered the commercial to clearly show the riders safely jumping over a wall onto visible land.

Writing for *The Irish Times*, Linehan (1999) relayed the Guinness Brand Director, Kenny Jamieson's response to the complaints about the ad:

> If you look at the commercial, there's a wall beyond the cliff-top, and you can see in previous shots that there's land beyond that wall, so there's an element of suspense about whether they managed to stop in time. If it had come through strongly as an issue in research, we just wouldn't air it, but it didn't.

He does not refer to the version of the ad that was broadcast without a wall at the edge of the cliff. However, the increasingly regulatory environment of the 1990s meant that Guinness had entered a new era, when on occasion it was forced to defend its ads, or ideally, create them in such a way that they would not raise concerns from the general public.

Conclusion

In a decade that launched *Riverdance* to an unsuspecting global audience, it is fitting that Guinness concluded the 1990s with a dance-themed ad. 'The Dance with it' series of ads features 'ordinary' people of various ethnicities, male and female, young and old, dancing very badly in an audition scenario. The purpose of the ad is to promote the new Guinness draught in a bottle, so some of the dancers use the new bottle as a prop. Bearing in mind the notoriety it had enjoyed with 'Anticipation', it is fitting that it returned to dancing, a universal signifier, enjoyed all over the world. The creators of the ad are confident that the audience will understand the provenance of the dance motif. Also, Ireland was in the throes, metaphorically speaking, of enjoying one big party with many people, particularly younger people, working hard and partying hard.

The backing track, 'Burke's Law', is by the Jamaican ska pioneer Prince Buster and, in keeping with most of Guinness's ads from 'Anticipation' onwards, comes from an international, non-Irish artist. By the time this ad was broadcast, the MTV generation that emerged in Ireland during the 1980s had fully assimilated global culture. Overt references to Ireland and Irishness are absent from the ad, with the exception of the final scene, which has echoes of *Riverdance.*

The ad exudes happiness and a carefree spirit. Despite the clumsiness of the dancers, they are confident and show no signs of self-consciousness. Their diversity provides a snapshot of Ireland's population at the end of the 1990s. By then, the Celtic Tiger economy had taken hold and in sharp contrast with the 1980s, the tide of emigration had been reversed. Ireland was a destination for economic migrants and fittingly, their presence was represented in the 'Dance with it' series. Immigrants and Irish people alike, they were emboldened by the success of the economy, thus enabling them to shake off their insecurities, for the time being in any case. Unlike 'Journey', which marked the end of the 1980s with a question mark over the merits of globalisation, Guinness's final series of ads in the 1990s represented a much more optimistic view of it. Compared to the previous decade, the 1990s had been good to Ireland, which helped allay the fears of living in a global economy.

Guinness's ads mirrored the seismic change that occurred in Ireland in the millennium's final decade. They started with a 'business as usual' approach, possibly facilitated by the continued use of its long-term advertising agency, Arks. Without realising it at the time, the agency reached its peak in 1994 with McKinney's 'Dancing Man,' but its inability to hold onto the Guinness account in 1996 was perhaps inevitable. The appointment of a series of internationally aligned agencies was in sync with the wider changes that occurred in society, from the Irish electorate voting in favour of divorce to the fallout of the scandals in the Catholic Church. With the widespread availability of contraceptives and the decriminalisation of homosexuality, the sexual revolution officially arrived in Ireland, some decades after it had taken hold in other Western societies. If Irish society was unrecognisable, so too was its economy, which was beholden to the vagaries of global forces. Therefore, the assimilation of Guinness into Diageo was unavoidable and replacing Arks with globally connected agencies paved the way for the implementation of internationally uniform communications platforms that could be adapted for Irish audiences. As demonstrated by much of 'The Big Pint' campaign, Guinness and its London-based agency did not always get this right at the start but by the end of the decade, the ads suggest that it understood the realities of life for Irish consumers. However, this does not mean that it understood Guinness and its very specific brand identity.

Concluding thoughts

The period under scrutiny in this study was a pivotal time in the Republic of Ireland's short history. It commences in 1959 when Ireland had just taken its first steps on the road to internationalisation. It concludes forty years later in 1999, by which time Ireland had metamorphosed into one of the most globalised countries in the world. Inevitably, this journey challenged and diluted some of the country's cultural and societal norms. Many of the changes that occurred in Ireland over the course of those years are clearly charted by piecing together a large number of the ads held in the Guinness Archive. Just as signs of Irishness, cultural specificity and the provenance of Guinness were inferred from these ads, so too was the growing prevalence of international cultural tropes.

Stories and storytelling are intrinsic ingredients in memorable advertising. Therefore, when crafting ads, agencies often interrogate clients so as to unearth nuggets from a brand's past. When woven into the narrative of an ad, they have the ability to bestow upon the message authenticity and distinction, thus building trust among consumers. There is ample evidence in the ads that were analysed for this book that Guinness's backstory and heritage not only featured in many of its Irish-oriented campaigns, but that it formed the basis of some of its most memorable ads. By the time it first started advertising in Ireland, Guinness was 200 years old. At this stage, it was firmly embedded in many facets of Irish life by virtue of the fact that it was a major employer, renowned for its benevolence to its employees, their families and the local community in Dublin. Musicians, poets, writers and politicians guaranteed its posterity by incorporating its name and famous porter into their writings. Therefore, by 1959 those 200 years had endowed upon the brand a rich history that placed it at a distinct advantage, particularly in later years when attempting to achieve cut-through in an increasingly crowded market place.

The most frequently used signs in Guinness's ads relate to its provenance. The first ever ad in Ireland drew attention to its longevity (200 years) and its legendary founder. The copy in that first ad contextualised Guinness's legacy when it invited readers to reflect: 'Do you imagine that our great-great-great grandfathers when they tasted their first Guinness two hundred years ago, realised that it was to become Ireland's favourite drink?' From then on, age and longevity are themes that were revisited in every decade.

The core elements of Guinness's visual identity were established more than 250 years ago and while they did evolve, such was the evolutionary nature of the changes that the elements employed in the 1960s and 1970s are still instantly recognisable as Guinness. First and foremost, the name has survived economic turmoil, changing consumer preferences, corporate takeovers, globalisation and the intensification of competition. Similarly, the rendering of the logotype in the name has remained much the same. Audiences are so familiar with the lettering that the mere hint of just one of the letters is sufficient to suggest 'Guinness'. This was put to the test in the 1986 ad, 'Logo'. Similarly, the brand's contrasting colours, black and gold, were evident in the vast majority of the ads under scrutiny.

In 1876, Guinness had the foresight to register the harp as a trademark. Since it is a mirror image of the State's official emblem, this further embedded the brand into Irish culture and heritage. Since the 1960s, its visibility in the ads was guaranteed because it was almost always on the glass that contained the settling, settled or partially consumed pint. The exception to this was in the second half of the 1990s and early noughties when for some ill-advised reason, the logo was not always used in the ads. Under Irish International's stewardship in the early noughties, not only did the harp reappear but it was flanked by the year 1759, once again reminding consumers of the brand's long heritage. More subtle references were often made to the musical instrument, such as the harp-shaped Carrick-a-Rede rope-bridge in 'Logo' and the harps in the 1982 ads that featured The Chieftains and Clannad. The final, long-standing visual element of the identity is the signature of Arthur Guinness, which was deployed in the ads less frequently than the aforementioned elements but when it was included, it established a connection between the founder and the product.

Guinness also recounted stories about its past through a number of ads, often resorting to hyperbole so as to make them more memorable. Recurring themes in many of the ads relate to place (St James's Gate and

Dublin), the time it takes to pour a pint, the settle, the significance of the year 1759, and the counter-intuitive way in which the head of the pint is always consumed last. The first ads in 1959 were based on facts taken from the annals of the Brewery. In the 1970s, a number of print ads focused on many of these themes and promoted them as a point of difference. With the growing use of TV advertising, stories about Guinness in bygone years were played out in historical, slice-of-life scenarios. The history and longevity of the brand were foregrounded in the 'Timelessness of Guinness' series (1974–6). 'Island' (1977) eulogised 'the wait', an aspect of Guinness that had become a hindrance when attracting new customers. Similarly, the more cheery but no less memorable 1994 ad, 'Anticipation' celebrated Guinness time, the time it takes for a pint to settle. 'The Big Pint' series in the 1990s attempted to perpetuate the mystery surrounding the pour but the obscurity of the ads did not resonate with the target audience.

Changes in the cultural signs used in Guinness's advertising in Ireland are evident over the forty-year period under examination. Up until the mid- to late 1960s, overtly Irish cultural signs dominated but thereafter the growing influence of international culture was apparent. In all decades, the pub was the setting for many of the print and TV ads. At first, it was always a traditional Irish pub, unless the story in the ad necessitated the creation of a futuristic, space-age hostelry. By the 1990s, the pubs in the ads were often represented as sleek, urban establishments, typical of the Celtic Tiger era when global culture pervaded all aspects of Irish life. In some instances, the pub in question was located in another country, a reference to two of Ireland's most famous exports, the Irish pub and its people. The propensity of the Irish to use drink and the pub as social lubricants comes through in many ads. For example, the campaigns, 'Get together with a Guinness' (1971–4) and 'Have a Guinness tonight' (1978–81) encapsulate the enjoyment that Irish people take from socialising with friends in a pub.

The copy in some of the 1960s print ads was in Irish. The voiceover in the TV ad 'Festival' (1968/9) was recorded in Irish as well as English. In the 1970s, a small number of print ads were produced in Irish but it was the 1977 ad 'Island' that really resonated with audiences because of its nostalgic imagery and the memorable line, '*Tá siad ag teacht*.' These four words aligned the Guinness brand with one of the most unique signifiers of Irish culture and the ad is still remembered by many people. There is very little evidence of the language in later decades but in 1996 two versions of 'Chinaman' were made. One of them used English subtitles to translate the Chinese voiceover and the other had Irish subtitles.

Music is one of the mainstays of Irish culture and Ireland has a proud tradition of songwriters, composers and performers. However, when the country opened its borders in 1958, international popular music was adopted with great enthusiasm. In the 1960s, music was not always used in Guinness's TV ads but when it was, it tended to be very neutral and was not suggestive of indigenous Irish culture. This trend continued in the 1970s but by the end of that decade, the influence of American and British soft rock and pop dominated the bespoke Guinness songs. The 'No beer comes near campaign' (1982) featured The Chieftains and Clannad. Both bands, particularly The Chieftains are known for their strong ties to traditional Irish music and this formed the soundtrack to the ads. However, English artists Elkie Brooks and Mike Oldfield also featured in the campaign. Their inclusion emphasised just how comfortable Irish people were with international artists. In the 1990s, music was central in many of the ads. Invariably, the tracks were by artists from all over the world and they appealed to cosmopolitan consumers in Ireland who were part of a global community.

The arrival of television in Ireland in the 1950s had a very significant impact on Irish culture and from the 1970s on, many of Guinness's ads incorporated themes that were instantly recognised by audiences who were familiar with British and American programmes. Kearney (1988b) referred to this development as culture without frontiers. Guardians of Irish culture had no way of halting its infiltration and when combined with the ubiquity of international cinema and popular music, its dilution was unavoidable.

Places are very much part of Irish culture and the Guinness brand. Unidentifiable rural landscapes, synonymous with Irishness, featured in many of its ads and conjured up thoughts of Ireland. The sea was a recurring theme in many of the ads, a reminder of its close relationship with Irish culture. It signifies the restlessness of the Irish and was used in ads like 'Island' (1977) and 'Big Wave', 1981/2 to symbolise the movement in a pint of Guinness when it has been poured. One of Ireland's most visited tourist attractions, the Cliffs of Moher was in 'Horses' (1999). Representations of place were not confined to the sea and rural landscapes. As globalisation took hold, ads were based in international cities. This started as far back as 1981 when a group of friends travelled to New York in 'Fireworks' but it became a more regular occurrence in the 1990s. Even if Irish people had never lived outside Ireland, exposure to international influences through popular culture, holidays, the availability of global brands meant that they could be quite cosmopolitan in their outlook (Inglis 2008).

For centuries, sport has been at the heart of Irish culture and many historians believe this dates back to the ancient Tailteann Games. From the start, Guinness featured a variety of sports in its ads, including horse racing, greyhound racing, cross-country running, Gaelic football, hurling and rugby. The Archive has many more examples of print ads from the 1960s and 1970s that were based on other sports such as cricket, bowls, golf and tennis. Clearly, it recognised sport as a way of connecting with its Irish audiences. The pub is fundamental to sporting life in Ireland, a place to socialise with teammates and opponents after participating in sport. This ritual was captured in 'Sporting Series' (1963 to 1965), Guinness's first ever series of TV ads. In 1995, its eighteen-year sponsorship of the GAA's Hurling Championship presented Guinness with the opportunity to align itself with a high profile signifier of Irish culture. This sponsorship would go on to be eclipsed in the noughties when Guinness strengthened its relationship with the IRFU, at a time when rugby was growing in popularity and assuming a greater role in modern-day Irish culture.

When pieced together, many of the ads analysed in this study provide a social and economic commentary about Ireland between 1959 and 1999. There is substantive proof that Guinness frequently drew on contemporary societal and economic issues in many of its ads. However, it did not stray into politics. Therefore, when the Irish electorate found itself in the midst of divisive campaigns on abortion and divorce in the 1980s and 1990s, no reference was made to them in the ads. Similarly, Northern Irish politics was never alluded to. Instead, stories were more often constructed around observations relating to the economy, women's role in society, migration within Ireland, emigration, evolving sexual mores, consumerism and globalisation.

The first decade of ads reflected Ireland's growing interest in the economy. Guinness appeared keen to position itself at the vanguard of the transition from a protectionist regime to an open economy. Its ads relayed news of its contribution to exports, taxes and employment. While the economy was less prevalent in the ads in the 1970s, it could not be avoided in the 1980s when the country entered a deep recession. A series of ads focused on the value of a pint of Guinness for hard-pressed consumers. Meanwhile, the emotive issue of emigration was usually couched in success and symbolised by well-to-do emigrants returning to Ireland or living prosperous lives abroad. Even when emigration was not as prevalent during the Celtic Tiger years, the Irish diaspora was not ignored and formed the basis of the stories in 'Drummer Boy' (1997) and 'Water Tower' (1998). The concept of globalisation was dealt with directly in some ads, not least the sombre, thought-provoking 'Journey' (1989). It also brought about a major shake-up in the international advertising industry. When combined with the formation of Diageo, this heralded greater centralisation of the brand's communications strategies.

The rise in consumerism was evident in many of the ads from the late 1960s. In response to this, Guinness advertising did not just focus on the product but picked up on the concepts of pleasure and enjoyment. Overall, the ads in the 1970s placed far more emphasis on lifestyle themes such as holidays and hobbies. The characters in the ads wore casual and fashionable clothes and aspirational lifestyles formed part of the narrative in many of the ads, particularly from the end of the 1970s. Due to the emphasis that consumers placed on appearances, many paid greater attention to the calories in products, not least beer. Ads in the 1970s and 1980s compared the calorie count in a Guinness with competing products and while some of these ads were aimed at women, men were sometimes targeted with this message too. Evolving trends in the consumption of alcohol were evident in some of the ads too. As far back as the mid-1960s, more alcohol was consumed in the home. From then on, Guinness created ads to promote its take-out beer. This was much more pressing from the 1990s when off-trade alcohol consumption increased at a very fast rate.

Significant societal shifts can be traced in many of the ads that were analysed. Visual triggers signified rural Ireland's demise, the expanding middle class and the changing role of women. It was evident in some of the ads from 1966 onwards that women were slowly starting to participate more in Irish life. Prior to that they were largely absent from the ads and when they were present, they were very much in the background. From 1966 onwards, they assumed more significant roles in the Guinness ads. This continued in the 1970s when they even starred in some on their own too. This coincided with the removal of the ban that prevented married women from working in public and civil service employment. Some ads deliberately imbued in the women sexual appeal and levels of confidence that would have been unconscionable in the 1960s. These traits were communicated in a variety of ways, including clothing and behaviour that suggested sexual intimacy between the man and woman in the ad.

In general though, it was apparent that Guinness ads did not court controversy. However, in the 1990s, a relaxation of sexual mores in Ireland accompanied the legalisation of homosexuality, divorce and contraception and this came through in some of the ads. 'Oysters' (1999) was sexually explicit but remained under the ASAI's radar. Ireland did not join the EEC until 1973 and up to then, advertising regulation was the sole responsibility of Irish legislators. Since advertising was still relatively undeveloped in Ireland, it was largely left to its own devices. However, the Single European Act (1992) led to the harmonisation of regulations in relation to the marketing of products like alcohol and tobacco. Consequently, the increasingly prescriptive regulatory framework that governed alcohol advertising was discernible in the Guinness ads. Images of men smoking and drinking Guinness in the pub were quite literally consigned to the archives, as was any suggestion that Guinness was good for consumers.

The question of the extent to which Guinness's advertising might have influenced Irish culture and society is very much open to conjecture. As stated in the introduction, archival research is not without bias, so when addressing a question like this, it invites the researcher to state their opinion without necessarily having the support of unequivocal evidence. Undoubtedly, Guinness occupies a place in the hearts and minds of the Irish in a way that no other brands can do. The ubiquity of 'the pint' and the recognition that the brand garners from Irish people and tourists alike affirms that Guinness is very much part of Irish culture. 'Big Wave'

(1981/2) inspired a line in Christy Moore's ballad from 1985, 'Delerium Tremens' when he wondered how the surfer in the ad managed to remain standing on his surfboard after fourteen pints of stout. The backing track in 'Anticipation' (1994) went on to become a big hit in Ireland and McKinney's dance moves were mimicked on dance-floors across Ireland. However, this was really no more than a fad with a finite shelf life and did not make a lasting impression on Irish culture. However, as long as it is creative and memorable, Guinness's advertising instils in Irish people a sense of pride and the impression that it is a very important part of Irish culture.

Archival research affords the researcher a view of society at a particular point in time. It cannot always explain why the material is the way it is, thereby necessitating an ethnographic approach. Whether or not Guinness ads have been a catalyst for change in Irish society is very difficult, if not impossible, to prove. However, in my opinion, it is conceivable that some ads from the first decade helped stimulate change in relation to the status of women in Irish society. My reason for subscribing to this view is that when compared to subsequent decades, there were very few media options available to Irish consumers at that time. Hence, a small number of outlets vied for their attention and they were more likely to notice the ads. Guinness's print ads in the first decade were laden with copy, which leads one to conclude that they were consumed very differently and that people took the time to read them. Television was a relatively new medium and unlike today, it was difficult to avoid the commercial breaks. The women's movement in Ireland did not gather momentum in Ireland until the 1970s, so when Guinness included women in non-typical scenarios in its ads in the second half of the 1960s, it was ahead of the curve. It is difficult to conclude that Guinness was responsible for the gradual change in the status of women in society. However, its ads probably supported the movement by normalising images of women in pubs or engaging in activities traditionally associated with men.

Bibliography

Archives Task Force (2004). *Listening to the Past, Speaking to the Future*. London: Archives Task Force.

Arning, Chris, and Gordon, Alex (2006). 'Sonic semiotics – the role of music in marketing communications.' *ESOMAR Conference Papers*. Annual Congress, London, September. Downloaded from WARC.

ASAI (1989). *Code of Advertising Standards for Ireland*. 3rd edn. Dublin: Advertising Standards Association for Ireland.

ASAI (1995). *Code of Advertising Standards for Ireland*. 4th edn. Dublin: Advertising Standards Association for Ireland.

ASAI (1999). 'Case Report.' *Advertising Standards Association for Ireland*. Batch number 116, Reference AC/9906/486, 25 August.

Balmer, John M. T. (2001). 'Corporate Identity, Corporate Branding and Corporate Marketing: Seeing through the Fog.' *European Journal of Marketing* 35 (3/4), 248–91.

Barthes, R. (1972). *Mythologies*. 1957. Trans. Annette Lavers. New York: Hill and Wang.

BBC (1954). '1954: Housewives Celebrate End of Rationing,' BBC News, *On This Day: 1950–2005*, 4 July [online]. Available at <http://news.bbc.co.uk/onthisday/hi/dates/stories/july/4/newsid_3818000/3818563.stm> [accessed on 1 March 2016].

BBC Good Food (n.d.). 'Glossary: Oyster' [online]. Available at <http://www.bbcgoodfood.com/glossary/oyster> [accessed on 23 February 2016].

Bell, D. (1985). 'Proclaiming the Republic: Broadcasting Policy and the Corporate State in Ireland.' *West European Politics*, Vol. 8, Issue 2 (Broadcasting and Politics in Western Europe), pp. 27–49.

Binet, L., Müllensiefen, D., and Edwards, P. (2013). 'The Power of Music.' *Admap*, October. Downloaded from WARC.

Boddewyn, J. J., Soehl, R., and Picard, J. (1986). 'Standardization in International Marketing: Is Ted Levitt in Fact Right?' *Business Horizons*, November–December, pp. 69–75.

Bourdieu, P. (1984). *Distinction*. Abingdon: Routledge.

Bradley, J. (2000). 'The Irish Economy in Comparative Perspective,' in Nolan, B., O'Connell, P. J., and Whelan, C. T. (eds). *Bust to Boom? The Irish Experience of Growth and Inequality*. Dublin: The Institute of Public Administration.

Brown, T. (2004) *Ireland: A Social and Cultural History 1922–2002*. London: Harper Perennial.

Buvelot, Q. (2017). 'The Food of Love,' in Waiboer, A. E. (ed.). *Vermeer and the Masters of Genre Painting*. New Haven, CT: Yale University Press (copyright by the National Gallery of Ireland).

Buzzell, R. D. (1968). 'Can you standardize multinational marketing?' *Harvard Business Review*, November–December, pp. 102–13.

Byrne, J. D. (1995). 'Strategic Corporate Identity and Corporate-Image Research in Ireland,' in Meenaghan, T., and O'Sullivan, P. (eds). *Marketing Communications in Ireland*. Dublin: Oak Tree Press.

Central Statistics Office (a) (n.d.). [Online.] Available at <http://www.cso.ie/px/pxeirestat/statire/SelectVarVal/saveselections.asp> [accessed on 11 August 2017].

Central Statistics Office (b) (n.d.). [Online.] Available at <http://www.cso.ie/en/media/csoie/releasespublications/documents/statisticalyearbook/2004/ireland&theeu.pdf> [accessed on 11 August 2017].

Central Statistics Office (c) (n.d.). [Online.] Available at <http://www.cso.ie/en/media/csoie/census/documents/vol12_entire.pdf> [accessed on 14 August 2017].

Chandler, D. (1994). *Semiotics for beginners* [online]. Available at <https://s3.amazonaws.com/academia.edu.documents/34512504/Semiotics_for_Beginners.pdf> [accessed on 11 May 2018].

Conniffe, D., and McCoy, D. (1993). *Alcohol Use in Ireland: Some Economic and Social Implications*. Dublin: Economic and Social Research Institute. General Research Series, paper number 160.

Connolly, F. (ed.) (1984). *The Christy Moore Songbook*. Dingle: Brandon.

Connolly, L. (2003) *The Irish Women's Movement: From Revolution to Devolution*. Dublin: The Lilliput Press Ltd.

Corcoran, M. P. (2000). 'Mall City,' in Slater, E., and Peillon, M. (eds). *Memories of the Present: A Sociological Chronicle of Ireland, 1997–8*. Dublin: Institute of Public Administration.

Cosgrave, B. (1998). 'Mass Attendance: Reflections on a Recent Survey.' *The Furrow*, Volume 49, Number 12 (December), 681–9.

Coulter, C. (2003). 'The end of Irish history? An introduction to the book,' in Coulter, C., and Coleman, S. (eds). *The end of Irish history? Critical approaches to the Celtic Tiger*. Manchester: Manchester University Press.

Craven, L. (2008). 'From the Archivist's Cardigan to the Very Dead Sheep: What are Archives? What are Archivists? What do they do?', Craven, L. (ed.). *What are Archives?* Ashgot Publishing.

Cronin, A. M. (2004). 'Regimes of mediation: advertising practitioners as cultural intermediaries?' *Consumption Markets and Culture*, 7: 4, pp. 349–69.

Daly, T. (2003) *The Rás: The Story of Ireland's Unique Bike Race*. Cork: The Collins Press.

Daniels, P. W. (1995). 'The Internationalisation of Advertising Services in a Changing Regulatory Environment.' *The Service Industries Journal*, 15(3), 276–94.

Delamere, M. (2000). 'Tourism and Transport,' in Redmond, A. (ed.). *That was then, This is now: Change in Ireland, 1949–1999. A publication to mark the 50th anniversary of the Central Statistics Office*. Dublin: The Stationery Office/Central Statistics Office.

Department of Health and Children (1996). *National Alcohol Policy*. September. Dublin: The Stationery Office.

Douglas, S. P., and Wind, Y. (1987). 'The Myth of Globalization.' *Columbia Journal of World Business*, Winter, pp. 19–29.

Elder, G. H., Pavalko, E. K., and Clipp, E. C. (2011). *Working with Archival Data*. Thousand Oaks, CA: SAGE Publications Inc. [online]. Available at <http://dx.doi.org/104135/9781412986519> [accessed on 3 September 2018].

Escher, M. C. (2000). *MC Escher: The Graphic Work*. Cologne: Taschen.

Ewen, S. (1976). *Captains of Consciousness: Advertising and the Social Roots of the Consumer Culture*. New York: McGraw-Hill.

Fagan, G. H. (2003). 'Globalised Ireland, or, contemporary transformations of national identity?' in Coulter, C., and Coleman, S. (eds). *The end of Irish history? Critical approaches to the Celtic Tiger*. Manchester: Manchester University Press.

Fahey, T., and Duffy, D. (2007). 'The Housing Boom,' in Fahey, T., Russell, H., and Whelan, C. T. (eds). *Best of Times? The Social Impact of the Celtic Tiger*. Dublin: Institute of Public Administration.

Fahey, T., and Layte, R. (2007). 'Family and Sexuality,' in Fahey, T., Russell, H., and Whelan, C. T. (eds). *Best of Times? The Social Impact of the Celtic Tiger*. Dublin: Institute of Public Administration.

Fanning, J. (1999). 'Tell Me a Story: The Future of Branding.' *Irish Marketing Review* 12 (2), 3–15.

Fanning, J. (2006). *The Importance of Being Branded: an Irish Perspective*. Dublin: The Liffey Press.

Felton, B., and Devlin, B. (1983). 'In Defence of Sally O'Brien.' *The Crane Bag*, Volume 7, Number 2, The Forum Issue, pp. 202–4. Richard Kearney. [Online.] Available at <http://www.jstor.org/stable/30060618> [accessed on 14 February 2017].

Fennell, D. (1986). 'Creating a New Irish Identity.' *Studies: An Irish Quarterly Review*, Vol. 75, No. 300 (Winter). Irish Province of the Society of Jesus [online]. Available at <http://www.jstor.org/stable/30090792> [accessed on 22 November 2015].

Ferriter, D. (2005) *The Transformation of Ireland 1900–2000*. London: Profile Books Ltd.

Fisher, D. (1978) *Broadcasting in Ireland*. London: Routledge and Kegan Paul Ltd.

Fiske, J. (1987). *Television Culture*. London: Routledge.

Fitzgerald, J. (1999). 'The Irish Economic Boom.' *Les Etudes du Centre d'Études et de Recherches Internationales*, November, No. 56.

Fitzgerald, J. (2000). 'The Story of Ireland's Failure – and Belated Success,' in Nolan, B., O'Connell, P. J., and Whelan, C. T. (eds). *Bust to Boom? The Irish Experience of Growth and Inequality*. Dublin: The Institute of Public Administration.

Foucault, M. (1972). *The Archaeology of Knowledge*. Trans. A. M. Sheridan Smith. New York: Pantheon.

Fox, S. (1997). *The Mirror Makers: A History of American Advertising and its Creators*. Urbana: University of Illinois Press.

Gadsby, N. (2010). 'Semiotics can make brands magical,' *Admap*, April, pp. 40–41 [online]. Available at <http://0-www.warc.com.millennium.it-tallaght.ie/Content/PrintViewer.aspx?MasterContentRef–e47bf07b-4f10-43a2-844f-038612614e43> [accessed on 27 July 2017].

Galligan, Y. (1998). *Women and Politics in Contemporary Ireland: From the Margins to the Mainstream*. London: Pinter.

Galway Oyster Festival (n.d.). 'History of the Galway Oyster and Seafood Festival' [online]. Available at <http://www.galwayoysterfest.com/> [accessed on 23 February 2016].

Gardiner, K. (1994). 'The Irish Economy: A Celtic Tiger,' *Morgan Stanley Euroletter*, 31 August.

Garrett, J. (2000). 'Guinness to return to TV screens with four new ads.' *The Guardian*, 14 November [online]. Available at <https://www.theguardian.com/media/2000/nov/14/advertising2> [accessed on 7 August 2017].

Gibbons, L. (1988). 'Coming out of Hibernation? The Myth of Modernity in Irish Culture' in Kearney, R. (ed.). *Across the Frontiers: Ireland in the 1990s*. Dublin: Wolfhound Press.

Gluckman, D. (2017). 'Why Guinness Light failed in 1979. An insider's confession.' *The Irish Times*, 3 October [online]. Available at <https://www.irishtimes.com/culture/books/why-guinness-light-failed-in-1979–an-insiders-confession-1.3242416> [accessed on 24 October 2017].

Goldman, R. (1992). *Reading Ads Socially*. London: Routledge.

Goodyear, M. (1991). 'Global advertising: the five stages of advertising literacy.' *Admap*, March. Downloaded from WARC.

Green, H. (1997). 'HHCL serves up twins Guinness drive.' *Campaign*. July 18 [online]. Available at <http://www.campaignlive.co.uk/article/hhcl-serves-twins-guinness-drive/35804> [accessed on 30 July 2017].

Guinness (1987). *Guinness PLC Report and Accounts 1987*. London: Guinness PLC.

Guinness (1988). *Guinness PLC Report and Accounts 1988* London: Guinness PLC.

Guinness (1996). *Annual Report and Accounts 1996*. London: Guinness PLC.

Guinness (2009a). *Guinness: An Official Celebration of 250 Remarkable Years*. London: Hamlyn.

Guinness, R. (2009b). *The World of Guinness*. London: Scala.

Guinness Storehouse (n.d.). 'Guinness and Food.' *Archive Fact Sheet* [online]. Available at <https://www.guinness-storehouse.com/Content/pdf/archive-factsheets/advertising/guinness-and-food.pdf> [accessed on 26 April 2018].

Harris, N. (2009). 'Great Sporting Moments: Dennis Taylor defeats Steve Davis 18–17 at the Crucible.' *The Independent*. Saturday, 11 July [online]. Available at <http://www.independent.co.uk/sport/general/others/great-sporting-moments- dennis-taylor-defeats-steve-davis-18–17–at-the-crucible-1741225.html> [accessed on 1 October 2017].

Haughton, J. (1987). 'The Historical Background', in O'Hagan, John W. (ed.). *The Economy of Ireland: Policy and Performance*. 5th edn. Dublin: Irish Management Institute.

Hearn, D. (2003). 'Macroeconomic policy in the Celtic Tiger: a critical reassessment,' in Coulter, C., and Coleman, S. (eds). *The end of Irish history? Critical approaches to the Celtic Tiger*. Manchester: Manchester University Press.

Hesmondhalgh, D. (2012). *The Culture Industries*. 3rd edn. London: Sage Publications.

Hewson, P., Durcan, P., Jordan, N., and Ballagh, R. (1988). 'Migrant Minds' in Kearney, R. (ed.). *Across the Frontiers: Ireland in the 1990s*. Dublin: Wolfhound Press.

HL Debate (25 November 1953). Volume 184, column 632 [online]. Available at <https://api.parliament.uk/historic-hansard/lords/1953/nov/25/television-policy#S5LV0184P0_19531125_HOL_128> [accessed on 4 June 2019].

Hughes, G., McGinnity, F., O'Connell, P., and Quinn, E. (2007). 'The Impact of Immigration,' in Fahey, T., Russell, H., and Whelan, C. T. (eds). *Best of Times? The Social Impact of the Celtic Tiger*. Dublin: Institute of Public Administration.

Inglis, T. (2008). *Global Ireland: Same Difference*. New York: Routledge.

International Commission for the Study of Communication Problems (1980). *Many Voices, One World: Towards a new more just and more efficient world information and communication order*. London: Kogan Page.

The Irish Independent (1997). 'Religious are divided on President's Communion,' 8 August [online]. Available at <http://www.independent.ie/irish-news/

religious-are-divided-on-presidents-communion-26200652.html> [accessed on 8 August 2017].

The Irish Times (1954). 'Eve Ireland, shopping for meat, finds a new meaning for the old phrase.' 8 June, p. 6 [online]. Available at <http://0–www.irishtimes.com.millennium.it-tallaght.ie/newspaper/archive/1954/0608/Pg006.html#Ar00608:5A41CA5C61E455A1CA59E1E45E71CA60F1E462B07763E0BC55B1895641A56311866391A35EE19E5F61BA5BE2355C624F57631E57D3350001B45791D157C1B657E1D057F1B45B21D15E71B560F1CF55E0815810BE58007D5940C15940805B40BD5DE1886031A56151B56391CF6162496392635D72FA5E93125EA2FA5F53125C01B55E01CF> [accessed on 31 July 2016].

Jhally, S. (2003). 'Image-Based Culture: Advertising and Popular Culture,' in Dines, G., and Humez, J. M. (eds). *Gender, Race, and Class in Media: A Text-Reader*. 2nd edn, pp. 249–57, Boston, MA: Sage.

Kearney, R. (1988a). 'Postmodern Ireland' in Hederman, M. (ed.). *The Clash of Ideas: Essays in Honour of Patrick Lynch*. Dublin: Gill and Macmillan.

Kearney, R. (ed.) (1988b). *Across the Frontiers: Ireland in the 1990s*. Dublin: Wolfhound Press.

Kennedy, F. (1989). *Family, Economy and Government in Ireland*. Dublin: Economic and Social Research Institute, General Research Series, paper number 143.

Kennedy, F. (2001). *Cottage to Crèche: Family Change in Ireland*. Dublin: Institute of Public Administration.

Kennedy, K. A., and Giblin, T. (1987). 'Employment', in O'Hagan, J. W. (ed.). *The Economy of Ireland: Policy and Performance*. 5th edn. Dublin: Irish Management Institute.

Kennedy, S. (2003). 'Irish women and the Celtic Tiger economy,' in Coulter, C., and Coleman, S. (eds). *The end of Irish history? Critical approaches to the Celtic Tiger*. Manchester: Manchester University Press.

Keohane, K., and Kuhling, C. (2006). 'The Happiest Country in the World?' in Corcoran, M. P., and Peillon, M. (eds). *Uncertain Ireland: A Sociological Chronicle, 2003–2004*. Dublin: The Institute of Public Administration.

Kiberd, D. (1984). 'Inventing Irelands.' *The Crane Bag*, Volume 8, Number 1, pp. 11–23. Richard Kearney. [Online.] Available at <http://www.jstor.org/stable/30059548> [accessed on 14 February 2017].

King, L. (2000). 'Advertising Ireland: Irish Graphic Design in the 1950s under the Patronage of Aer Lingus.' *Circa 92*, Summer, pp. 16–19.

Kiriakidou, O., and Millward, L. F. (2000). 'Corporate Identity: External Reality or Internal Fit?' *Corporate Communications: An International Journal* 5 (1), 49–58.

Lannon, J. (1992). 'Asking the right questions – what do people do with advertising?' *Admap*, March. Downloaded from WARC.

Lawes, R. (2002). 'De-mystifying Semiotics: Some Key Questions Answered.' *Market Research Society: Annual Conference*, 2002. Downloaded from WARC.

Lee, J. (1982). 'Society and Culture'. *Administration* 30 (2), 1–18.

Leiss, W., Kline, S., Jhally, S., and Botterill, J. (2005). *Social Communication in Advertising: Consumption in the Mediated Marketplace*. 3rd edn. New York: Routledge, Taylor and Francis.

Leslie, D. A. (1995). 'Global Scan: The Globalization of Advertising Agencies, Concepts and Campaigns.' *Economic Geography*, 71(4), 402–26.

Levitt, T. (1983). 'The Globalization of Markets.' *Harvard Business Review*, May/June, pp. 92–102.

Linehan, H. (1997). 'Barman, this beer ad is flat.' *The Irish Times*, 22 February [online]. Available at <https://www.irishtimes.com/news/barman-this-beer-ad-is-flat-1.45729> [accessed on 29 July 2017].

Linehan, H. (1999). 'Plain Erotic.' *The Irish Times*, 10 July [online]. Available at <https://www.irishtimes.com/news/plain-erotic-1.205295?mode=print&ot=example.AjaxPageLayout.ot> [accessed on 31 July 2017].

McCormack, K., and Meany, P. (2000). 'Consumer Prices and Expenditure,' in Redmond, A. (ed.). *That was then, This is now: Change in Ireland, 1949–1999. A publication to mark the 50th anniversary of the Central Statistics Office*. Dublin: The Stationery Office/Central Statistics Office.

McCoy, D. (1991). 'Issues for Irish Alcohol Policy: A Historical Perspective with Some Lessons for the Future.' *Journal of the Statistical and Social Inquiry Society of Ireland*, Vol. XXVI, Part IV.

McMahon, T. (2000). 'Industry and Construction,' in Redmond, A. (ed.). *That was then, This is now: Change in Ireland, 1949–1999. A publication to mark the 50th anniversary of the Central Statistics Office*. Dublin: The Stationery Office/Central Statistics Office.

Madden, J. (2000). 'The Services Sector,' in Redmond, A. (ed.). *That was then, This is now: Change in Ireland, 1949–1999. A publication to mark the 50th anniversary of the Central Statistics Office*. Dublin: The Stationery Office/Central Statistics Office.

Maguire, J., and Tuck, J. (2005). 'National Identity, Rugby Union and Notions of Ireland and the Irish.' *Irish Journal of Sociology* (14.1), 86–109.

Marchand, R. (1985). *Advertising the American Dream: Making Way for Modernity, 1920–40*. Berkeley: University of California Press.

Meenaghan, T. (1995). 'Marketing Communications in Transition,' in Meenaghan, T., and O'Sullivan, P. (eds). *Marketing Communications in Ireland*. Dublin: Oak Tree Press.

Melewar, T. C., and Saunders, J. (2000). 'Global corporate visual identity systems: using an extended marketing mix.' *European Journal of Marketing* 34 (5/6), 538–50.

Mennell, S. (1996). *All Manners of Food: Eating and Taste in England and France from the Middle Ages to the Present*. 2nd edn. Urbana: University of Illinois Press.

Moore, N., Salter, A., Stanley, L., and Tamboukou, M. (2017). 'In Other Archives and Beyond,' in Moore, N., Salter, A., Stanley, L., and Tamboukou, M. (eds). *The Archive Project: Archival Research in Social Sciences*, pp. 1–30. Kindle edition. Abingdon: Routledge.

Moran, C. (1984). 'The Advertising Agency View of Ireland: Conservative Mono-Culture.' *The Crane Bag*, Volume 8, Number 2, pp. 84–89. Richard Kearney [online]. Available at <http://www.jstor.org/stable/30023283> [accessed on 14 February 2017].

Muniz, A. M., Jr, and O'Guinn, T. C. (2001). 'Brand Community.' *Journal of Consumer Research*, Vol. 27, March, 412–32.

Murphy, B. (2014). 'A hundred thousand welcomes,' in Maher, E., and O'Brien, E. (eds). *From Prosperity to Austerity*. Manchester: Manchester University Press.

Muzellec, L., and Lambkin, M. (2007). 'Does Diageo make your Guinness taste better?' *Journal of Product & Brand Management* 16 (5), pp. 321–33.

Muzellec, L., and Lambkin, M. (2008). 'Corporate rebranding and the implications for brand architecture management: The case of Guinness (Diageo) Ireland.' *Journal of Strategic Marketing* 16 (4), pp. 283–99.

Negra, D. (2010). 'Urban Space, Luxury Retailing and The New Irishness.' *Cultural Studies*, 24(6), November, pp. 836–53.

NESC (1986). *A Strategy for Development 1986 to 1990: Growth, Employment and Fiscal Balance*. Number 83. Dublin: National Economic & Social Council.

NESC (1989). *Ireland in the European Community: Performance, Prospects and Strategy*. Number 88. Dublin: National Economic & Social Council.

NESC (1991). *The Economic and Social Implications of Emigration*. Number 90. Dublin: National Economic & Social Council.

Nolan, S. (1987). 'Economic Growth: Theory and Analysis,' in O'Hagan, J. W. (ed.). *The Economy of Ireland: Policy and Performance*. 5th edn. Dublin: Irish Management Institute.

O'Boyle, N. (2011). *New Vocabularies, Old Ideas: Culture, Irishness and the Advertising Industry*. Bern: Peter Lang.

O'Brien, C. (2009). 'Joyce and Bloomsday capture "soul of a people"', *The Irish Times*, 17 June [online]. Available at <https://www.irishtimes.com/news/joyce-and-bloomsday-capture-soul-of-a-people-1.785488?mode=print&ot=example.AjaxPageLayout.ot> [accessed on 22 November, 2017].

O'Brien, E. (2009). *Kicking Bishop Brennan up the Arse: negotiating texts and contexts in contemporary Irish studies*. Bern: Peter Lang.

O'Brien, E. (2014). 'Bloomsday and Arthur's Day – Secular Sacraments as Symbolic and Cultural Capital,' in MacConIomaire, M., and Maher, E. (eds). *'Tickling the Palate': Gastronomy in Irish Culture, Literature and the Public Imagination*. Oxford: Peter Lang.

O'Connell, P. J., and Russell, H. (2007). 'Employment and the Quality of Work,' in Fahey, T., Russell, H., and Whelan, C. T. (eds). *Best of Times? The Social Impact of the Celtic Tiger*. Dublin: Institute of Public Administration.

O'Connor, N. (1991). *Bringing It All Back Home: The Influence of Irish Music*. London: BBC Books.

O'Connor, P. (1998). *Emerging Voices: Women in Contemporary Irish Society*. Dublin: Institute of Public Administration.

O'Donnell, R. (1993). 'Ireland and Europe: Challenges for a New Century.' *Economic and Social Research Institute (ESRI) Research Series*, Paper number 17, March.

O'Hearn, D. (1998). *Inside the Celtic Tiger: The Irish Economy and the Asian Model*. London: Pluto Press.

O'Leary, R. (2000). 'The President's Communion,' in Slater, E., and Peillon, M. (eds). *Memories of the Present: A Sociological Chronicle of Ireland, 1997–8*. Dublin: Institute of Public Administration.

Ollins, W. (1989). *Corporate Identity: Making Business Strategy Visible through Design*. London: Thames & Hudson.

O'Riordan, A. (2009). 'Fresh draughts of literary history', *The Irish Times*, 28 September [online]. Available at <https://www.irishtimes.com/culture/fresh-draughts-of-literary-history-1.746464?mode=print&ot=example.AjaxPageLayout.ot> [accessed on 22 November 2017].

Packard, V. (1957) *The Hidden Persuaders*. London: Penguin Books. (Reprinted with Introduction and Epilogue in 1981.)

Patterson, A. (2009). 'Brand Ireland.' *Irish Marketing Review* 20 (2), 89–98.

Peillon, M. (2000). 'Carnival Ireland,' in Slater, E., and Peillon, M. (eds). *Memories of the Present: A Sociological Chronicle of Ireland, 1997–8*. Dublin: Institute of Public Administration.

Pope, C. (2018). 'Ireland's most popular tourist attractions named,' *The Irish Times*, 7 June [online]. Available at <https://www.irishtimes.com/life-and-style/travel/ireland/ireland-s-most-popular-tourist-attractions-named-1.3522528> [accessed on 10 June 2018].

Prue, T. (1998). 'An all-embracing theory of how advertising works?' *Admap*, *33*, pp. 18–23.

Quelch, J. A., and Hoff, E. J. (1986). 'Customizing global marketing.' *Harvard Business Review*, May–June, pp. 59–68.

Redmond, A., and Heanue, M. (2000). 'Aspects of Society,' in Redmond, A. (ed.). *That was then, This is now: Change in Ireland, 1949–1999. A publication to mark the 50th anniversary of the Central Statistics Office.* Dublin: The Stationery Office/Central Statistics Office.

Rottman, D. B., and O'Connell, P. J. (1982). 'The Changing Social Structure.' *Administration*, January (30), (2), 63–88.

Rowley, R. (1988). 'Thinking Globally and Acting Locally' in Kearney, R. (ed.). *Across Frontiers: Ireland in the 1990s.* Dublin: Wolfhound Press.

Ryanair (n.d.). 'History of Ryanair.' Ryanair [online]. Available at <https://corporate.ryanair.com/about-us/history-of-ryanair/> [accessed on 14 March 2017].

Salter, A. (2017). 'Reading Time Backwards? Archival Research and Temporal Order,' in Moore, N., Salter, A., Stanley, L., and Tamboukou, M. (eds). *The Archive Project: Archival Research in Social Sciences*, pp. 99–126. Kindle edition. Abingdon: Routledge.

Scahill, A. (2009). 'Riverdance: representing Irish traditional music.' *New Hibernia Review* 13 (2), pp. 70–76.

Scannell, Y. (1988). 'The constitution and the role of women,' in Farrell, B. (ed.). *De Valera's Constitution and Ours.* Dublin: Gill and Macmillan.

Schramm, W. (1955). 'Information theory and mass communication.' *Journalism Quarterly* 32 (2), pp. 131–46.

Shannon, C., and Weaver, W. (1949). *The Mathematical Theory of Communications.* Champaign: University of Illinois Press.

Sheffield, T. (2006). *The Religious Dimensions of Advertising.* New York: Palgrave Macmillan.

Smyth, G. (2014). 'Popular Music and the Celtic Tiger,' in Maher, E., and O'Brien, E. (eds). *From Prosperity to Austerity: A Socio-Cultural Critique of the Celtic Tiger and Its Aftermath.* Manchester: Manchester University Press.

Sorenson, R. Z. (1975). 'How multinationals view marketing standardization.' *Harvard Business Review*, May–June, 53(3), pp. 38–54.

Stanley, L. (2017). 'Archival Methodology Inside the Blackbox,' in Moore, N., Salter, A., Stanley, L., and Tamboukou, M. (eds), *The Archive Project: Archival Research in Social Sciences*, pp. 33–68. Kindle edition. Abingdon: Routledge.

Stern, B. B. (1991). 'Two Pornographies: A Feminist View of Sex in Advertising.' *Advances in Consumer Research*, Volume 18, 384–91.

Stivers, R. (2000). *Hair of the Dog: Irish Drinking and Its American Stereotype.* New York: The Continuum International Publishing Group Inc., new revised edn.

Thompson, C. (2004). 'Marketplace Mythology and Discourses of Power.' *Journal of Consumer Research* (31), June, 162–80.

Thornley, D. (1964). 'The End of an Era?' *Studies: An Irish Quarterly Review* 53 (209), Spring, 1–17.

Treacy, J., and O'Connell, N. (2000). 'Labour Market,' in Redmond, A. (ed.). *That was then, This is now: Change in Ireland, 1949–1999. A publication to mark the 50th anniversary of the Central Statistics Office*. Dublin: The Stationery Office/ Central Statistics Office.

Upshaw, L. B. (1997). 'Transferable Truths of Brand Identity.' *Design Management Journal*, Winter, 9–14.

Van Raaij, W. F. (1997). 'Globalisation of marketing communication?' *Journal of Economic Psychology* 18 (2), pp. 259–70.

Ventresca, M. J., and Mohr, J. W. (2002). 'Archival Research Methods', in Baum, J. A. C. (ed.), *The Blackwell Companion to Organizations*. Oxford: Blackwell Publishers.

Vignoles, J. (1984). 'What Is Irish Popular Music.' *The Crane Bag*, Volume 8, Number 2, pp. 70–72. Richard Kearney [online]. Available at <http://www.jstor.org/stable/30023280> [accessed on 14 February 2017].

Walker, D. (1984). 'Visual Aspects of Popular Culture.' *The Crane Bag*, Volume 8, Number 2, pp. 125–29. Richard Kearney [online]. Available at <http://www.jstor.org/stable/30023292> [accessed on 14 February 2017].

Walsh, B. M. (1972). 'Ireland's Demographic Transformation, 1958–70.' *The Economic and Social Review* 3 (2), 251–75.

Walsh, B. M. (1980). *Drinking in Ireland: A Review of Trends in Alcohol Consumption, Alcohol Related Problems and Policies towards Alcohol*. Dublin: The Economic and Social Research Institute.

Ward, T. (2009). 'Sport and National Identity.' *Soccer and Society* 10 (5), 518–31.

Ware, R., and Branthwaite, A. (1997). 'The Role of Music in Advertising.' *Admap*, July.

Waters, K. (1997). 'Dual and Extension Branding: Using Research to Guide Design Decisions and Branding Strategy.' *Design Management Journal*, Winter, 26–33.

Weber, R. P. (1990). *Basic Content Analysis*. Volume 49, Sage Publications.

Whelan, C. T., Breen, R., and Whelan, B. J. (1990). 'Industrialisation, Class Formation and Social Mobility in Ireland.' *Proceedings of the British Academy*, Volume 79, pp. 105–28.

Williamson, J. (1978). *Decoding Advertisements: Ideology and Meaning in Advertising*. London: Marion Boyars Publishers Ltd.

Winterman, D. (2012). 'Breakfast, lunch and dinner: Have we always eaten them?' *BBC News Magazine*, 15 November [online]. Available at <http://www.bbc.com/news/magazine-20243692> [accessed on 29 February 2016].

Wyman, B., and Havers, R. (2001). *Bill Wyman's Blues Odyssey: A Journey to Music's Heart & Soul*. London: Dorling Kindersley Limited.

Yenne, B. (2007). *Guinness: The 250–Year Quest for the Perfect Pint.* Hoboken, NJ: Wiley.

Yeshin, T. (2006). *Advertising.* London: Thomson Learning.

Yuval-Davis, N. (1993). 'Gender and Racial Studies.' *Ethnic and Racial Studies*, 16: 4, 621–32.

Zachary, G. P. (1999). 'Letter from Ireland.' *Washington Quarterly* 22 (4), pp. 127–40.

Index

Reimagining Ireland

Series Editor: Dr. Eamon Maher, Technological University Dublin

The concepts of Ireland and 'Irishness' are in constant flux in the wake of an ever-increasing reappraisal of the notion of cultural and national specificity in a world assailed from all angles by the forces of globalisation and uniformity. Reimagining Ireland interrogates Ireland's past and present and suggests possibilities for the futureby looking at Ireland's literature, culture and history and subjecting them to the most up-to-date critical appraisals associated with sociology, literary theory, historiography, political science and theology.

Some of the pertinent issues include, but are not confined to, Irish writing in English and Irish, Nationalism, Unionism, the Northern 'Troubles', the Peace Process, economic development in Ireland, the impact and decline of the Celtic Tiger, Irish spirituality, the rise and fall of organised religion, the visual arts, popular cultures, sport, Irish music and dance, emigration and the Irish diaspora, immigration and multiculturalism, marginalisation, globalisation, modernity/postmodernity and postcolonialism. The series publishes monographs, comparative studies, interdisciplinary projects, conference proceedings and edited books.

Proposals should be sent either to Dr Eamon Maher at eamon.maher@ittdublin.ie or to ireland@peterlang.com.

Vol. 1 Eugene O'Brien: 'Kicking Bishop Brennan up the Arse': Negotiating Texts and Contexts in Contemporary Irish Studies
ISBN 978-3-03911-539-6. 219 pages. 2009.

Vol. 2 James P. Byrne, Padraig Kirwan and Michael O'Sullivan (eds): Affecting Irishness: Negotiating Cultural Identity Within and Beyond the Nation
ISBN 978-3-03911-830-4. 334 pages. 2009.

Vol. 3 Irene Lucchitti: The Islandman: The Hidden Life of Tomás O'Crohan
ISBN 978-3-03911-837-3. 232 pages. 2009.

Vol. 4 Paddy Lyons and Alison O'Malley-Younger (eds): No Country for Old Men: Fresh Perspectives on Irish Literature
ISBN 978-3-03911-841-0. 289 pages. 2009.

Vol. 5 Eamon Maher (ed.): Cultural Perspectives on Globalisation and Ireland
ISBN 978-3-03911-851-9. 256 pages. 2009.

Vol. 6 Lynn Brunet: 'A Course of Severe and Arduous Trials': Bacon, Beckett and Spurious Freemasonry in Early Twentieth-Century Ireland
ISBN 978-3-03911-854-0. 218 pages. 2009.

Vol. 7 Claire Lynch: Irish Autobiography: Stories of Self in the Narrative of a Nation
ISBN 978-3-03911-856-4. 234 pages. 2009.

Vol. 8 Victoria O'Brien: A History of Irish Ballet from 1927 to 1963
ISBN 978-3-03911-873-1. 208 pages. 2011.

Vol. 9 Irene Gilsenan Nordin and Elin Holmsten (eds): Liminal Borderlands in Irish Literature and Culture
ISBN 978-3-03911-859-5. 208 pages. 2009.

Vol. 10 Claire Nally: Envisioning Ireland: W.B. Yeats's Occult Nationalism
ISBN 978-3-03911-882-3. 320 pages. 2010.

Vol. 11 Raita Merivirta: The Gun and Irish Politics: Examining National History in Neil Jordan's *Michael Collins*
ISBN 978-3-03911-888-5. 202 pages. 2009.

Vol. 12 John Strachan and Alison O'Malley-Younger (eds): Ireland: Revolution and Evolution
ISBN 978-3-03911-881-6. 248 pages. 2010.

Vol. 13 Barbara Hughes: Between Literature and History: The Diaries and Memoirs of Mary Leadbeater and Dorothea Herbert
ISBN 978-3-03911-889-2. 255 pages. 2010.

Vol. 14 Edwina Keown and Carol Taaffe (eds): Irish Modernism: Origins, Contexts, Publics
ISBN 978-3-03911-894-6. 256 pages. 2010.

Vol. 15 John Walsh: Contests and Contexts: The Irish Language and Ireland's Socio-Economic Development
ISBN 978-3-03911-914-1. 492 pages. 2011.

Vol. 16 Zélie Asava: The Black Irish Onscreen: Representing Black and Mixed-Race Identities on Irish Film and Television
ISBN 978-3-0343-0839-7. 213 pages. 2013.

Vol. 17 Susan Cahill and Eóin Flannery (eds): This Side of Brightness: Essays on the Fiction of Colum McCann
ISBN 978-3-03911-935-6. 189 pages. 2012.

Vol. 18 Brian Arkins: The Thought of W.B. Yeats
ISBN 978-3-03911-939-4. 204 pages. 2010.

Vol. 19 Maureen O'Connor: The Female and the Species: The Animal in Irish Women's Writing
ISBN 978-3-03911-959-2. 203 pages. 2010.

Vol. 20 Rhona Trench: Bloody Living: The Loss of Selfhood in the Plays of Marina Carr
ISBN 978-3-03911-964-6. 327 pages. 2010.

Vol. 21 Jeannine Woods: Visions of Empire and Other Imaginings: Cinema, Ireland and India, 1910–1962
ISBN 978-3-03911-974-5. 230 pages. 2011.

Vol. 22 Neil O'Boyle: New Vocabularies, Old Ideas: Culture, Irishness and the Advertising Industry
ISBN 978-3-03911-978-3. 233 pages. 2011.

Vol. 23 Dermot McCarthy: John McGahern and the Art of Memory
ISBN 978-3-0343-0100-8. 344 pages. 2010.

Vol. 24 Francesca Benatti, Sean Ryder and Justin Tonra (eds): Thomas Moore: Texts, Contexts, Hypertexts
ISBN 978-3-0343-0900-4. 220 pages. 2013.

Vol. 25 Sarah O'Connor: No Man's Land: Irish Women and the Cultural Present
ISBN 978-3-0343-0111-4. 230 pages. 2011.

Vol. 26 Caroline Magennis: Sons of Ulster: Masculinities in the Contemporary Northern Irish Novel
ISBN 978-3-0343-0110-7. 192 pages. 2010.

Vol. 27 Dawn Duncan: Irish Myth, Lore and Legend on Film
ISBN 978-3-0343-0140-4. 181 pages. 2013.

Vol. 28 Eamon Maher and Catherine Maignant (eds): Franco-Irish Connections in Space and Time: Peregrinations and Ruminations
ISBN 978-3-0343-0870-0. 295 pages. 2012.

Vol. 29 Holly Maples: Culture War: Conflict, Commemoration and the Contemporary Abbey Theatre
ISBN 978-3-0343-0137-4. 294 pages. 2011.

Vol. 30 Maureen O'Connor (ed.): Back to the Future of Irish Studies: Festschrift for Tadhg Foley
ISBN 978-3-0343-0141-1. 359 pages. 2010.

Vol. 31 Eva Urban: Community Politics and the Peace Process in Contemporary Northern Irish Drama
ISBN 978-3-0343-0143-5. 303 pages. 2011.

Vol. 32 Mairéad Conneely: Between Two Shores / *Idir Dhá Chladach*: Writing the Aran Islands, 1890–1980
ISBN 978-3-0343-0144-2. 299 pages. 2011.

Vol. 33 Gerald Morgan and Gavin Hughes (eds): Southern Ireland and the Liberation of France: New Perspectives
ISBN 978-3-0343-0190-9. 250 pages. 2011.

Vol. 34 Anne MacCarthy: Definitions of Irishness in the 'Library of Ireland' Literary Anthologies
ISBN 978-3-0343-0194-7. 271 pages. 2012.

Vol. 35 Irene Lucchitti: Peig Sayers: In Her Own Write
ISBN 978-3-0343-0253-1. Forthcoming.

Vol. 36 Eamon Maher and Eugene O'Brien (eds): Breaking the Mould: Literary Representations of Irish Catholicism
ISBN 978-3-0343-0232-6. 249 pages. 2011.

Vol. 37 Mícheál Ó hAodha and John O'Callaghan (eds): Narratives of the Occluded Irish Diaspora: Subversive Voices
ISBN 978-3-0343-0248-7. 227 pages. 2012.

Vol. 38 Willy Maley and Alison O'Malley-Younger (eds): Celtic Connections: Irish–Scottish Relations and the Politics of Culture
ISBN 978-3-0343-0214-2. 247 pages. 2013.

Vol. 39 Sabine Egger and John McDonagh (eds): Polish–Irish Encounters in the Old and New Europe
ISBN 978-3-0343-0253-1. 322 pages. 2011.

Vol. 40 Elke D'hoker, Raphaël Ingelbien and Hedwig Schwall (eds): Irish Women Writers: New Critical Perspectives
ISBN 978-3-0343-0249-4. 318 pages. 2011.

Vol. 41 Peter James Harris: From Stage to Page: Critical Reception of Irish Plays in the London Theatre, 1925–1996
ISBN 978-3-0343-0266-1. 311 pages. 2011.

Vol. 42 Hedda Friberg-Harnesk, Gerald Porter and Joakim Wrethed (eds):
Beyond Ireland: Encounters Across Cultures
ISBN 978-3-0343-0270-8. 342 pages. 2011.

Vol. 43 Irene Gilsenan Nordin and Carmen Zamorano Llena (eds): Urban and Rural Landscapes in Modern Ireland: Language, Literature and Culture
ISBN 978-3-0343-0279-1. 238 pages. 2012.

Vol. 44 Kathleen Costello-Sullivan: Mother/Country: Politics of the Personal in the Fiction of Colm Tóibín
ISBN 978-3-0343-0753-6. 247 pages. 2012.

Vol. 45 Lesley Lelourec and Gráinne O'Keeffe-Vigneron (eds): Ireland and Victims: Confronting the Past, Forging the Future
ISBN 978-3-0343-0792-5. 331 pages. 2012.

Vol. 46 Gerald Dawe, Darryl Jones and Nora Pelizzari (eds): Beautiful Strangers: Ireland and the World of the 1950s
ISBN 978 -3- 0343-0801-4. 207 pages. 2013.

Vol. 47 Yvonne O'Keeffe and Claudia Reese (eds): New Voices, Inherited Lines: Literary and Cultural Representations of the Irish Family
ISBN 978-3-0343-0799-4. 238 pages. 2013.

Vol. 48 Justin Carville (ed.): Visualizing Dublin: Visual Culture, Modernity and the Representation of Urban Space
ISBN 978-3-0343-0802-1. 326 pages. 2014.

Vol. 49 Gerald Power and Ondřej Pilný (eds): Ireland and the Czech Lands: Contacts and Comparisons in History and Culture
ISBN 978-3-0343-1701-6. 243 pages. 2014.

Vol. 50 Eoghan Smith: John Banville: Art and Authenticity
ISBN 978-3-0343-0852-6. 199 pages. 2014.

Vol. 51 María Elena Jaime de Pablos and Mary Pierse (eds): George Moore and the Quirks of Human Nature
ISBN 978-3-0343-1752-8. 283 pages. 2014.

Vol. 52 Aidan O'Malley and Eve Patten (eds): Ireland, West to East: Irish Cultural Connections with Central and Eastern Europe
ISBN 978-3-0343-0913-4. 307 pages. 2014.

Vol. 53 Ruben Moi, Brynhildur Boyce and Charles I. Armstrong (eds): The Crossings of Art in Ireland
ISBN 978-3-0343-0983-7. 319 pages. 2014.

Vol. 54 Sylvie Mikowski (ed.): Ireland and Popular Culture
ISBN 978-3-0343-1717-7. 257 pages. 2014.

Vol. 55 Benjamin Keatinge and Mary Pierse (eds): France and Ireland in the Public Imagination
ISBN 978-3-0343-1747-4. 279 pages. 2014.

Vol. 56 Raymond Mullen, Adam Bargroff and Jennifer Mullen (eds): John McGahern: Critical Essays
ISBN 978-3-0343-1755-9. 253 pages. 2014.

Vol. 57 Máirtín Mac Con Iomaire and Eamon Maher (eds): 'Tickling the Palate': Gastronomy in Irish Literature and Culture
ISBN 978-3-0343-1769-6. 253 pages. 2014.

Vol. 58 Heidi Hansson and James H. Murphy (eds): Fictions of the Irish Land War
ISBN 978-3-0343-0999-8. 237 pages. 2014.

Vol. 59 Fiona McCann: A Poetics of Dissensus: Confronting Violence in Contemporary Prose Writing from the North of Ireland
ISBN 978-3-0343-0979-0. 238 pages. 2014.

Vol. 60 Marguérite Corporaal, Christopher Cusack, Lindsay Janssen and Ruud van den Beuken (eds): Global Legacies of the Great Irish Famine: Transnational and Interdisciplinary Perspectives
ISBN 978-3-0343-0903-5. 357 pages. 2014.

Vol. 61 Katarzyna Ojrzyn'ska: 'Dancing As If Language No Longer Existed': Dance in Contemporary Irish Drama
ISBN 978-3-0343-1813-6. 318 pages. 2015.

Vol. 62 Whitney Standlee: 'Power to Observe': Irish Women Novelists in Britain, 1890–1916
ISBN 978-3-0343-1837-2. 288 pages. 2015.

Vol. 63 Elke D'hoker and Stephanie Eggermont (eds): The Irish Short Story: Traditions and Trends
ISBN 978-3-0343-1753-5. 330 pages. 2015.

Vol. 64 Radvan Markus: Echoes of the Rebellion: The Year 1798 in Twentieth-Century Irish Fiction and Drama
ISBN 978-3-0343-1832-7. 248 pages. 2015.

Vol. 65 B. Mairéad Pratschke: Visions of Ireland: Gael Linn's *Amharc Éireann* Film Series, 1956–1964
ISBN 978-3-0343-1872-3. 301 pages. 2015.

Vol. 66 Una Hunt and Mary Pierse (eds): France and Ireland: Notes and Narratives
ISBN 978-3-0343-1914-0. 272 pages. 2015.

Vol. 67 John Lynch and Katherina Dodou (eds): The Leaving of Ireland: Migration and Belonging in Irish Literature and Film
ISBN 978-3-0343-1896-9. 313 pages. 2015.

Vol. 68 Anne Goarzin (ed.): New Critical Perspectives on Franco-Irish Relations
ISBN 978-3-0343-1781-8. 271 pages. 2015.

Vol. 69 Michel Brunet, Fabienne Gaspari and Mary Pierse (eds): George Moore's Paris and His Ongoing French Connections
ISBN 978-3-0343-1973-7. 279 pages. 2015.

Vol. 70 Carine Berbéri and Martine Pelletier (eds): Ireland: Authority and Crisis
ISBN 978-3-0343-1939-3. 296 pages. 2015.

Vol. 71 David Doolin: Transnational Revolutionaries: The Fenian Invasion of Canada, 1866
ISBN 978-3-0343-1922-5. 348 pages. 2016.

Vol. 72 Terry Phillips: Irish Literature and the First World War: Culture, Identity and Memory
ISBN 978-3-0343-1969-0. 297 pages. 2015.

Vol. 73 Carmen Zamorano Llena and Billy Gray (eds): Authority and Wisdom in the New Ireland: Studies in Literature and Culture
ISBN 978-3-0343-1833-4. 263 pages. 2016.

Vol. 74 Flore Coulouma (ed.): New Perspectives on Irish TV Series: Identity and Nostalgia on the Small Screen
ISBN 978-3-0343-1977-5. 222 pages. 2016.

Vol. 75 Fergal Lenehan: Stereotypes, Ideology and Foreign Correspondents: German Media Representations of Ireland, 1946–2010
ISBN 978-3-0343-2222-5. 306 pages. 2016.

Vol. 76 Jarlath Killeen and Valeria Cavalli (eds): 'Inspiring a Mysterious Terror': 200 Years of Joseph Sheridan Le Fanu
ISBN 978-3-0343-2223-2. 260 pages. 2016.

Vol. 77 Anne Karhio: 'Slight Return': Paul Muldoon's Poetics of Place
ISBN 978-3-0343-1986-7. 272 pages. 2017.

Vol. 78 Margaret Eaton: Frank Confessions: Performance in the Life-Writings of Frank McCourt
ISBN 978-1-906165-61-1. 294 pages. 2017.

Vol. 79 Marguérite Corporaal, Christopher Cusack and Ruud van den Beuken (eds): Irish Studies and the Dynamics of Memory: Transitions and Transformations
ISBN 978-3-0343-2236-2. 360 pages. 2017

Vol. 80 Conor Caldwell and Eamon Byers (eds): New Crops, Old Fields: Reimagining Irish Folklore
ISBN 978-3-0343-1912-6. 200 pages. 2017

Vol. 81 Sinéad Wall: Irish Diasporic Narratives in Argentina: A Reconsideration of Home, Identity and Belonging
ISBN 978-1-906165-66-6. 282 pages. 2017

Vol. 82 Ute Anna Mittermaier: Images of Spain in Irish Literature, 1922–1975
ISBN 978-3-0343-1993-5. 386 pages. 2017

Vol. 83 Lauren Clark: Consuming Irish Children: Advertising and the Art of Independence, 1860–1921
ISBN 978-3-0343-1989-8. 288 pages. 2017

Vol. 84 Lisa FitzGerald: Re-Place: Irish Theatre Environments
ISBN 978-1-78707-359-3. 222 pages. 2017

Vol. 85 Joseph Greenwood: 'Hear My Song': Irish Theatre and Popular Song in the 1950s and 1960s
ISBN 978-3-0343-1915-7. 320 pages. 2017

Vol. 86 Nils Beese: Writing Slums: Dublin, Dirt and Literature
ISBN 978-1-78707-959-5. 250 pages. 2018

Vol. 87 Barry Houlihan (ed): Navigating Ireland's Theatre Archive: Theory, Practice, Performance
ISBN 978-1-78707-372-2. 306 pages. 2019.

Vol. 88 María Elena Jaime de Pablos (ed.): Giving Shape to the Moment: The Art of Mary O'Donnell: Poet, Novelist and Short Story Writer
ISBN 978-1-78874-403-4. 228 pages. 2018

Vol. 89 Marguérite Corporaal and Peter Gray (eds): The Great Irish Famine and Social Class: Conflicts, Responsibilities, Representations
ISBN 978-1-78874-166-8. 330 pages. 2019

Vol. 90 Patrick Speight: Irish-Argentine Identity in an Age of Political Challenge and Change, 1875–1983
ISBN 978-1-78874-417-1. 368 pages. 2019.

Vol. 91 Fionna Barber, Heidi Hansson, and Sara Dybris, McQuaid (eds): Ireland and the North
ISBN 978-1-78874-289-4. 338 pages. 2019.

Vol. 92 Ruth Sheehy: The Life and Work of Richard King: Religion, Nationalism and Modernism
ISBN 978-1-78707-246-6. 482 pages. 2019.

Vol. 93 Brian Lucey, Eamon Maher and Eugene O'Brien (eds): Recalling the Celtic Tiger
ISBN 978-1-78997-286-3. 386 pages. 2019.

Vol. 94 Melania Terrazas Gallego (ed.): Trauma and Identity in Contemporary Irish Culture
ISBN 978-1-78997-557-4. 316 pages. 2019

Vol. 95 Patricia Medcalf: Advertising the Black Stuff in Ireland 1959–1999
ISBN 978-1-78874-289-4. 224 pages. 2019.

Lightning Source UK Ltd.
Milton Keynes UK
UKHW021901190920
370189UK00005B/143

9 781789 973457